Fear and Loathing in Las Vegas

and

Other American Stories

Hunter S. Thompson

Fear and Loathing in Las Vegas

and

Other American Stories

ILLUSTRATED BY RALPH STEADMAN

THE MODERN LIBRARY
NEW YORK

1996 Modern Library Edition

Biographical note copyright © 1996 by Random House, Inc.
Copyright © 1971 by Hunter S. Thompson

All rights reserved under International and Pan-American Copyright
Conventions. Published in the United States by Random House, Inc., New York,
and simultaneously in Canada by Random House of Canada Limited, Toronto.

MODERN LIBRARY and colophon are registered trademarks of Random House, Inc.

This work was originally published in hardcover by Random House, Inc., in 1972,
and in paperback by Vintage Books, a division of Random House, Inc., in 1989.

Fear and Loathing in Las Vegas by "Raoul Duke" first appeared in *Rolling Stone*,
issue 95, November 11, 1971, and issue 96, November 25, 1971.

Grateful acknowledgment is made to the following for permission to reprint
previously published material:

SIMON AND SCHUSTER: pages 105–11 from *The Great Shark Hunt* by Hunter S.
Thompson, reprinted here as "Jacket Copy for *Fear and Loathing in Las Vegas: A
Savage Journey to the Heart of the American Dream.*" Copyright © 1971, 1979 by
Hunter S. Thompson. Reprinted by permission of Simon and Schuster.

STRAIGHT ARROW PUBLISHERS, INC.: "Strange Rumblings in Aztlan" by Hunter S.
Thompson, from the April 29, 1971, issue of *Rolling Stone*. Copyright © 1971 by
Straight Arrow Publishers, Inc. Reprinted by permission of Straight Arrow
Publishers, Inc.

Jacket photograph: Raoul Duke in Las Vegas, April 26, 1971,
by "Dusty" in bar of Caesar's Palace

LIBRARY OF CONGRESS CATALOGING-IN-PUBLICATION DATA
Thompson, Hunter S.
Fear and loathing in Las Vegas and other American stories/Hunter S. Thompson;
illustrated by Ralph Steadman.—1998 Modern Library ed.
p.   cm.
ISBN 0-679-60298-4
1. Thompson, Hunter S. 2. Journalists—United States—Biography. I. Title.
PN4874.T44A3   1998
070´.92—dc21   98-12001

Modern Library website address: www.modernlibrary.com

Printed in the United States of America on acid-free paper

19 20 18

HUNTER S. THOMPSON

Hunter S. Thompson, creator of the aggressively subjective approach to reporting, found his niche early. Born in Louisville, Kentucky, in 1937, by the age of ten he was writing for his own two-page, four-cent neighborhood newspaper. While attending Louisville Male High School Thompson was inducted into the city's prestigious Athenaeum Literary Association in recognition of his fiction and poetry. He continued to pursue his chosen vocation after enlisting in the United States Air Force, where he wrote a weekly sports column for his base newspaper.

After two years' service Thompson took to freelance writing for various publications until he became Caribbean correspondent for the New York *Herald Tribune*. In 1962 he began reporting on South America for the *National Observer*. Upon returning to the United States a year later Thompson became a national correspondent for *The Reporter*, *The Nation*, and *Spyder* magazine, the voice of the Free Speech movement at Berkeley.

The time was right and Thompson put himself in place to be the living historian of the counterculture. In 1967 he published his first book, *Hell's Angels*, a brutal and eloquent account of the year he spent riding with the notorious biker gang, then a symbol of everything that made middle America nervous. "Hunter Thompson has presented us with a close view of a world most of us would never encounter," said *The New York Times Book Review*. "His language is brilliant, his eye remarkable." Studs Terkel called *Hell's Angels* "superb and terrifying."

In 1969 *Scanlan's Monthly* commissioned Thompson to return to his hometown to cover America's premier Thoroughbred horse race. The result was "The Kentucky Derby Is Decadent and Depraved," in which traditional reportage is skewed through Thompson's wildly funny first-person perspective. Accompanied by Ralph Steadman's perversely exact illustrations, the piece won immediate acclaim.

The appearance of *Fear and Loathing in Las Vegas* in two issues of *Rolling Stone* in 1971 sealed Thompson's reputation as an outlaw genius. As the subtitle warns, the work takes readers on "a savage journey to the heart of the American Dream." *The New York Times* said, "What goes on in these pages makes Lenny Bruce seem angelic. . . . The whole book boils down to a kind of mad, corrosive prose poetry." Tom Wolfe pronounced it "a scorching epochal sensation."

Thompson's incisive coverage of the 1972 Nixon-McGovern presidential race for *Rolling Stone* became his next book, *Fear and Loathing on the Campaign Trail '72*. As the self-confessed "political junkie" explained on the jacket flap, "This book is nothing more or less than a scrambled account of what it was like for one human being to cover (more or less journalistically) a presidential campaign run by other human beings. . . . Every year I feel more like a wino turned loose in the tasting room." *The New York Times Book Review* dubbed the book "the best account yet published of what it feels like to be out there in the middle of the American political process."

By the time *The Great Shark Hunt* came out in 1979, Thompson was firmly entrenched as the voice of what used to be called the demimonde before the rest of the world came to meet it halfway. The first volume of "Gonzo Papers" tracking the Death of the American Dream, *The Great Shark Hunt* tears through the sixties and seventies with acid analysis of everything from Nixon and napalm to Carter and cocaine. "No other reporter reveals how much we have to fear and loathe," said the *Chicago Tribune*.

In 1983 Thompson wrote *The Curse of Lono*, a brain-curdling South Sea odyssey that did for Hawaii what he had done earlier for Las Vegas. Commented *The Washington Post*: "*The Curse of Lono* dispenses pages rabid with his hilarious, frenzied rantings, gusts of sixties madness for the stuffy eighties."

His wrath erupted quite brutally with the second volume of Gonzo Papers, *Generation of Swine* in 1988, which was nominated for the Pulitzer Prize. The book collects Thompson's *San Francisco Examiner* columns keeping score on the eighties with the Book of Revelation as scorecard; as Thompson explained, "Most smart people tend to feel queasy when the conversation turns to things like 'certain death' and 'total failure' and the idea of a 'doomed generation.' But not me. I am comfortable with these themes."

The third volume of Gonzo Papers, *Songs of the Doomed*, ushered in 1990 with a sampling of Thompson's apocalyptic musings for the end of the millennium. Filled with accounts of how he and we made the long, strange trip from Kennedy to Nixon to Clinton, the book ends with the grim tale of a bizarre and ultimately doomed government police action against Thompson.

His latest book, 1994's *Better Than Sex*, subjected the 1992 presidential campaign to Thompson's gut-ripping powers of observation. Wandering again into the savage vortex of political power, he somehow managed to emerge with the bizarre tale of life "within the Belly of the Great American Beast," leading the *Daily News* to hail him for delivering "yet another of his cocktail mixes of unbelievable tales and dark observations."

Thompson lives in a fortified compound near Aspen, Colorado, where he ran for sheriff on the Freak Power ticket in 1970 and has been locked in a blood feud with local authorities ever since. His son, Juan, graduated summa cum laude from the University of Colorado in English, computer science, and religious studies. He currently heads the university's computerized fund-raising arm.

Contents

To Bob Geiger,
for reasons that need
not be explained here
—and to Bob Dylan,
for *Mister Tambourine Man*

"He who makes a beast of
himself gets rid of the pain of
being a man."

—DR. JOHNSON

We were somewhere around Barstow on the edge of the desert when the drugs began to take hold. I remember saying something like "I feel a bit lightheaded; maybe you should drive. . . ." And suddenly there was a terrible roar all around us and the sky was full of what looked like huge bats, all swooping and screeching and diving around the car, which was going about a hundred miles an hour with the top down to Las Vegas. And a voice was screaming: "Holy Jesus! What are these goddamn animals?"

Then it was quiet again. My attorney had taken his shirt off and was pouring beer on his chest, to facilitate the tanning process. "What the hell are you yelling about?" he muttered, staring up at the sun with his eyes closed and covered with wraparound Spanish sunglasses. "Never mind," I said. "It's your turn to drive." I hit the brakes and aimed the Great Red Shark toward the shoulder of the highway. No point mentioning those bats, I thought. The poor bastard will see them soon enough.

It was almost noon, and we still had more than a hundred miles to go. They would be tough miles. Very soon, I knew, we would both be completely twisted. But there was no going back, and no time to rest. We would have to ride it out. Press registration for the fabulous Mint 400 was already underway, and we had to get there by four to claim our sound-proof suite. A fashionable sporting magazine in New York had taken care of the reservations, along with this huge red Chevy convertible we'd just rented off a lot on the Sunset

Strip . . . and I was, after all, a professional journalist; so I had an obligation to *cover the story*, for good or ill.

The sporting editors had also given me $300 in cash, most of which was already spent on extremely dangerous drugs. The trunk of the car looked like a mobile police narcotics lab. We had two bags of grass, seventy-five pellets of mescaline, five sheets of high-powered blotter acid, a salt shaker half full of cocaine, and a whole galaxy of multi-colored uppers, downers, screamers, laughers . . . and also a quart of tequila, a quart of rum, a case of Budweiser, a pint of raw ether and two dozen amyls.

All this had been rounded up the night before, in a frenzy of high-speed driving all over Los Angeles County—from Topanga to Watts, we picked up everything we could get our hands on. Not that we *needed* all that for the trip, but once you get locked into a serious drug collection, the tendency is to push it as far as you can.

The only thing that really worried me was the ether. There is nothing in the world more helpless and irresponsible and depraved than a man in the depths of an ether binge. And I knew we'd get into that rotten stuff pretty soon. Probably at the next gas station. We had sampled almost everything else, and now—yes, it was time for a long snort of ether. And then do the next hundred miles in a horrible, slobbering sort of spastic stupor. The only way to keep alert on ether is to do up a lot of amyls—not all at once, but steadily, just enough to maintain the focus at ninety miles an hour through Barstow.

"Man, this is the way to travel," said my attorney. He leaned over to turn the volume up on the radio, humming along with the rhythm section and kind of moaning the words: "One toke over the line, Sweet Jesus . . . One toke over the line . . ."

One toke? You poor fool! Wait till you see those goddamn bats. I could barely hear the radio . . . slumped over on the far side of the seat, grappling with a tape recorder turned all the way up on "Sympathy for the Devil." That was the only tape we had, so we played it constantly, over and over, as a kind of demented counterpoint to the radio. And also to maintain our rhythm on the road. A constant speed is good for gas mileage—and for some reason that seemed important at the time. Indeed. On a trip like this one *must* be careful about gas consumption. Avoid those quick bursts of acceleration that drag blood to the back of the brain.

My attorney saw the hitchhiker long before I did. "Let's give this boy a lift," he said, and before I could mount any argument he was stopped and this poor Okie kid was running up to the car with a big grin on his face, saying, "Hot damn! I never rode in a convertible before!"

"Is that right?" I said. "Well, I guess you're about ready, eh?"

The kid nodded eagerly as we roared off.

"We're your friends," said my attorney. "We're not like the others."

O Christ, I thought, he's gone around the bend. "No more of that talk," I said sharply. "Or I'll put the leeches on you." He grinned, seeming to understand. Luckily, the noise in the car was so awful—between the wind and the radio and the tape machine—that the kid in the back seat couldn't hear a word we were saying. Or could he?

How long can we *maintain?* I wondered. How long before one of us starts raving and jabbering at this boy? What will he think then? This same lonely desert was the last known home of the Manson family. Will he make that grim connection when my attorney starts screaming about bats and huge manta rays coming down on the car? If so—well, we'll just have to cut his head off and bury him somewhere. Because it goes without saying that we can't turn him loose. He'll report us at once to some kind of outback nazi law enforcement agency, and they'll run us down like dogs.

Jesus! Did I *say* that? Or just think it? Was I talking? Did they hear me? I glanced over at my attorney, but he seemed oblivious—watching the road, driving our Great Red Shark along at a hundred and ten or so. There was no sound from the back seat.

Maybe I'd better have a chat with this boy, I thought. Perhaps if I *explain* things, he'll rest easy.

Of course. I leaned around in the seat and gave him a fine big smile . . . admiring the shape of his skull.

"By the way," I said. "There's one thing you should probably understand."

He stared at me, not blinking. Was he gritting his teeth?

"Can you *hear* me?" I yelled.

He nodded.

"That's good," I said. "Because I want you to know that we're on our way to Las Vegas to find the American Dream." I smiled. "That's why we rented this car. It was the only way to do it. Can you grasp that?"

He nodded again, but his eyes were nervous.

"I want you to have all the background," I said. "Because this is a very ominous assignment—with overtones of extreme personal danger. . . . Hell, I forgot all about this beer; you want one?"

He shook his head.

"How about some ether?" I said.

"What?"

"Never mind. Let's get right to the heart of this thing. You see, about twenty-four hours ago we were sitting in the Polo Lounge of the Beverly Hills Hotel—in the patio section, of course—and we were just sitting there under a palm tree when this uniformed dwarf came up to me with a pink telephone and said, 'This must be the call you've been waiting for all this time, sir.' "

I laughed and ripped open a beer can that foamed all over the back seat while I kept talking. "And you know? He was right! I'd been *expecting* that call, but I didn't know who it would come from. Do you follow me?"

The boy's face was a mask of pure fear and bewilderment.

I blundered on: "I want you to understand that this man at the wheel is my *attorney!* He's not just some dingbat I found on the Strip. Shit, *look* at him! He doesn't look like you or me, right? That's because he's a foreigner. I think he's probably

Samoan. But it doesn't matter, does it? Are you prejudiced?"

"Oh, hell *no!*" he blurted.

"I didn't think so," I said. "Because in spite of his race, this man is extremely valuable to me." I glanced over at my attorney, but his mind was somewhere else.

I whacked the back of the driver's seat with my fist. "This is *important*, goddamnit! This is a *true story!*" The car swerved sickeningly, then straightened out. "Keep your hands off my fucking neck!" my attorney screamed. The kid in the back looked like he was ready to jump right out of the car and take his chances.

Our vibrations were getting nasty—but why? I was puzzled, frustrated. Was there no communication in this car? Had we deteriorated to the level of *dumb beasts?*

Because my story *was* true. I was certain of that. And it was extremely important, I felt, for the *meaning* of our journey to be made absolutely clear. We had actually been sitting there in the Polo Lounge—for many hours—drinking Singapore Slings with mescal on the side and beer chasers. And when the call came, I was ready.

The Dwark approached our table cautiously, as I recall, and when he handed me the pink telephone I said nothing, merely listened. And then I hung up, turning to face my attorney. "That was headquarters," I said. "They want me to go to Las Vegas at once, and make contact with a Portuguese photographer named Lacerda. He'll have the details. All I have to do is check into my suite and he'll seek me out."

My attorney said nothing for a moment, then he suddenly came alive in his chair. "God *hell!*" he exclaimed. "I think I see the *pattern*. This one sounds like real trouble!" He tucked his khaki undershirt into his white rayon bellbottoms and called for more drink. "You're going to need plenty of legal advice before this thing is over," he said. "And my first advice is that you should rent a very fast car with no top and get the hell out of L.A. for at least forty-eight hours." He shook his head sadly. "This blows my weekend, because naturally I'll have to go with you—and we'll have to arm ourselves."

"Why not?" I said. "If a thing like this is worth doing at all, it's worth doing right. We'll need some decent equipment and plenty of cash on the line—if only for drugs and a super-sensitive tape recorder, for the sake of a permanent record."

"What kind of a story is this?" he asked.

"The Mint 400," I said. "It's the richest off-the-road race for motorcycles and dune-buggies in the history of organized sport—a fantastic spectacle in honor of some fatback *grossero* named Del Webb, who owns the luxurious Mint Hotel in the heart of downtown Las Vegas . . . at least that's what the press release says; my man in New York just read it to me."

"Well," he said, "as your attorney I advise you to buy a motorcycle. How else can you cover a thing like this righteously?"

"No way," I said. "Where can we get hold of a Vincent Black Shadow?"

"What's that?"

"A fantastic bike," I said. "The new model is something like two thousand cubic inches, developing two hundred brake-horsepower at four thousand revolutions per minute on a magnesium frame with two styrofoam seats and a total curb weight of exactly two hundred pounds."

"That sounds about right for this gig," he said.

"It is," I assured him. "The fucker's not much for turning, but it's pure hell on the straightaway. It'll outrun the F-111 until takeoff."

"Takeoff?" he said. "Can we handle that much torque?"

"Absolutely," I said. "I'll call New York for some cash."

2.
The Seizure of $300 from a Pig Woman in Beverly Hills

The New York office was not familiar with the Vincent Black Shadow: they referred me to the Los Angeles bureau--which is actually in Beverly Hills just a few long blocks from the Polo Lounge—but when I got there, the money-woman refused to give me more than $300 in cash. She had no idea who I was, she said, and by that time I was pouring sweat. My blood is too thick for California: I have never been able to properly explain myself in this climate. Not with the soaking sweats . . . wild red eyeballs and trembling hands.

So I took the $300 and left. My attorney was waiting in a bar around the corner. "This won't make the nut," he said, "unless we have unlimited credit."

I assured him we would. "You Samoans are all the same," I told him. "You have no faith in the essential decency of the white man's culture. Jesus, just one hour ago we were sitting over there in that stinking baiginio, stone broke and paralyzed for the weekend, when a call comes through from some total stranger in New York, telling me to go to Las Vegas and expenses be damned—and then he sends me over to some office in Beverly Hills where another total stranger gives me $300 raw cash for no reason at all . . . I tell you, my man, this is the American Dream in action! We'd be fools not to ride this strange torpedo all the way out to the end."

"Indeed," he said. "We *must* do it."

"Right," I said. "But first we need the car. And after that, the cocaine. And then the tape recorder, for special music,

11

and some Acapulco shirts." The only way to prepare for a trip like this, I felt, was to dress up like human peacocks and get crazy, then screech off across the desert and *cover the story*. Never lose sight of the primary responsibility.

But what *was* the story? Nobody had bothered to say. So we would have to drum it up on our own. Free Enterprise. The American Dream. Horatio Alger gone mad on drugs in Las Vegas. Do it *now:* pure Gonzo journalism.

There was also the socio-psychic factor. Every now and then when your life gets complicated and the weasels start closing in, the only real cure is to load up on heinous chemicals and then drive like a bastard from Hollywood to Las Vegas. To *relax*, as it were, in the womb of the desert sun. Just roll the roof back and screw it on, grease the face with white tanning butter and move out with the music at top volume, and at least a pint of ether.

Getting hold of the drugs had been no problem, but the car and the tape recorder were not easy things to round up at 6:30 on a Friday afternoon in Hollywood. I already had one car, but it was far too small and slow for desert work. We went to a Polynesian bar, where my attorney made seventeen calls before locating a convertible with adequate horsepower and proper coloring.

"Hang onto it," I heard him say into the phone. "We'll be over to make the trade in thirty minutes." Then after a pause, he began shouting: "What? *Of course* the gentleman has a major credit card! Do you realize who the fuck you're talking to?"

"Don't take any guff from these swine," I said as he slammed the phone down. "Now we need a sound store with the finest equipment. Nothing dinky. We want one of those new Belgian Heliowatts with a voice-activated shotgun mike, for picking up conversations in oncoming cars."

We made several more calls and finally located our equipment in a store about five miles away. It was closed, but the salesman said he would wait, if we hurried. But we were delayed en route when a Stingray in front of us killed a pedestrian on Sunset Boulevard. The store was closed by the time we got there. There were people inside, but they refused to come to the double-glass door until we gave it a few belts and made ourselves clear.

Finally two salesmen brandishing tire irons came to the door and we managed to negotiate the sale through a tiny slit. Then they opened the door just wide enough to shove the equipment out, before slamming and locking it again. "Now take that stuff and get the hell away from here," one of them shouted through the slit.

My attorney shook his fist at them. "We'll be back," he yelled. "One of these days I'll toss a fucking bomb into this place! I have your name on this sales slip! I'll find out where you live and burn your house down!"

"That'll give him something to think about," he muttered as we drove off. "That guy is a paranoid psychotic, anyway. They're easy to spot."

We had trouble, again, at the car rental agency. After signing all the papers, I got in the car and almost lost control of it while backing across the lot to the gas pump. The rental-man was obviously shaken.

"Say there . . . uh . . . you fellas are going to be *careful* with this car, aren't you?"

"Of course."

"Well, good god!" he said. "You just backed over that two-foot concrete abutment and you didn't even slow down! Forty-five in reverse! And you barely missed the pump!"

"No harm done," I said. "I always test a transmission that way. The *rear end*. For stress factors."

Meanwhile, my attorney was busy transferring rum and ice from the Pinto to the back seat of the convertible. The rental-man watched him nervously.

"Say," he said. "Are you fellas *drinking?*"

"Not me," I said.

"Just fill the goddamn tank," my attorney snapped. "We're in a hell of a hurry. We're on our way to Las Vegas for a desert race."

"What?"

"Never mind," I said. "We're responsible people." I watched him put the gas cap on, then I jammed the thing into low gear and we lurched into traffic.

"There's another worrier," said my attorney. "He's probably all cranked up on speed."

"Yeah, you should have given him some reds."

"Reds wouldn't help a pig like that," he said. "To hell with him. We have a lot of business to take care of, before we can get on the road."

"I'd like to get hold of some priests' robes," I said. "They might come in handy in Las Vegas."

But there were no costume stores open, and we weren't up to burglarizing a church. "Why bother?" said my attorney. "And you have to remember that a lot of cops are good vicious Catholics. Can you imagine what those bastards would do to us if we got busted all drugged-up and drunk in stolen vestments? Jesus, they'd castrate us!"

"You're right," I said. "And for christ's sake don't smoke that pipe at stoplights. Keep in mind that we're exposed."

He nodded. "We need a big hookah. Keep it down here on the seat, out of sight. If anybody sees us, they'll think we're using oxygen."

We spent the rest of that night rounding up materials and packing the car. Then we ate the mescaline and went swimming in the ocean. Somewhere around dawn we had breakfast in a Malibu coffee shop, then drove very carefully across town and plunged onto the smog-shrouded Pasadena Freeway, heading East.

3.
Strange Medicine
on the Desert...
a Crisis of
Confidence

I am still vaguely haunted by our hitchhiker's remark about how he'd "never rode in a convertible before." Here's this poor geek living in a world of convertibles zipping past him on the highways all the time, and he's never even *ridden* in one. It made me feel like King Farouk. I was tempted to have my attorney pull into the next airport and arrange some kind of simple, common-law contract whereby we could just *give* the car to this unfortunate bastard. Just say: "Here, sign this and the car's yours." Give him the keys and then use the credit card to zap off on a jet to some place like Miami and rent another huge fireapple-red convertible for a drug-addled, top-speed run across the water all the way out to the last stop in Key West . . . and then trade the car off for a boat. Keep moving.

But this manic notion passed quickly. There was no point in getting this harmless kid locked up—and, besides, I had *plans* for this car. I was looking forward to flashing around Las Vegas in the bugger. Maybe do a bit of serious drag-racing on the Strip: Pull up to that big stoplight in front of the Flamingo and start screaming at the traffic:

"Alright, you chickenshit wimps! You pansies! When this goddamn light flips green, I'm gonna stomp down on this thing and blow every one of you gutless punks off the road!"

Right. Challenge the bastards on their own turf. Come screeching up to the crosswalk, bucking and skidding with a bottle of rum in one hand and jamming the horn to drown out the music . . . glazed eyes insanely dilated behind tiny black, gold-rimmed greaser shades, screaming gibberish . . . a genuinely *dangerous* drunk, reeking of ether and terminal psychosis. Revving the engine up to a terrible high-pitched chattering whine, waiting for the light to change . . .

How often does a chance like that come around? To jangle the bastards right down to the core of their spleens. Old elephants limp off to the hills to die; old Americans go out to the highway and drive themselves to death with huge cars.

But our trip was different. It was a classic affirmation of everything right and true and decent in the national character. It was a gross, physical salute to the fantastic *possibilities* of life in this country—but only for those with true grit. And we were chock full of that.

My attorney understood this concept, despite his racial handicap, but our hitchhiker was not an easy person to reach. He *said* he understood, but I could see in his eyes that he didn't. He was lying to me.

The car suddenly veered off the road and we came to a sliding halt in the gravel. I was hurled against the dashboard. My attorney was slumped over the wheel. "What's wrong?" I yelled. "We can't stop *here*. This is bat country!"

"My heart," he groaned. "Where's the medicine?"

"Oh," I said. "The medicine, yes, it's right here." I reached into the kit-bag for the amyls. The kid seemed petrified. "Don't worry," I said. "This man has a bad heart—Angina Pectoris. But we have the cure for it. Yes, here they are." I picked four amyls out of the tin box and handed two of them to my attorney. He immediately cracked one under his nose, and I did likewise.

He took a long snort and fell back on the seat, staring straight up at the sun. "Turn up the fucking music!" he screamed. "My heart feels like an alligator!

"Volume! Clarity! Bass! We must have bass!" He flailed his naked arms at the sky. "What's *wrong* with us? Are we goddamn *old ladies?*"

I turned both the radio and the tape machine up full bore. "You scurvy shyster bastard," I said. "Watch your language! You're talking to a doctor of journalism!"

He was laughing out of control. "What the fuck are we *doing* out here on this desert?" he shouted. "Somebody call the police! We need help!"

"Pay no attention to this swine," I said to the hitchhiker. "He can't handle the medicine. Actually, we're *both* doctors of journalism, and we're on our way to Las Vegas to cover the main story of our generation." And then I began laughing. . . .

My attorney hunched around to face the hitchhiker. "The truth is," he said, "we're going to Vegas to croak a scag baron named Savage Henry. I've known him for years, but he ripped us off—and you know what that means, right?"

I wanted to shut him off, but we were both helpless with laughter. What the fuck *were* we doing out here on this desert, when we both had bad hearts?

"Savage Henry has cashed his check!" My attorney snarled at the kid in the back seat. "We're going to rip his lungs out!"

"And eat them!" I blurted. "That bastard won't get away with this! What's going on in this country when a scumsucker like that can get away with sandbagging a doctor of journalism?"

Nobody answered. My attorney was cracking another amyl and the kid was climbing out of the back seat, scrambling down the trunk lid. "Thanks for the ride," he yelled. "Thanks a *lot*. I *like* you guys. Don't worry about *me*." His feet hit the asphalt and he started running back towards Baker. Out in the middle of the desert, not a tree in sight.

"Wait a minute," I yelled. "Come back and get a beer." But apparently he couldn't hear me. The music was very loud, and he was moving away from us at good speed.

"Good riddance," said my attorney. "We had a real freak on our hands. That boy made me nervous. Did you see his *eyes?*" He was still laughing. "Jesus," he said. "This is good medicine!"

I opened the door and reeled around to the driver's side. "Move over," I said. "I'll drive. We have to get out of California before that kid finds a cop."

"Shit, that'll be hours," said my attorney. "He's a hundred miles from anywhere."

"So are we," I said.

"Let's turn around and drive back to the Polo Lounge," he said. "They'll never look for us there."

I ignored him. "Open the tequila," I yelled as the wind-scream took over again; I stomped on the accelerator as we hurtled back onto the highway. Moments later he leaned over with a map. "There's a place up ahead called Mescal Springs," he said. "As your attorney, I advise you to stop and take a swim."

I shook my head. "It's absolutely imperative that we get to the Mint Hotel before the deadline for press registration," I said. "Otherwise, we might have to pay for our suite."

He nodded. "But let's forget that bullshit about the American Dream," he said. "The *important* thing is the Great Samoan Dream." He was rummaging around in the kit-bag. "I think it's about time to chew up a blotter," he said. "That cheap mescaline wore off a long time ago, and I don't know if I can stand the smell of that goddamn ether any longer."

"I *like* it," I said. "We should soak a towel with the stuff and then put it down on the floorboard by the accelerator, so the fumes will rise up in my face all the way to Las Vegas."

He was turning the tape cassette over. The radio was screaming: "Power to the People—Right On!" John Lennon's political song, ten years too late. "That poor fool should have stayed where he was," said my attorney. "Punks like that just get in the way when they try to be serious."

"Speaking of serious," I said. "I think it's about time to get into the ether and the cocaine."

"Forget ether," he said. "Let's save it for soaking down the rug in the suite. But here's this. Your half of the sunshine blotter. Just chew it up like baseball gum."

I took the blotter and ate it. My attorney was now fumbling with the salt shaker containing the cocaine. Opening it. Spilling it. Then screaming and grabbing at the air, as our fine white dust blew up and out across the desert highway. A very expensive little twister rising up from the Great Red Shark. "Oh, *jesus!*" he moaned. "Did you see what God just did to us?"

"God didn't do that!" I shouted. "*You* did it. You're a fucking narcotics agent! I was on to your stinking act from the start, you pig!"

"You better be careful," he said. And suddenly he was waving a fat black .357 magnum at me. One of those snubnosed Colt Pythons with the beveled cylinder. "Plenty of vultures out here," he said. "They'll pick your bones clean before morning."

"You whore," I said. "When we get to Las Vegas I'll have you chopped into hamburger. What do you think the Drug Bund will do when I show up with a Samoan narcotics agent?"

"They'll kill us both," he said. "Savage Henry knows who I am. Shit, I'm your *attorney*." He burst into wild laughter.

"You're full of acid, you fool. It'll be a goddamn miracle if we can get to the hotel and check in before you turn into a wild animal. Are you ready for that? Checking into a Vegas hotel under a phony name with intent to commit capital fraud and a head full of acid?" He was laughing again, then he jammed his nose down toward the salt shaker, aiming the thin green roll of a $20 bill straight into what was left of the powder.

"How long do we have?" I said.

"Maybe thirty more minutes," he replied. "As your attorney I advise you to drive at top speed."

Las Vegas was just up ahead. I could see the strip/hotel skyline looming up through the blue desert ground-haze: The Sahara, the landmark, the Americana and the ominous Thunderbird—a cluster of grey rectangles in the distance, rising out of the cactus.

Thirty minutes. It was going to be very close. The objective was the big tower of the Mint Hotel, downtown—and if we didn't get there before we lost all control, there was also the Nevada State prison upstate in Carson City. I had been there once, but only for a talk with the prisoners—and I didn't want to go back, for any reason at all. So there was really no choice: We would have to run the gauntlet, and acid be damned. Go through all the official gibberish, get the car into the hotel garage, work out on the desk clerk, deal with the bellboy, sign in for the press passes—all of it bogus, totally illegal, a fraud on its face, but of course it would have to be done.

"KILL THE BODY AND THE HEAD WILL DIE"

This line appears in my notebook, for some reason. Perhaps some connection with Joe Frazier. Is he still alive? Still able to talk? I watched that fight in Seattle—horribly twisted about four seats down the aisle from the Governor. A very painful experience in every way, a proper end to the sixties: Tim Leary a prisoner of Eldridge Cleaver in Algeria, Bob Dylan clipping coupons in Greenwich Village, both Kennedys murdered by mutants, Owsley folding napkins on Terminal Island, and finally Cassius/Ali belted incredibly off his pedestal by a human hamburger, a man on the verge of death. Joe Frazier, like Nixon, had finally prevailed for reasons that people like me refused to understand—at least not out loud.

. . . But that was some other era, burned out and long gone from the brutish realities of this foul year of Our Lord, 1971. A lot of things had changed in those years. And now I was in Las Vegas as the motor sports editor of this fine slick magazine that had sent me out here in the Great Red Shark for some reason that nobody claimed to understand. "Just check it out," they said, "and we'll take it from there. . . ."

Indeed. Check it out. But when we finally arrived at the Mint Hotel my attorney was unable to cope artfully with the registration procedure. We were forced to stand in line with all the others—which proved to be extremely difficult under the circumstances. I kept telling myself: "Be quiet, be calm, say nothing . . . speak only when spoken to: name, rank and press affiliation, nothing else, ignore this terrible drug, pretend it's not happening. . . ."

There is no way to explain the terror I felt when I finally lunged up to the clerk and began babbling. All my well-rehearsed lines fell apart under that woman's stoney glare. "Hi there," I said. "My name is . . . ah, Raoul Duke . . . yes, *on the list*, that's for sure. Free lunch, final wisdom, total coverage. . . . why not? I have my attorney with me and I realize of course that *his* name is not on the list, but we *must* have that suite, yes, this man is actually my *driver*. We brought this Red Shark all the way from the Strip and now it's time for the desert, right? Yes. Just check the list and you'll see. Don't worry. What's the score here? What's next?"

The woman never blinked. "Your room's not ready yet," she said. "But there's somebody looking for you."

"No!" I shouted. "Why? We haven't *done* anything yet!" My legs felt rubbery. I gripped the desk and sagged toward her as she held out the envelope, but I refused to accept it. The woman's face was *changing:* swelling, pulsing . . . horrible green jowls and fangs jutting out, the face of a Moray Eel! Deadly poison! I lunged backwards into my attorney, who gripped my arm as he reached out to take the note. "I'll handle this," he said to the Moray woman. "This man has a bad heart, but I have plenty of medicine. My name is Doctor Gonzo. Prepare our suite at once. We'll be in the bar."

The woman shrugged as he led me away. In a town full of bedrock crazies, nobody even *notices* an acid freak. We struggled through the crowded lobby and found two stools at the bar. My attorney ordered two cuba libres with beer and mescal on the side, then he opened the envelope. "Who's Lacerda?" he asked. "He's waiting for us in a room on the twelfth floor."

I couldn't remember. Lacerda? The name rang a bell, but I couldn't concentrate. Terrible things were happening all around us. Right next to me a huge reptile was gnawing on a woman's neck, the carpet was a blood-soaked sponge—impossible to walk on it, no footing at all. "Order some golf shoes," I whispered. "Otherwise, we'll never get out of this place alive. You notice these lizards don't have any trouble moving around in this muck—that's because they have *claws* on their feet."

"Lizards?" he said. "If you think we're in trouble now, wait till you see what's happening in the elevators." He took off his Brazilian sunglasses and I could see he'd been crying. "I just went upstairs to see this man Lacerda," he said. "I told him we knew what he was up to. He *says* he's a photographer, but when I mentioned Savage Henry—well, that did it; he freaked. I could see it in his eyes. He knows we're onto him."

"Does he understand we have magnums?" I said.

"No. But I told him we had a Vincent Black Shadow. That scared the piss out of him."

"Good," I said. "But what about our room? And the golf shoes? We're right in the middle of a fucking reptile zoo! And somebody's giving *booze* to these goddamn things! It won't be long before they tear us to shreds. Jesus, look at the floor! Have you ever *seen* so much blood? How many have they killed *already?*" I pointed across the room to a group that seemed to be staring at us. "Holy shit, look at that bunch over there! They've spotted us!"

"That's the press table," he said. "That's where you have to sign in for our credentials. Shit, let's get it over with. You handle that, and I'll get the room."

4.
Hideous Music and the Sound of Many Shotguns... Rude Vibes on a Saturday Evening in Vegas

We finally got into the suite around dusk, and my attorney was immediately on the phone to room service—ordering four club sandwiches, four shrimp cocktails, a quart of rum and nine fresh grapefruits. "Vitamin C," he explained. "We'll need all we can get."

I agreed. By this time the drink was beginning to cut the acid and my hallucinations were down to a tolerable level. The room service waiter had a vaguely reptilian cast to his features, but I was no longer seeing huge pterodactyls lumbering around the corridors in pools of fresh blood. The only problem now was a gigantic neon sign outside the window, blocking our view of the mountains—millions of colored balls running around a very complicated track, strange symbols & filigree, giving off a loud hum. . . .

"Look outside," I said.

"Why?"

"There's a big . . . machine in the sky, . . . some kind of electric snake . . . coming straight at us."

"Shoot it," said my attorney.

"Not yet," I said. "I want to study its habits."

He went over to the corner and began pulling on a chain to close the drapes. "Look," he said, "you've got to stop this talk about snakes and leeches and lizards and that stuff. It's making me sick."

"Don't worry," I said.

"*Worry?* Jesus, I almost went crazy down there in the bar.

They'll never let us back in that place—not after your scene at the press table."

"What scene?"

"You bastard," he said. "I left you alone for *three minutes!* You scared the shit out of those people! Waving that god-damn marlin spike around and yelling about reptiles. You're lucky I came back in time. They were ready to call the cops. I said you were only drunk and that I was taking you up to your room for a cold shower. Hell, the only reason they gave us the press passes was to get you out of there."

He was pacing around nervously. "Jesus, that scene straightened me right out! I *must* have some drugs. What have you done with the mescaline?"

"The kit-bag," I said.

He opened the bag and ate two pellets while I got the tape machine going. "Maybe *you* should only eat *one* of these," he said. "That acid's still working on you."

I agreed. "We have to go out to the track before dark," I said. "But we have time to watch the TV news. Let's carve up this grapefruit and make a fine rum punch, maybe toss in a blotter . . . where's the car?"

"We gave it to somebody in the parking lot," he said. "I have the ticket in my briefcase."

"What's the number? I'll call down and have them wash the bastard, get rid of that dust and grime."

"Good idea," he said. But he couldn't find the ticket.

"Well, we're fucked," I said. "We'll never convince them to give us that car without proof."

He thought for a moment, then picked up the phone and asked for the garage. "This is Doctor Gonzo in eight-fifty," he said. "I seem to have lost my parking stub for that red convertible I left with you, but I want the car washed and ready to go in thirty minutes. Can you send up a duplicate stub? . . . What . . . Oh? . . . Well, that's fine." He hung up and reached for the hash pipe. "No problem," he said. "That man remembers my face."

"That's good," I said. "They'll probably have a big net

ready for us when we show up."

He shook his head. "As your attorney, I advise you not to worry about *me*."

The TV news was about the Laos Invasion—a series of horrifying disasters: explosions and twisted wreckage, men fleeing in terror, Pentagon generals babbling insane lies. "Turn that shit off!" screamed my attorney "Let's get *out* of here!"

A wise move. Moments after we picked up the car my attorney went into a drug coma and ran a red light on Main Street before I could bring us under control. I propped him up in the passenger seat and took the wheel myself . . . feeling fine, extremely sharp. All around me in traffic I could see people talking and I wanted to hear what they were saying. All of them. But the shotgun mike was in the trunk and I decided to leave it there. Las Vegas is not the kind of town where you want to drive down Main Street aiming a black bazooka-looking instrument at people.

Turn up the radio. Turn up the tape machine. Look into the sunset up ahead. Roll the windows down for a better taste of the cool desert wind. Ah yes. This is what it's all about. Total control now. Tooling along the main drag on a Saturday night in Las Vegas, two good old boys in a fireapple-red convertible . . . stoned, ripped, twisted . . . Good People.

Great God! What is this terrible music?
"The Battle Hymn of Lieutenant Calley":

> *". . . as we go marching on . . .*
> *When I reach my final campground, in that land*
>   *beyond the sun,*
> *and the Great Commander asks me . . ."*
>   (What did he ask you, Rusty?)
> *". . . Did you fight or did you run?"*
>   (and what did you tell him, Rusty?)
>   *". . . We responded to their rifle fire with everything*
>   *we had . . ."*

No! I *can't* be hearing this! It must be the drug. I glanced over at my attorney, but he was staring up at the sky, and I could see that his brain had gone off to that campground beyond the sun. Thank christ he can't hear this music, I thought. It would drive him into a racist frenzy.

Mercifully, the song ended. But my mood was already shattered . . . and now the fiendish cactus juice took over, plunging me into a sub-human funk as we suddenly came up on the turnoff to the Mint Gun Club. "One mile," the sign said. But even a mile away I could hear the crackling scream of two-stroke bike engines winding out . . . and then, coming closer, I heard another sound.

Shotguns! No mistaking that flat hollow boom.

I stopped the car. What the hell is going on down there? I rolled up all the windows and eased down the gravel road, hunched low on the wheel . . . until I saw about a dozen figures pointing shotguns into the air, firing at regular intervals.

Standing on a slab of concrete out here in the mesquite-desert, this scraggly little oasis in a wasteland north of Vegas . . . They were clustered, with their shotguns, about fifty yards away from a one-story concrete/block-house, half-shaded by ten or twelve trees and surrounded by cop-cars, bike-trailers and motorcycles.

Of course. The Mint *Gun Club!* These lunatics weren't letting *anything* interfere with their target practice. Here were about a hundred bikers, mechanics and assorted motorsport types milling around in the pit area, signing in for tomorrow's race, idly sipping beers and appraising each other's machinery—and right in the middle of all this, oblivious to everything but the clay pigeons flipping out of the traps every five seconds or so, the shotgun people never missed a beat.

Well, why not? I thought. The shooting provided a certain rhythm—sort of a steady bass-line—to the high-pitched chaos of the bike scene. I parked the car and wandered into the crowd, leaving my attorney in his coma.

I bought a beer and watched the bikes checking in. Many

405 Husquavarnas, high-tuned Swedish fireballs . . . also many Yamahas, Kawasakis, a few 500 Triumphs, Maicos, here & there a CZ, a Pursang . . . all very fast, super-light dirt bikes. No Hogs in this league, not even a Sportster . . . that would be like entering our Great Red Shark in the dune buggy competition.

Maybe I should *do* that, I thought. Sign my attorney up as the driver, then send him out to the starting line with a head full of ether and acid. How would they handle it?

Nobody would dare go out on the track with a person that crazy. He would roll on the first turn, and take out four or five dune buggies—a Kamikaze trip.

"What's the entry fee?" I asked the desk-man.

"Two fifty," he said.

"What if I told you I had a Vincent Black Shadow?"

He stared up at me, saying nothing, not friendly. I noticed he was wearing a .38 revolver on his belt. "Forget it," I said. "My driver's sick, anyway."

His eyes narrowed. "Your driver ain't the only one sick around here, buddy."

"He has a bone in his throat," I said.

"What?"

The man was getting ugly, but suddenly his eyes switched away. He was staring at something else . . .

My attorney; no longer wearing his Danish sunglasses, no longer wearing his Acapulco shirt . . . a very crazy looking person, half-naked and breathing heavily.

"What's the trouble here?" he croaked. "This man is my client. Are you prepared to go to court?"

I grabbed his shoulder and gently spun him around. "Never mind," I said. "It's the Black Shadow—they won't accept it."

"*Wait* a minute!" he shouted. "What do you *mean*, they won't *accept* it? Have you made a *deal* with these pigs?"

"Certainly not," I said, pushing him along toward the gate. "But you notice they're all armed. We're the only people here without guns. Can't you hear that *shooting* over there?"

He paused, listened for an instant, then suddenly began

running toward the car. "You cocksuckers!" he screamed over his shoulder. "We'll be back!"

By the time we got the shark back on the highway he was able to talk. "Jesus christ! How did we get mixed up with that gang of psychotic bigots? Let's get the fuck out of this town. Those scumbags were trying to *kill* us!"

5.
Covering the Story . . .
A Glimpse of the
Press in Action
. . . Ugliness & Failure

The racers were ready at dawn. Fine sunrise over the desert. Very tense. But the race didn't start until nine, so we had to kill about three long hours in the casino next to the pits, and that's where the trouble started.

The bar opened at seven. There was also a "koffee & donut canteen" in the bunker, but those of us who had been up all night in places like the Circus-Circus were in no mood for coffee & donuts. We wanted strong drink. Our tempers were ugly and there were at least two hundred of us, so they opened the bar early. By eight-thirty there were big crowds around the crap-tables. The place was full of noise and drunken shouting.

A boney, middle-aged hoodlum wearing a Harley-Davidson T-shirt boomed up to the bar and yelled: "God damn! What day is this—Saturday?"

"More like Sunday," somebody replied.

"Hah! That's a *bitch*, ain't it?" the H-D boomer shouted to nobody in particular. "Last night I was out home in Long Beach and somebody said they were runnin' the Mint 400 today, so I says to my old lady, 'Man, I'm goin'.'" He laughed. "So she gives me a lot of crap about it, you know . . . so I started slappin' her around and the next thing I knew two guys I never even seen before got me out on the sidewalk workin' me over. Jesus! They beat me stupid."

He laughed again, talking into the crowd and not seeming to care who listened. "Hell yes!" he continued. "Then one of 'em says, 'Where you going?' And I says, 'Las Vegas, to the Mint 400.' So they gave me ten bucks and drove me down to the bus station. . . ." He paused. "At least I *think* it was them. . . .

"Well, anyway, here I am. And I tell you that was one *hell* of a long night, man! Seven hours on that goddamn bus! But when I woke up it was dawn and here I was in downtown Vegas and for a minute I didn't know what the hell I was *doin'* here. All I could think was, 'O Jesus, here we go again: Who's divorced me this time?' "

He accepted a cigarette from somebody in the crowd, still grinning as he lit up. "But then I remembered, by God! I was here for the Mint 400 . . . and, man, that's all I needed to know. I tell you it's wonderful to be here, man. I don't give a damn who wins or loses. It's just wonderful to be here with you people. . . ."

Nobody argued with him. We all understood. In some circles, the "Mint 400" is a far, far better thing than the Super Bowl, the Kentucky Derby and the Lower Oakland Roller Derby Finals all rolled into one. This race attracts a very special breed, and our man in the Harley T-shirt was clearly one of them.

The correspondent from *Life* nodded sympathetically and screamed at the bartender: "Senzaman wazzyneeds!"

"Fast up with it," I croaked. "Why not five?" I smacked the bar with my open, bleeding palm. "Hell yes! Bring us ten!"

"I'll back it!" The *Life* man screamed. He was losing his grip on the bar, sinking slowly to his knees, but still speaking with definite authority: "This is a magic moment in sport! It may never come again!" Then his voice seemed to break. "I once did the Triple Crown," he muttered. "But it was nothing like this."

The frog-eyed woman clawed feverishly at his belt. "Stand up!" she pleaded. "*Please* stand up! You'd be a very handsome man if you'd just *stand* up!"

He laughed distractedly. "Listen, madam," he snapped.

"I'm damn near intolerably handsome down here where I am. You'd go *crazy* if I stood up!"

The woman kept pulling at him. She'd been mooning at his elbows for two hours, and now she was making her move. The man from *Life* wanted no part of it; he slumped deeper into his crouch.

I turned away. It was too horrible. We were, after all, the absolute cream of the national sporting press. And we were gathered here in Las Vegas for a very special assignment: to cover the Fourth Annual "Mint 400" . . . and when it comes to things like this, you don't fool around.

But now—even before the spectacle got under way—there were signs that we might be losing control of the situation. Here we were on this fine Nevada morning, this cool bright dawn on the desert, hunkered down at some greasy bar in a concrete blockhouse & gambling casino called the "Mint Gun Club" about ten miles out of Vegas . . . and with the race about to start, we were dangerously disorganized.

Outside, the lunatics were playing with their motorcycles, taping the headlights, topping off oil in the forks, last minute bolt-tightening (carburetor screws, manifold nuts, etc.) . . . and the first ten bikes blasted off on the stroke of nine. It was extremely exciting and we all went outside to watch. The flag went down and these ten poor buggers popped their clutches and zoomed into the first turn, all together, then somebody grabbed the lead (a 405 Husquavarna, as I recall), and a cheer went up as the rider screwed it on and disappeared in a cloud of dust.

"Well, that's that," somebody said. "They'll be back around in an hour or so. Let's go back to the bar."

But not yet. No. There were something like a hundred and ninety more bikes waiting to start. They went off ten at a time, every two minutes. At first it was possible to watch them out to a distance of some two hundred yards from the starting line. But this visibility didn't last long. The third brace of ten disappeared into the dust about a hundred yards from where we stood . . . and by the time they'd sent off the first hundred (with still *another* hundred to go), our visibility was down to something like fifty feet. We could see as far as the hay-bales at the end of the pits. . . .

Beyond that point the incredible dustcloud that would hang over this part of the desert for the next two days was already formed up solid. None of us realized, at the time, that this was the last we would see of the "Fabulous Mint 400"—

By noon it was hard to see the pit area from the bar/casino, one hundred feet away in the blazing sun. The idea of trying to "cover this race" in any conventional press-sense was absurd: It was like trying to keep track of a swimming meet in an Olympic-sized pool filled with talcum powder instead of water. The Ford Motor Company had come through, as promised, with a "press Bronco" and a driver, but after a few savage runs across the desert—looking for motorcycles and occasionally finding one—I abandoned this vehicle to the photographers and went back to the bar.

It was time, I felt, for an Agonizing Reappraisal of the whole scene. The race was definitely under way. I had witnessed the start; I was sure of that much. But what now? Rent a helicopter? Get back in that stinking Bronco? Wander out on that goddamn desert and *watch* these fools race past the checkpoints? One every thirteen minutes. . . . ?

By ten they were spread out all over the course. It was no longer a "race"; now it was an Endurance Contest. The only visible action was at the start/finish line, where every few minutes some geek would come speeding out of the dustcloud and stagger off his bike, while his pit crew would gas it up and then launch it back onto the track with a fresh driver . . . for another fifty-mile lap, another brutal hour of kidney-killing madness out there in that terrible dust-blind limbo.

Somewhere around eleven, I made another tour in the press-vehicle, but all we found were two dune-buggies full of what looked like retired petty-officers from San Diego. They cut us off in a dry-wash and demanded, "Where *is* the damn thing?"

"Beats me," I said. "We're just good patriotic Americans like yourselves." Both of their buggies were covered with ominous symbols: Screaming Eagles carrying American Flags in their claws, a slant-eyed snake being chopped to bits by a buzz-saw made of stars & stripes, and one of the vehicles had what looked like a machine-gun mount on the passenger side.

They were having a bang-up time—just crashing around the desert at top speed and hassling anybody they met. "What *outfit* you fellas with?" one of them shouted. The engines were all roaring; we could barely hear each other.

"The sporting press," I yelled. "We're friendlies—hired geeks."

Dim smiles.

"If you want a good chase," I shouted, "you should get after that skunk from CBS News up ahead in the big black jeep. He's the man responsible for *The Selling of the Pentagon.*"

"Hot damn!" two of them screamed at once. "A black jeep, you say?"

They roared off, and so did we. Bouncing across the rocks & scrub oak/cactus like iron tumbleweeds. The beer in my hand flew up and hit the top, then fell in my lap and soaked my crotch with warm foam.

"You're fired," I said to the driver. "Take me back to the pits."

It was time, I felt, to get grounded—to ponder this rotten assignment and figure out how to cope with it. Lacerda insisted on Total Coverage. He wanted to go back out in the dust storm and keep trying for some rare combination of film and lens that might penetrate the awful stuff.

"Joe," our driver, was willing. His name was not really "Joe," but that's what we'd been instructed to call him. I had talked to the FoMoCo boss the night before, and when he mentioned the driver he was assigning to us he said, "His real name is Steve, but you should call him Joe."

"Why not?" I said. "We'll call him anything he wants. How about 'Zoom'?"

"No dice," said the Ford man. "It has to be 'Joe.'"

Lacerda agreed, and sometime around noon he went out on the desert, again, in the company of our driver, Joe. I went back to the blockhouse bar/casino that was actually the Mint Gun Club—where I began to drink heavily, think heavily, and make many heavy notes. . . .

6.
A Night on the Town...
Confrontation at
the Desert Inn...
Drug Frenzy
at the Circus-Circus

Saturday midnight . . . Memories of this night are extremely hazy. All I have, for guide-pegs, is a pocketful of keno cards and cocktail napkins, all covered with scribbled notes. Here is one: "Get the Ford man, demand a Bronco for race-observation purposes . . . photos? . . . Lacerda/call . . . why not a helicopter? . . . Get on the phone, *lean* on the fuckers . . . heavy yelling."

Another says: "Sign on Paradise Boulevard—'Stopless and Topless' . . . bush-league sex compared to L.A.; *pasties* here —total naked public humping in L.A. . . . Las Vegas is a society of armed masturbators/gambling is the kicker here/sex is extra/weird trip for high rollers . . . house-whores for winners, hand jobs for the bad luck crowd."

A long time ago when I lived in Big Sur down the road from Lionel Olay I had a friend who liked to go to Reno for the crap-shooting. He owned a sporting-goods store in Carmel. And one month he drove his Mercedes highway-cruiser to Reno on three consecutive weekends—winning heavily each time. After three trips he was something like $15,000 ahead, so he decided to skip the fourth weekend and take some friends to dinner at Nepenthe. "Always quit winners," he explained. "And besides, it's a long drive."

On Monday morning he got a phone call from Reno—from the general manager of the casino he'd been working out on. "We missed you this weekend," said the GM. "The pit-men were bored."

"Shucks," said my friend.

So the next weekend he flew up to Reno in a private plane, with a friend and two girls—all "special guests" of the GM. Nothing too good for high rollers. . . .

And on Monday morning the same plane—the casino's plane—flew him back to the Monterey airport. The pilot lent him a dime to call a friend for a ride to Carmel. He was $30,000 in debt, and two months later he was looking down the barrel of one of the world's heaviest collection agencies.

So he sold his store, but that didn't make the nut. They could wait for the rest, he said—but then he got stomped, which convinced him that maybe he'd be better off borrowing enough money to pay the whole wad.

Mainline gambling is a very heavy business—and Las Vegas makes Reno seem like your friendly neighborhood grocery store. For a loser, Vegas is the meanest town on earth. Until about a year ago, there was a giant billboard on the outskirts of Las Vegas, saying:

DON'T GAMBLE WITH MARIJUANA!
IN NEVADA: POSSESSION—20 YEARS
SALE—LIFE!

So I was not entirely at ease drifting around the casinos on this Saturday night with a car full of marijuana and head full of acid. We had several narrow escapes: at one point I tried to drive the Great Red Shark into the laundry room of the Landmark Hotel—but the door was too narrow, and the people inside seemed dangerously excited.

We drove over to the Desert Inn, to catch the Debbie Reynolds/Harry James show. "I don't know about you," I told my attorney, "but in my line of business it's important to be Hep."

"Mine too," he said. "But as your attorney I advise you to drive over to the Tropicana and pick up on Guy Lombardo. He's in the Blue Room with his Royal Canadians."

"Why?" I asked.

"Why *what?*"

"Why should I pay out my hard-earned dollars to watch a fucking corpse?"

"Look," he said. "Why are we out here? To entertain ourselves, or to *do the job?*"

"The job, of course," I replied. We were driving around in circles, weaving through the parking lot of a place I thought was the Dunes, but it turned out to be the Thunderbird . . . or maybe it was the Hacienda . . .

My attorney was scanning *The Vegas Visitor*, looking for hints of action. "How about " 'Nickel Nick's Slot Arcade?' " he said. " 'Hot Slots,' that sounds heavy . . . Twenty-nine cent hotdogs . . ."

Suddenly people were screaming at us. We were in trouble. Two thugs wearing red–gold military overcoats were looming over the hood: "What the hell are you doing?" one screamed. "You can't park *here!*"

"Why not?" I said. It seemed like a reasonable place to park, plenty of space. I'd been looking for a parking spot for what seemed like a very long time. Too long. I was about ready to abandon the car and call a taxi . . . but then, yes, we found this *space.*

Which turned out to be the sidewalk in front of the main entrance to the Desert Inn. I had run over so many curbs by this time, that I hadn't even noticed this last one. But now we found ourselves in a position that was hard to explain . . . blocking the entrance, thugs yelling at us, bad confusion. . . .

My attorney was out of the car in a flash, waving a five-dollar bill. "We want this car parked! I'm an old friend of Debbie's. I used to *romp* with her."

For a moment I thought he had blown it . . . then one of

the doormen reached out for the bill, saying: "OK, OK. I'll take care of it, sir." And he tore off a parking stub.

"Holy shit!" I said, as we hurried through the lobby. "They almost had us there. That was quick thinking."

"What do you expect?" he said. "I'm your *attorney* . . . and you owe me five bucks. I want it now."

I shrugged and gave him a bill. This garish, deep-orlon carpeted lobby of the Desert Inn seemed an inappropriate place to be haggling about nickel/dime bribes for the parking lot attendant. This was Bob Hope's turf. Frank Sinatra's. Spiro Agnew's. The lobby fairly reeked of high-grade formica and plastic palm trees—it was clearly a high-class refuge for Big Spenders.

We approached the grand ballroom full of confidence, but they refused to let us in. We were too late, said a man in a wine-colored tuxedo; the house was already full—no seats left, at *any* price.

"Fuck seats," said my attorney. "We're old friends of Debbie's. We drove all the way from L.A. for this show, and we're goddamn well going in."

The tux-man began jabbering about "fire regulations," but my attorney refused to listen. Finally, after a lot of bad noise, he let us in for nothing—provided we would stand quietly in back and not smoke.

We promised, but the moment we got inside we lost control. The tension had been too great. Debbie Reynolds was yukking across the stage in a silver Afro wig . . . to the tune of "Sergeant Pepper," from the golden trumpet of Harry James.

"Jesus creeping shit!" said my attorney. "We've wandered into a time capsule!"

Heavy hands grabbed our shoulders. I jammed the hash pipe back into my pocket just in time. We were dragged across the lobby and held against the front door by goons until our car was fetched up. "OK, get lost," said the wine-tux-man. "We're giving you a break. If Debbie has friends like you guys, she's in worse trouble than I thought."

"We'll see about this!" my attorney shouted as we drove away. "You paranoid scum!"

I drove around to the Circus-Circus Casino and parked near the back door. "This is the place," I said. "They'll never fuck with us here."

"Where's the ether?" said my attorney. "This mescaline isn't working."

I gave him the key to the trunk while I lit up the hash pipe. He came back with the ether-bottle, un-capped it, then poured some into a kleenex and mashed it under his nose, breathing heavily. I soaked another kleenex and fouled my own nose. The smell was overwhelming, even with the top down. Soon we were staggering up the stairs towards the entrance, laughing stupidly and dragging each other along, like drunks.

This is the main advantage of ether: it makes you behave like the village drunkard in some early Irish novel . . . total loss of all basic motor skills: blurred vision, no balance, numb tongue—severance of all connection between the body and the brain. Which is interesting, because the brain continues to function more or less normally . . . you can actually *watch* yourself behaving in this terrible way, but you can't control it.

You approach the turnstiles leading into the Circus-Circus and you know that when you get there, you have to give the man two dollars or he won't let you inside . . . but when you get there, everything goes wrong: you misjudge the distance to the turnstile and slam against it, bounce off and grab hold of an old woman to keep from falling, some angry Rotarian shoves you and you think: What's happening here? What's going on? Then you hear yourself mumbling: "Dogs fucked the Pope, no fault of mine. Watch out! . . . Why money? My name is Brinks; I was born . . . born? Get sheep over side . . . women and children to armored car . . . orders from Captain Zeep."

Ah, devil ether—a total body drug. The mind recoils in horror, unable to communicate with the spinal column. The hands flap crazily, unable to get money out of the pocket . . . garbled laughter and hissing from the mouth . . . always smiling.

Ether is the perfect drug for Las Vegas. In this town they love a drunk. Fresh meat. So they put us through the turnstiles and turned us loose inside.

The Circus-Circus is what the whole hep world would be doing on Saturday night if the Nazis had won the war. This is the Sixth Reich. The ground floor is full of gambling tables, like all the other casinos . . . but the place is about four stories high, in the style of a circus tent, and all manner of strange County-Fair/Polish Carnival madness is going on up in this space. Right above the gambling tables the Forty Flying Carazito Brothers are doing a high-wire trapeze act, along with four muzzled Wolverines and the Six Nymphet Sisters from San Diego . . . so you're down on the main floor playing blackjack, and the stakes are getting high when suddenly you chance to look up, and there, right smack above your head is a half-naked fourteen-year-old girl being chased through the air by a snarling wolverine, which is suddenly locked in a death battle with two silver-painted Polacks who come swinging down from opposite balconies and meet in mid-air on the wolverine's neck . . . both Polacks seize the animal as they fall straight down towards the crap tables—but they bounce off the net; they separate and spring back up towards the roof in three different directions, and just as they're about to fall again they are grabbed out of the air by three Korean Kittens and trapezed off to one of the balconies.

This madness goes on and on, but nobody seems to notice. The gambling action runs twenty-four hours a day on the main floor, and the circus never ends. Meanwhile, on all the upstairs balconies, the customers are being hustled by every conceivable kind of bizarre shuck. All kinds of funhouse-type booths. Shoot the pasties off the nipples of a ten-foot bull-dyke and win a cotton-candy goat. Stand in front of this fantastic machine, my friend, and for just 99¢ your likeness will appear, two hundred feet tall, on a screen above downtown Las Vegas. Ninety-nine cents more for a voice message. "Say whatever you want, fella. They'll hear you, don't worry about that. Remember you'll be two hundred feet tall."

Jesus Christ. I could see myself lying in bed in the Mint Hotel, half-asleep and staring idly out the window, when suddenly a vicious nazi drunkard appears two hundred feet tall in the midnight sky, screaming gibberish at the world: *"Woodstock Über Alles!"*

We will close the drapes tonight. A thing like that could send a drug person careening around the room like a ping-pong ball. Hallucinations are bad enough. But after a while you learn to cope with things like seeing your dead grand-mother crawling up your leg with a knife in her teeth. Most acid fanciers can handle this sort of thing.

But *nobody* can handle that other trip—the possibility that any freak with $1.98 can walk into the Circus-Circus and suddenly appear in the sky over downtown Las Vegas twelve times the size of God, howling anything that comes into his head. No, this is not a good town for psychedelic drugs. Reality itself is too twisted.

Good mescaline comes on slow. The first hour is all waiting, then about halfway through the second hour you start cursing the creep who burned you, because nothing is happening . . . and then ZANG! Fiendish intensity, strange glow and vibrations . . . a very heavy gig in a place like the Circus-Circus.

"I hate to say this," said my attorney as we sat down at the Merry-Go-Round Bar on the second balcony, "but this place is getting *to* me. I think I'm getting the Fear."

"Nonsense," I said. "We came out here to find the American Dream, and now that we're right in the vortex you want to quit." I grabbed his bicep and squeezed. "You must *realize*," I said, "that we've found the main nerve."

"I know," he said. "That's what gives me the Fear."

The ether was wearing off, the acid was long gone, but the mescaline was running strong. We were sitting at a small round gold formica table, moving in orbit around the bartender.

"Look over there," I said. "Two women fucking a polar bear."

"Please," he said. "Don't *tell* me those things. Not now." He signaled the waitress for two more Wild Turkeys. "This is my last drink," he said. "How much money can you lend me?"

"Not much," I said. "Why?"

"I have to go," he said.

"Go?"

"Yes. Leave the country. Tonight."

"Calm down," I said. "You'll be straight in a few hours."

"No," he said. "This is serious."

"George Metesky was serious," I said. "And you see what they did to him."

"Don't fuck around!" he shouted. "One more hour in this town and I'll kill somebody!"

I could see he was on the edge. That fearful intensity that comes at the peak of a mescaline seizure. "OK," I said. "I'll lend you some money. Let's go outside and see how much we have left."

"Can we make it?" he said.

"Well . . . that depends on how many people we fuck with between here and the door. You want to leave quietly?"

"I want to leave *fast*," he said.

"OK. Let's pay this bill and get up very slowly. We're both out of our heads. This is going to be a long walk." I shouted at the waitress for a bill. She came over, looking bored, and my attorney stood up.

"Do they *pay* you to screw that bear?" he asked her.

"What?"

Ralph STEADman

"He's just kidding," I said, stepping between them. "Come on, Doc—let's go downstairs and gamble." I got him as far as the edge of the bar, the rim of the merry-go-round, but he refused to get off until it stopped turning.

"It won't stop," I said. "It's not *ever* going to stop." I stepped off and turned around to wait for him, but he wouldn't move . . . and before I could reach out and pull him off, he was carried away. "Don't move," I shouted. "You'll come around!" His eyes were staring blindly ahead, squinting with fear and confusion. But he didn't move a muscle until he'd made the whole circle.

I waited until he was almost in front of me, then I reached out to grab him—but he jumped back and went around the circle again. This made me very nervous. I felt on the verge of a freakout. The bartender seemed to be watching us.

Carson City, I thought. Twenty years.

I stepped on the merry-go-round and hurried around the bar, approaching my attorney on his blind side—and when we came to the right spot I pushed him off. He staggered into the aisle and uttered a hellish scream as he lost his balance and went down, thrashing into the crowd . . . rolling like a log, then up again in a flash, fists clenched, looking for somebody to hit.

I approached him with my hands in the air, trying to smile. "You fell," I said. "Let's go."

By this time people *were* watching us. But the fool wouldn't move, and I knew what would happen if I grabbed him. "OK," I said. "You stay here and go to jail. I'm leaving." I started walking fast towards the stairs, ignoring him.

This moved him.

"Did you see that?" he said as he caught up with me. "Some sonofabitch kicked me in the back!"

"Probably the bartender," I said. "He wanted to stomp you for what you said to the waitress."

"Good *god!* Let's get out of here. Where's the elevator?"

"Don't go *near* that elevator," I said. "That's just what they *want* us to do . . . trap us in a steel box and take us down to the basement." I looked over my shoulder, but nobody was following.

"Don't run," I said. "They'd like an excuse to shoot us." He nodded, seeming to understand. We walked fast along the big indoor midway—shooting galleries, tattoo parlors, moneychangers and cotton-candy booths—then out through a bank of glass doors and across the grass downhill to a parking lot where the Red Shark waited.

"You drive," he said. "I think there's something wrong with me."

7.
Paranoid Terror...
and the Awful Specter
of Sodomy...
A Flashing of Knives
and Green Water

When we got to the Mint I parked on the street in front of the casino, around a corner from the parking lot. No point risking a scene in the lobby, I thought. Neither one of us could pass for drunk. We were both hyper-tense. Extremely menacing vibrations all around us. We hurried through the casino and up the rear escalator.

We made it to the room without meeting anybody—but the key wouldn't open the door. My attorney was struggling desperately with it. "Those bastards have changed the lock on us," he groaned. "They probably searched the room. Jesus, we're finished."

Suddenly the door swung open. We hesitated, then hurried inside. No sign of trouble. "Bolt everything," said my attorney. "Use all chains." He was staring at two Mint Hotel Room keys in his hand. "Where did *this* one come from?" he said, holding up a key with number 1221 on it.

"That's Lacerda's room," I said.

He smiled. "Yeah, that's right. I thought we might need it."

"What for?"

"Let's go up there and blast him out of bed with the fire hose," he said.

"No," I said. "We should leave the poor bastard alone, I get the feeling he's avoiding us for some reason."

"Don't kid yourself," he said. "That Portuguese son of bitch is *dangerous*. He's watching us like a hawk." He squinted at me. "Have you made a deal with him?"

"I talked with him on the phone," I said, "while you were out getting the car washed. He said he was turning in early, so he can get out there to the starting line at dawn."

My attorney was not listening. He uttered an anguished cry and smacked the wall with both hands. "That dirty bastard!" he shouted. "I *knew* it! He got hold of my woman!"

I laughed. "That little blonde groupie with the film crew? You think he sodomized her?"

"That's right—*laugh* about it!" he yelled. "You goddamn honkies are all the same." By this time he'd opened a new bottle of tequila and was quaffing it down. Then he grabbed a grapefruit and sliced it in half with a Gerber Mini-Magnum— a stainless-steel hunting knife with a blade like a fresh-honed straight razor.

"Where'd you get that knife?" I asked.

"Room service sent it up," he said. "I wanted something to cut the limes."

"What limes?"

"They didn't have any," he said. "They don't grow out here in the desert." He sliced the grapefruit into quarters . . . then into eighths . . . then sixteenths . . . then he began slashing aimlessly at the residue. "That dirty toad bastard," he groaned. "I *knew* I should have taken him out when I had the chance. Now he *has* her."

I remembered the girl. We'd had a problem with her on the elevator a few hours earlier: my attorney had made a fool of himself.

"You must be a rider," she'd said. "What class are you in?"

"Class?" he snapped. "What the fuck do you mean?"

"What do you *ride?*" she asked with a quick smile. "We're filming the race for a TV series—maybe we can use you."

"*Use* me?"

Mother of God, I thought. Here it comes. The elevator was crowded with race people: it was taking a long time to get from floor to floor. By the time we'd stopped at Three, he was trembling badly. Five more to go. . . .

"I ride the *big ones!*" he shouted suddenly. "The really *big* fuckers!"

I laughed, trying to de-fuse the scene. "The Vincent Black Shadow," I said. "We're with the factory team."

This brought a murmur of rude dissent from the crowd. "Bullshit," somebody behind me muttered.

"Wait a minute!" my attorney shouted . . . and then to the girl: "Pardon me, lady, but I think there's some kind of ignorant chicken-sucker in this car who needs his face cut open." He plunged his hand into the pocket of his black plastic jacket and turned to face the people crowded into the rear of the elevator. "You cheap honky faggots," he snarled. "Which one of you wants to get cut?"

I was watching the overhead floor-indicator. The door opened at Seven, but nobody moved. Dead silence. The door closed. Up to Eight . . . then open again. Still no sound or movement in the crowded car. Just as the door began to close I stepped off and grabbed his arm, jerking him out just in time. The doors slid shut and the elevator light dinged Nine.

"Quick! Into the room," I said. "Those bastards will have the pigs on us!" We ran around the corner to the room. My attorney was laughing wildly. "Spooked!" he shouted. "Did you

see *that?* They were *spooked*. Like rats in a death-cage!"
Then, as we bolted the door behind us, he stopped laughing.
"God damn," he said. "It's *serious* now. That girl understood.
She fell in love with me."

Now, many hours later, he was convinced that Lacerda—
the so-called photographer—had somehow got his hands on
the girl. "Let's go up there and *castrate* that fucker," he said,
waving his new knife around in quick circles in front of his
teeth. "Did *you* put him onto her?"

"Look," I said, "you'd better put that goddamn blade away
and get your head straight. I have to put the car in the lot." I
was backing slowly towards the door. One of the things you
learn, after years of dealing with drug people, is that *everything* is serious. You can turn your back on a person, but
never turn your back on a drug—especially when it's waving
a razor-sharp hunting knife in your eyes.

"Take a shower," I said. "I'll be back in twenty minutes." I
left quickly, locking the door behind me and taking the key to
Lacerda's room—the one my attorney had stolen earlier. That
poor geek, I thought, as I hurried down the escalator. They
sent him out here on this perfectly reasonable assignment—
just a few photos of motorcycles and dune buggies racing
around the desert—and now he was plunged, without real-
izing it, into the maw of some world beyond his ken. There
was no way he could possibly understand what was happening.

What were we doing out here? What was the meaning of
this trip? Did I actually have a big red convertible out there
on the street? Was I just roaming around these Mint Hotel es-
calators in a drug frenzy of some kind, or had I really come
out here to Las Vegas to work on a *story?*

I reached in my pocket for the room key; "1850," it said. At
least that much was real. So my immediate task was to deal
with the car and get back to that room . . . and then hope-

fully get straight enough to cope with whatever might happen at dawn.

Now off the escalator and into the casino, big crowds still tight around the crap tables. Who *are* these people? These faces! Where do they come from? They look like caricatures of used-car dealers from Dallas. But they're *real*. And, sweet Jesus, there are a hell of a *lot* of them—still screaming around these desert-city crap tables at four-thirty on a Sunday morning. Still humping the American Dream, that vision of the Big Winner somehow emerging from the last-minute pre-dawn chaos of a stale Vegas casino.

Big strike in Silver City. Beat the dealer and go home rich. Why not? I stopped at the Money Wheel and dropped a dollar on Thomas Jefferson—a $2 bill, the straight Freak ticket, thinking as always that some idle instinct bet might carry the whole thing off.

But no. Just another two bucks down the tube. You bastards!

No. Calm down. Learn to *enjoy* losing. The important thing is to cover this story on its own terms; leave the other stuff to *Life* and *Look*—at least for now. On the way down the escalator I saw the *Life* man twisted feverishly into the telegraph booth, chanting his wisdom into the ear of some horny robot in a cubicle on that other coast. Indeed: "LAS VEGAS AT DAWN—The racers are still asleep, the dust is still on the desert, $50,000 in prize money slumbers darkly in the office safe at Del Webb's fabulous Mint Hotel in the bright heart of *Casino Center*. Extreme tension. And our *Life* team is here (as always, with a sturdy police escort. . .)." Pause. "Yes, operator, that word was *police*. What else? This is, after all, a *Life* Special. . . ."

The Red Shark was out on Fremont where I'd left it. I drove around to the garage and checked it in—Dr. Gonzo's car, no problem, and if any of your men fall idle we can use a total wax job before morning. Yes, of course—just bill the room.

• • •

My attorney was in the bathtub when I returned. Submerged in green water—the oily product of some Japanese bath salts he'd picked up in the hotel gift shop, along with a new AM/FM radio plugged into the electric razor socket. Top volume. Some gibberish by a thing called "Three Dog Night," about a frog named Jeremiah who wanted "Joy to the World."

First Lennon, now this, I thought. Next we'll have Glenn Campbell screaming "Where Have All the Flowers Gone?"

Where indeed? No flowers in this town. Only carnivorous plants. I turned the volume down and noticed a hunk of chewed-up white paper beside the radio. My attorney seemed not to notice the sound-change. He was lost in a fog of green steam; only half his head was visible above the water line.

"You ate this?" I asked, holding up the white pad.

He ignored me. But I knew. He would be very difficult to reach for the next six hours. The whole blotter was chewed up.

"You evil son of a bitch," I said. "You better hope there's some thorazine in that bag, because if there's not you're in bad trouble tomorrow."

"Music!" he snarled. "Turn it up. Put that tape on."

"What tape?"

"The new one. It's right there."

I picked up the radio and noticed that it was also a tape recorder—one of those things with a cassette-unit built in. And the tape, *Surrealistic Pillow*, needed only to be flipped over. He had already gone through side one—at a volume that must have been audible in every room within a radius of one hundred yards, walls and all.

" 'White Rabbit,' " he said. "I want a *rising* sound."

"You're doomed," I said. "I'm leaving here in two hours—and then they're going to come up here and beat the mortal shit out of you with big saps. Right there in the tub."

"I dig my own graves," he said. "Green water and the White Rabbit . . . put it on; don't make me use this." His arm lashed out of the water, the hunting knife gripped in his fist.

"Jesus," I muttered. And at that point I figured he was beyond help—lying there in the tub with a head full of acid and the sharpest knife I've ever seen, totally incapable of reason, demanding the White Rabbit. This is it, I thought. I've gone as far as I can with this waterhead. This time it's a suicide trip. This time he wants it. He's ready. . . .

"OK," I said, turning the tape over and pushing the "play" button. "But do me one last favor, will you? Can you give me two hours? That's all I ask—just two hours to sleep before tomorrow. I suspect it's going to be a very difficult day."

"Of course," he said. "I'm your *attorney*. I'll give you all the time you need, at my normal rates: $45 an hour—but you'll be wanting a cushion, so why don't you just lay one of those $100 bills down there beside the radio, and fuck off?"

"How about a check?" I said. "On the Sawtooth National Bank. You won't need any ID to cash it there. They know me."

"Whatever's right," he said, beginning to jerk with the music. The bathroom was like the inside of a huge defective woofer. Heinous vibrations, overwhelming sound. The floor was full of water. I moved the radio as far from the tub as it would go, then I left and closed the door behind me.

Within seconds he was shouting at me. "Help! You bastard! I need help!"

I rushed back inside, thinking he'd sliced off an ear by accident.

But no . . . he was reaching across the bathroom toward the white formica shelf where the radio sat. "I want that fuckin radio," he snarled.

I grabbed it away from his hand. "You fool!" I said. "Get back in that tub! Get away from that goddamn radio!" I shoved it back from his hand. The volume was so far up that it was hard to know what was playing unless you knew *Surrealistic Pillow* almost note for note . . . which I did, at the time, so I knew that "White Rabbit" had finished; the peak had come and gone.

But my attorney, it seemed, had not made it. He wanted more. "Back the tape up!" he yelled. "I need it again!" His eyes were full of craziness now, unable to focus. He seemed on the verge of some awful psychic orgasm . . .

"Let it roll!" he screamed. "Just as high as the fucker can go! And when it comes to that fantastic note where the rabbit bites its own head off, I want you to throw that fuckin radio into the tub with me."

I stared at him, keeping a firm grip on the radio. "Not me," I said finally. "I'd be happy to ram a goddamn 440-volt cattle prod into that tub with you right now, but *not* this radio. It would blast you right through the wall—stone-dead in ten seconds." I laughed. "Shit, they'd make me *explain* it—drag me down to some rotten coroner's inquest and grill me about . . . yes . . . the *exact details*. I don't need that."

"Bullshit!" he screamed. "Just tell them I wanted to get *Higher!*"

I thought for a moment. "Okay," I said finally. "You're right. This is probably the only solution." I picked up the tape/radio—which was still plugged in—and held it over the tub. "Just let me make sure I have it all lined up," I said. "You want me to throw this thing into the tub when 'White Rabbit' peaks—is that it?"

He fell back in the water and smiled gratefully. "Fuck yes," he said. "I was beginning to think I was going to have to go out and get one of the goddamn *maids* to do it."

"Don't worry," I said. "Are you ready?" I hit the "play" button and "White Rabbit" started building again. Almost immediately he began to howl and moan . . . another fast run up that mountain, and thinking, this time, that he would finally get over the top. His eyes were gripped shut and only his head and both kneecaps poked up through the oily green water.

I let the song build while I sorted through the pile of fat ripe grapefruit next to the basin. The biggest one of the lot weighed almost two pounds. I got a good Vida Blue fastball grip on the fucker—and just as "White Rabbit" peaked I lashed it into the tub like a cannonball.

My attorney screamed crazily, thrashing around in the tub like a shark after meat, churning water all over the floor as he struggled to get hold of something.

I jerked the AC cord out of the tape/radio and moved out of the bathroom very quickly . . . the machine kept on playing, but now it was back on its own harmless battery power. I could hear the beat cooling down as I moved across the room to my kitbag and fetched up the Mace can . . . just as my attorney ripped the bathroom door open and started out. His eyes were still unfocused, but he was waving the blade out in front of him like a man who meant to cut something.

"Mace!" I shouted. "You want *this?*" I waved the Mace bomb in front of his watery eyes.

He stopped, "You bastard!" he hissed. "You'd *do* that, wouldn't you?"

I laughed, still waving the bomb at him. "Why worry? You'll *like* it. Shit, there's nothing in the world like a Mace high—forty-five minutes on your knees with the dry heaves, gasping for breath. It'll calm you right down."

He stared in my general direction, trying to focus. "You cheap honky sonofabitch," he muttered. "You'd *do* it, wouldn't you?"

"Why not?" I said. "Hell, just a minute ago you were asking me to *kill* you! And now you want to kill *me!* What I should do, goddamnit, is call the *police!*"

He sagged. "The cops?"

I nodded. "Yeah, there's no choice. I wouldn't dare go to sleep with you wandering around in this condition—with a head full of acid and wanting to slice me up with that goddamn knife."

He rolled his eyes for a moment, then tried to smile. "Who said anything about slicing you up?" he mumbled. "I just wanted to carve a little Z on your forehead—nothing serious." He shrugged and reached for a cigarette on top of the TV set.

I menaced him again with the Mace can. "Get back in that tub," I said. "Eat some reds and try to calm down. Smoke some grass, shoot some smack—shit, do whatever you *have* to do, but let me get some rest."

He shrugged and smiled distractedly, as if everything I'd said made perfect sense. "Hell yes," he said very earnestly. "You really *need* some sleep. You have to *work* tomorrow." He shook his head sadly and turned back toward the bathroom. "God damn! What a bummer." He waved me off. "Try to rest," he said. "Don't let me keep you up."

I nodded, and watched him shuffle back into the bathroom —still holding the blade, but now he seemed unaware of it. The acid had shifted gears on him; the next phase would probably be one of those hellishly intense introspection nightmares. Four hours or so of catatonic despair; but nothing physical, nothing dangerous. I watched the door close behind him, then I quietly slid a heavy, sharp-angled chair up in front of the bathroom knob and put the Mace can beside the alarm clock.

The room was very quiet. I walked over to the TV set and turned it on to a dead channel—white noise at maximum decibels, a fine sound for sleeping, a powerful continuous hiss to drown out everything strange.

8.
"Genius 'Round the World Stands Hand in Hand, and One Shock of Recognition Runs the Whole Circle 'Round"

I live in a quiet place, where any sound at night means something is about to happen: You come awake fast—thinking, what does *that* mean?

Usually nothing. But sometimes . . . it's hard to adjust to a city gig where the night is full of sounds, all of them comfortably routine. Cars, horns, footsteps . . . no way to relax; so drown it all out with the fine white drone of a cross-eyed TV set. Jam the bugger between channels and doze off nicely. . . .

Ignore that nightmare in the bathroom. Just another ugly refugee from the Love Generation, some doom-struck gimp who couldn't handle the pressure. My attorney has never been able to accept the notion—often espoused by reformed drug abusers and especially popular among those on probation—that you can get a lot higher without drugs than with them.

And neither have I, for that matter. But I once lived down the hill from Dr. —— on —— Road,* a former acid guru who later claimed to have made that long jump from chemical frenzy to preternatural consciousness. One fine afternoon in the first rising curl of what would soon become the Great San Francisco Acid Wave I stopped by the Good Doctor's house with the idea of asking him (since he was even then a known drug authority) what sort of advice he might have for a neighbor with a healthy curiosity about LSD.

I parked on the road and lumbered up his gravel driveway,

* Names deleted at insistence of publisher's lawyer.

pausing enroute to wave pleasantly at his wife, who was working in the garden under the brim of a huge seeding hat . . . a good scene, I thought: The old man is inside brewing up one of his fantastic drug-stews, and here we see his woman out in the garden, pruning carrots, or whatever . . . humming while she works, some tune I failed to recognize.

Humming. Yes . . . but it would be nearly ten years before I would recognize that sound for what it was: Like Ginsberg far gone in the Om, —— was trying to *humm me off*. That was no old lady out there in that garden; it was the good doctor *himself*—and his humming was a frantic attempt to block me out of his higher consciousness.

I made several attempts to make myself clear: Just a neighbor come to call and ask the doctor's advice about gobbling some LSD in my shack just down the hill from his house. I did, after all, have weapons. And I liked to shoot them—especially at night, when the great blue flame would leap out, along with all that noise . . . and, yes, the bullets, too. We couldn't ignore that. Big balls of lead/alloy flying around the valley at speeds up to 3700 feet per second. . . .

But I always fired into the nearest hill or, failing that, into blackness. I meant no harm; I just liked the explosions. And I was careful never to kill more than I could eat.

"Kill?" I realized I could never properly explain that word to this creature toiling here in its garden. Had it ever eaten meat? Could it conjugate the verb "hunt?" Did it understand hunger? Or grasp the awful fact that my income averaged around $32 a week that year?

No . . . no hope of communication in this place. I recognized that—but not soon enough to keep the drug doctor from humming me all the way down his driveway and into my car and down the mountain road. Forget LSD, I thought. Look what it's done to *that* poor bastard.

So I stuck with hash and rum for another six months or so, until I moved into San Francisco and found myself one night in a place called "The Fillmore Auditorium." And that was that. One grey lump of sugar and BOOM. In my mind I was right back there in the doctor's garden. Not on the surface, but *underneath*—poking up through that finely cultivated earth like some kind of mutant mushroom. A victim of the Drug Explosion. A natural street freak, just eating whatever came by. I recall one night in the Matrix, when a road-person came in with a big pack on his back, shouting: "Anybody want some L . . . S . . . D . . . ? I got all the makin's right here. All I need is a place to cook."

The manager was on him at once, mumbling, "Cool it, cool it, come on back to the office." I never saw him after that night, but before he was taken away, the road-person distributed his samples. Huge white spansules. I went into the men's room to eat mine. But only *half* at first, I thought. Good thinking, but a hard thing to accomplish under the circumstances. I ate the first half, but spilled the rest on the sleeve of my red Pendleton shirt . . . And then, wondering what to do with it, I saw one of the musicians come in. "What's the trouble," he said.

"Well," I said. "All this white stuff on my sleeve is LSD."

He said nothing: Merely grabbed my arm and began sucking on it. A very gross tableau. I wondered what would happen if some Kingston Trio/young stockbroker type might wander in and catch us in the act. Fuck him, I thought. With a bit of luck, it'll ruin his life—forever thinking that just behind some narrow door in all his favorite bars, men in red Pendleton shirts are getting incredible kicks from things he'll never know. Would he dare to suck a sleeve? Probably not. Play it safe. Pretend you never saw it. . . .

Strange memories on this nervous night in Las Vegas. Five years later? Six? It seems like a lifetime, or at least a Main Era—the kind of peak that never comes again. San Francisco in the middle sixties was a very special time and place to be a part of. Maybe it *meant something*. Maybe not, in the long run . . . but no explanation, no mix of words or music or memories can touch that sense of knowing that you were

there and alive in that corner of time and the world. Whatever it meant. . . .

History is hard to know, because of all the hired bullshit,
but even without being sure of "history" it seems entirely
reasonable to think that every now and then the energy of a
whole generation comes to a head in a long fine flash, for reasons that nobody really understands at the time—and which
never explain, in retrospect, what actually happened.

My central memory of that time seems to hang on one or
five or maybe forty nights—or very early mornings—when I
left the Fillmore half-crazy and, instead of going home,
aimed the big 650 Lightning across the Bay Bridge at a
hundred miles an hour wearing L. L. Bean shorts and a Butte
sheepherder's jacket . . . booming through the Treasure
Island tunnel at the lights of Oakland and Berkeley and Rich-
mond, not quite sure which turn-off to take when I got to the
other end (always stalling at the toll-gate, too twisted to find
neutral while I fumbled for change) . . . but being absolutely
certain that no matter which way I went I would come to a
place where people were just as high and wild as I was: No
doubt at all about that. . . .

There was madness in any direction, at any hour. If not
across the Bay, then up the Golden Gate or down 101 to Los

Altos or La Honda. . . . You could strike sparks anywhere. There was a fantastic universal sense that whatever we were doing was *right*, that we were winning. . . .

And that, I think, was the handle—that sense of inevitable victory over the forces of Old and Evil. Not in any mean or military sense; we didn't need that. Our energy would simply *prevail*. There was no point in fighting—on our side or theirs. We had all the momentum; we were riding the crest of a high and beautiful wave. . . .

So now, less than five years later, you can go up on a steep hill in Las Vegas and look West, and with the right kind of eyes you can almost *see* the high-water mark—that place where the wave finally broke and rolled back.

9.
No Sympathy
for the Devil
... Newsmen Tortured? ...
Flight into Madness

The decision to flee came suddenly. Or maybe not. Maybe I'd planned it all along—subconsciously waiting for the right moment. The bill was a factor, I think. Because I had no money to pay it. And no more of these devilish credit-card/reimbursement deals. Not after dealing with Sidney Zion. They seized my American Express card after that one, and now the bastards are suing me—along with the Diner's Club and the IRS. . . .

And besides, the magazine is legally responsible. My attorney saw to that. We signed nothing. Except those room service tabs. We never knew the total, but—just before we left—my attorney figured we were running somewhere between $29 and $36 per hour, for forty-eight consecutive hours.

"Incredible," I said. "How could it happen?"

But by the time I asked this question, there was nobody around to answer. My attorney was gone.

He must have sensed trouble. On Monday evening he ordered up a set of fine cowhide luggage from room service, then told me he had reservations on the next plane for L.A. We would have to hurry, he said, and on the way to the airport he borrowed $25 for the plane ticket.

I saw him off, then I went back to the airport souvenir counter and spent all the rest of my cash on garbage—complete shit, souvenirs of Las Vegas, plastic fake-Zippo-lighters with a built-in roulette wheel for $6.95, JFK half-dollar money clips for $5 each, tin apes that shook dice for $7.50 . . .

I loaded up on this crap, then carried it out to the Great Red Shark and dumped it all in the back seat . . . and then I stepped into the driver's seat in a very dignified way (the white top was rolled back, as always) and I sat there and turned the radio on and began thinking.

How would Horatio Alger handle this situation?

One toke over the line, sweet Jesus . . . one toke over the line.

Panic. It crept up my spine like the first rising vibes of an acid frenzy. All these horrible realities began to dawn on me: Here I was all alone in Las Vegas with this goddamn incredibly expensive car, completely twisted on drugs, no attorney, no cash, no story for the magazine—and on top of everything else I had a gigantic goddamn hotel bill to deal with. We had ordered everything into that room that human hands could carry—including about six hundred bars of translucent Neutrogena soap.

The whole car was full of it—all over the floors, the seats, the glove compartment. My attorney had worked out some kind of arrangement with the mestizo maids on our floor to have this soap delivered to us—six hundred bars of this weird, transparent shit—and now it was all mine.

Along with this plastic briefcase that I suddenly noticed right beside me on the front seat. I lifted the fucker and knew immediately what was inside. No Samoan attorney in his right mind is going to stomp through the metal-detector gates of a commercial airline with a fat black .357 Magnum on his person. . . .

So he had left it with me, for delivery—if I made it back to L.A. Otherwise . . . well, I could almost hear myself talking to the California Highway Patrol:

What? This weapon? This loaded, unregistered, concealed and maybe hot .357 Magnum? What am I doing with it? Well, you see, officer, I pulled off the road near Mescal Springs—on the advice of my attorney, who subsequently disappeared—and all of a sudden while I was just sort of walking around that deserted waterhole by myself for no reason at all when this little

*fella with a beard came up to me, out of nowhere, and he had
this horrible linoleum knife in one hand and this huge black
pistol in the other hand . . . and he offered to carve a big X on
my forehead, in memory of Lieutenant Calley . . . but when I
told him I was a doctor of journalism his whole attitude
changed. Yes, you probably won't believe this, officer, but he
suddenly hurled that knife into the brackish mescal waters
near our feet, and then he gave me this revolver. Right, he just
shoved it into my hands, butt-first, and then he ran off into the
darkness.*

*So that's why I have this weapon, officer. Can you believe
that?*

No.

But I wasn't about to throw the bastard away, either. A
good .357 is a hard thing to get, these days.

So I figured, well, just get this bugger back to Malibu, and
it's *mine*. My risk—my gun: it made perfect sense. And if
that Samoan pig wanted to argue, if he wanted to come yelling around the house, give him a taste of the bugger about
midway up the femur. Indeed. 158 grains of half-jacketed
lead/alloy, traveling 1500 feet per second, equals about forty
pounds of Samoan hamburger, mixed up with bone splinters.
Why not?

Madness, madness . . . and meanwhile all alone with the
Great Red Shark in the parking lot of the Las Vegas airport.
To hell with this panic. Get a grip. *Maintain.* For the next
twenty-four hours this matter of personal control will be critical. Here I am sitting out here alone on this fucking desert,
in this nest of armed loonies, with a very dangerous carload
of hazards, horrors and liabilities that I *must* get back to L.A.
Because if they nail me out here, I'm doomed. Completely
fucked. No question about that. No future for a doctor of
journalism editing the state pen weekly. Better to get the hell
out of this atavistic state at high speed. Right. But, first—
back to the Mint Hotel and cash a $50 check, then up to the
room and call down for two club sandwiches, two quarts of

milk, a pot of coffee and a fifth of Bacardi Anejo.

Rum will be absolutely necessary to get through this night —to polish these notes, this shameful diary . . . keep the tape machine screaming all night long at top volume: "Allow me to introduce myself . . . I'm a man of wealth and taste."

Sympathy?

Not for me. No mercy for a criminal freak in Las Vegas. This place is like the Army: the shark ethic prevails—eat the wounded. In a closed society where everybody's guilty, the only crime is getting caught. In a world of thieves, the only final sin is stupidity.

It is a weird feeling to sit in a Las Vegas hotel at four in the morning—hunkered down with a notebook and a tape recorder in a $75-a-day suite and a fantastic room service bill, run up in forty-eight hours of total madness—knowing that just as soon as dawn comes up you are going to flee without paying a fucking penny . . . go stomping out through the lobby and call your red convertible down from the garage and stand there waiting for it with a suitcase full of marijuana and illegal weapons . . . trying to look casual, scanning the first morning edition of the Las Vegas *Sun*.

This was the final step. I had taken all the grapefruit and other luggage out to the car a few hours earlier.

Now it was only a matter of slipping the noose: Yes, extremely casual behavior, wild eyes hidden behind these Saigon-mirror sun glasses . . . waiting for the Shark to roll up. Where is it? I gave that evil pimp of a carboy $5, a prime investment right now.

Stay calm, keep reading the paper. The lead story was a screaming blue headline across the top of the page:

Trio Re-arrested
in Beauty's Death

An overdose of heroin was listed as the official cause of death for pretty Diane Hamby, 19, whose body was found stuffed in a refrigerator last week, according to the Clark County Coroner's office. Investigators of the sheriff's homicide team who went to arrest the suspects said that one, a 24-year-old woman, attempted to fling herself through the glass doors of her trailer before being stopped by deputies. Officers said she was apparently hysterical and shouted, 'You'll never take me alive.' But officers handcuffed the woman and she apparently was not injured. . . .

GI DRUG DEATHS CLAIMED

WASHINGTON (AP)—A House Subcommittee report says illegal drugs killed 160 American GI's last year—40 of them in Vietnam . . . Drugs were suspected, it said, in another 56 military deaths in Asia and the Pacific Command . . . It said the heroin problem in Vietnam is increasing in seriousness, primarily because of processing laboratories in Laos, Thailand and Hong Kong. "Drug suppression in Vietnam is almost completely ineffective," the report said, "partially because of an ineffective local police force and partially because some presently unknown corrupt officials in public office are involved in the drug traffic."

To the left of that grim notice was a four-column center-page photo of Washington, D.C., cops fighting with "young anti-war demonstrators who staged a sit-in and blocked the entrance to Selective Service Headquarters."

And next to the photo was a large black headline: TORTURE TALES TOLD IN WAR HEARINGS.

WASHINGTON—Volunteer witnesses told an informal congressional panel yesterday that while serving as military interrogators they routinely used electrical telephone hookups and helicopter drops to torture and kill Vietnamese prisoners. One Army intelligence specialist said the pistol slaying of his Chinese interpreter was defended by a superior who said, "She was just a slope, anyway," meaning she was an Asiatic. . . .

Right underneath that story was a headline saying: FIVE WOUNDED NEAR NYC TENEMENT . . . by an unidentified gunman who fired from the roof of a building, for no apparent reason. This item appeared just above a headline that said: PHARMACY OWNER ARRESTED IN PROBE . . . "a result," the article explained, "of a preliminary investigation (of a Las Vegas pharmacy) showing a shortage of over 100,000 pills considered dangerous drugs. . . ."

Reading the front page made me feel a lot better. Against that heinous background, my crimes were pale and meaningless. I was a relatively respectable citizen—a multiple felon, perhaps, but certainly not dangerous. And when the Great Scorer came to write against my name, that would surely make a difference.

Or would it? I turned to the sports page and saw a small item about Muhammad Ali; his case was before the Supreme Court, the final appeal. He'd been sentenced to five years in prison for *refusing* to kill "slopes."

"I ain't got nothin' against them Viet Congs," he said.

Five years.

10.
Western Union Intervenes: A Warning from Mr. Heem ... New Assignment from the Sports Desk and a Savage Invitation from the Police

Suddenly I felt guilty again. The Shark! Where was it? I tossed the paper aside and began to pace. Losing control. I felt my whole act slipping . . . and then I saw the car, swooping down a ramp in the next-door garage.

Deliverance! I grasped my leather satchel and moved forward to meet my wheels.

"MISTER DUKE!"

The voice came from over my shoulder.

"Mister Duke! We've been looking for you!"

I almost collapsed on the curb. Every cell in my brain and body sagged. No! I thought. I must be hallucinating. There's nobody back there, nobody calling . . . it's a paranoid delusion, amphetamine psychosis . . . just keep walking towards the car, always smiling. . . .

"MISTER DUKE! Wait!"

Well . . . why not? Many fine books have been written in prison. And it's not like I'll be a total stranger up there in Carson City. The warden will recognize me; and the Con Boss—I once interviewed them for *The New York Times*. Along with a lot of other cons, guards, cops and assorted hustlers who got ugly, by mail, when the article never appeared.

Why not? They asked. They wanted their stories told. And

it was hard to explain; in those circles, that everything they told me went into the wastebasket or at least the dead-end file because the lead paragraphs I wrote for that article didn't satisfy some editor three thousand miles away—some nervous drone behind a grey formica desk in the bowels of a journalistic bureaucracy that no con in Nevada will ever understand—and that the article finally died on the vine, as it were, because I refused to rewrite the lead. For reasons of my own . . .

None of which would make much sense in The Yard. But what the hell? Why worry about details? I turned to face my accuser, a small young clerk with a big smile on his face and a yellow envelope in his hand. "I've been calling your room," he said. "Then I saw you standing outside."

I nodded, too tired to resist. By now the Shark was beside me, but I saw no point in even tossing my bag into it. The game was up. They had me.

The clerk was still smiling. "This telegram just came for you," he said. "But actually it *isn't* for you. It's for somebody named Thompson, but it says '*care of* Raoul Duke'; does that make sense?"

I felt dizzy. It was too much to absorb all at once. From freedom, to prison, and then back to freedom again—all in thirty seconds. I staggered backwards and leaned on the car, feeling the white folds of the canvas top beneath my trembling hand. The clerk, still smiling, was poking the telegram at me.

I nodded, barely able to speak. "Yes," I said finally, "it makes sense." I accepted the envelope and tore it open:

URGENT SPEED LETTER

HUNTER S. THOMPSON
  C/O RAOUL DUKE
SOUNDPROOF SUITE 1850
MINT HOTEL LAS VEGAS

CALL ME AT ONCE REPEAT AT ONCE WE HAVE A NEW ASSIGNMENT BEGINNING TOMORROW ALSO VEGAS DONT

LEAVE STOP THE NATIONAL CONFERENCE OF DISTRICT ATTORNEYS INVITES YOU TO THEIR FOUR DAY SEMINAR ON NARCOTICS AND DANGEROUS DRUGS AT DUNES HOTEL STOP ROLLING STONE CALLED THEY WANT 50 THOUSAND WORDS MASSIVE PAYMENT TOTAL EXPENSES INCLUDING ALL SAMPLES STOP WE HAVE RESERVATIONS AT HOTEL FLAMINGO AND WHITE CADDY CONVERTIBLE STOP EVERYTHING IS ARRANGED CALL IMMEDIATELY FOR DETAILS URGENT REPEAT URGENT STOP

DOCTOR GONZO

"Holy shit!" I muttered. "This can't be true!"

"You mean it's not for you?" the clerk asked, suddenly nervous. "I checked the register for this man Thompson. We don't show him, but I thought he was part of your team."

"He is," I said quickly. "Don't worry, I'll get it to him." I tossed my bag into the front seat of the Shark, wanting to leave before my stay of execution ran out. But the clerk was still curious.

"What about Doctor Gonzo?" he said.

I stared at him, giving him a full taste of the mirrors. "He's fine," I said. "But he has a vicious temper. The Doctor handles our finances, makes all our *arrangements*." I slid into the driver's seat and prepared to leave.

The clerk leaned into the car. "What confused us," he said, "was Doctor Gonzo's signature on this telegram from Los Angeles—when we knew he was here in the hotel." He shrugged. "And then to have the telegram addressed to some guest we couldn't account for . . . well, this delay was unavoidable. You understand, I hope. . . ."

I nodded, impatient to flee. "You did the right thing," I said. "Never try to understand a press message. About half the time we use codes—especially with Doctor Gonzo."

He smiled again, but this time it seemed a trifle odd. "Tell me," he said, "when will the doctor be awake?"

I tensed at the wheel. "Awake? What do you mean?"

He seemed uncomfortable. "Well . . . the manager, Mister

Heem, would like to *meet* him." Now his grin was definitely malevolent. "Nothing unusual. Mr. Heem likes to meet all our *large* accounts . . . put them on a personal basis . . . just a chat and a handshake, you understand."

"Of course," I said. "But if I were you I'd leave the doctor alone until after he's eaten breakfast. He's a very crude man."

The clerk nodded warily. "But he *will* be available. . . . Perhaps later this morning?"

I saw what he was getting at. "Look," I said. "That telegram was all scrambled. It was actually *from* Thompson, not *to* him. Western Union must have got the names reversed." I held up the telegram, knowing he'd already read it. "What this *is*," I said, "is a speed message to Doctor Gonzo, upstairs, saying Thompson is on his way out from L.A. with a new assignment—a new work order." I waved him off the car. "See you later," I snapped. "I have to get out to the track."

He backed away as I eased the car into low gear. "There's no hurry," he called after me. "The race is *over*."

"Not for me," I said, tossing him a quick friendly wave.

"Let's have lunch!" he shouted as I turned into the street.

"Righto!" I yelled. And then I was off into traffic. After a few blocks in the wrong direction on Main Street, I doubled back and aimed south, towards L.A. But with all deliberate speed. Keep cool and slow, I thought. Just *drift* to the city limits. . . .

What I needed was a place to get safely off the road, out of sight, and ponder this incredible telegram from my attorney. It was true; I was certain of that. There was a definite valid urgency in the message. The tone was unmistakable. . . .

But I was in no mood or condition to spend another week in Las Vegas. Not *now*. I had pushed my luck about as far as it was going to carry me in this town . . . all the way out to the edge. And now the weasels were closing in; I could *smell* the ugly brutes.

Yes, it was definitely time to leave. My margin had shrunk to nothing.

Now idling along Las Vegas Boulevard at thirty miles an hour, I wanted a place to rest and formalize the decision. It was settled, of course, but I needed a beer or three to seal the bargain and stupefy that one rebellious nerve end that kept vibrating negative. . . .

It would have to be dealt with. Because there *was* an argument, of sorts, for staying on. It was treacherous, stupid and demented in every way—but there was no avoiding the stench of twisted humor that hovered around the idea of a gonzo journalist in the grip of a potentially terminal drug episode being invited to cover the National District Attorneys' Conference on Narcotics and Dangerous Drugs.

There was also a certain bent appeal in the notion of running a savage burn on one Las Vegas Hotel and then—instead of becoming a doomed fugitive on the highway to L.A. —just wheeling across town, trading in the red Chevy convertible for a white Cadillac and checking into *another* Vegas hotel, with press credentials to mingle with a thousand ranking cops from all over America, while they harangued each other about the Drug Problem.

It was dangerous lunacy, but it was also the kind of thing a real connoisseur of edge-work could make an argument for. Where, for instance, was the *last* place the Las Vegas police would look for a drug-addled fraud-fugitive who just ripped off a downtown hotel?

Right. In the middle of a National District Attorneys' Drug Conference at an elegant hotel on the strip. . . . Arriving at Caesar's Palace for the Tom Jones dinner show in a flashing white Coupe de Ville . . . At a cocktail party for narcotics agents and their wives at the Dunes?

Indeed, what better place to hide? For *some* people. But not for me. And certainly not for my attorney—a very conspicuous person. Separately, we might pull it off. But together, no —we would blow it. Too much aggressive chemistry in that mix; the temptation to run a deliberate freakout would be too heavy.

And that of course would finish us. They would show us no mercy. To infiltrate the infiltrators would be to accept the fate of all spies: "As always, if you or any member of your organization is apprehended by the enemy, the Secretary will deny any Knowledge, etc. . . ."

No, it was too much. The line between madness and masochism was already hazy; the time had come to pull back . . . to retire, hunker down, back off and "cop out," as it were. Why not? In every gig like this, there comes a time to either cut your losses or consolidate your winnings—whichever fits.

I drove slowly, looking for a proper place to sit down with an early morning beer and get my head together . . . to plot this unnatural retreat.

11.
Aaawww, Mama,
Can This Really
Be the End? . . .
Down and Out in Vegas,
with Amphetamine
Psychosis Again?

Tuesday, 9:00 A.M. . . . Now, sitting in "Wild Bill's Cafe" on the outskirts of Las Vegas, I saw it all very clearly. There is only one road to L.A.—US Interstate 15, a straight run with no backroads or alternate routes, just a flat-out high-speed burn through Baker and Barstow and Berdoo and then on the Hollywood Freeway straight into frantic oblivion: safety, obscurity, just another freak in the Freak Kingdom.

But in the meantime, for the next five or six hours, I'd be the most conspicuous thing on this goddamn evil road—the only fireapple-red shark convertible between Butte and Tijuana . . . blazing along this desert highway with a half-naked hillbilly mental case at the wheel. Is it better to wear my purple and green Acapulco shirt, or nothing at all?

No way to hide in this monster.

This will not be a happy run. Not even the Sun God wants to watch. He has gone behind a cloud for the first time in three days. No sun at all. The sky is grey and ugly.

Just as I pulled into Wild Bill's back-street, half-hidden parking lot I heard a roar overhead and looked up to see a big silver smoke-trailing DC-8 taking off—about two thousand feet above the highway. Was Lacerda aboard? The man from *Life*? Did they have all the photos they needed? All the facts? Had they fulfilled their responsibilities?

I didn't even know who'd won the race. Maybe nobody. For all I knew, the whole spectacle had been aborted by a terrible riot—an orgy of senseless violence, kicked off by drunken hoodlums who refused to abide by the rules.

I wanted to plug this gap in my knowledge at the earliest opportunity: Pick up the L.A. *Times* and scour the sports section for a Mint 400 story. Get the details. Cover myself. Even on the Run, in the grip of a serious Fear . . .

I knew it was Lacerda in that plane, heading back to New York. He told me last night that he meant to catch the first flight.

So there he goes . . . and here I am, with no attorney, slumped on a red plastic stool in Wild Bill's Tavern, nervously sipping a Budweiser in a bar just coming awake to an early morning rush of pimps and pinball hustlers . . . with a huge Red Shark just outside the door so full of felonies that I'm afraid to even look at it.

But I can't abandon the fucker. The only hope is to somehow get it across three hundred miles of open road between here and Sanctuary. But, sweet Jesus, I am *tired!* I'm scared. I'm crazy. This culture has beaten me down. What the fuck am I *doing* out here? This is not even the story I was supposed to be working on. My agent warned me against it. All signs were negative—especially that evil Dwark with the pink telephone in the Polo Lounge. I should have stayed there . . . anything but *this.*

> *Aaaww . . . Mama*
> *can this really be the end?*

No!

Who played that song? Did I actually *hear* that fucking thing on the jukebox just now? At 9:19 on this filthy grey morning in Wild Bill's Tavern?

No. That was only in my brain, some long-lost echo of a painful dawn in Toronto . . . a long time ago, half-mad in another world. . . . but no different.

HELP!

How many more nights and weird mornings can this terrible shit go on? How long can the body and the brain *tolerate* this doom-struck craziness? This grinding of teeth, this pouring of sweat, this pounding of blood in the temples . . . small blue veins gone amok in front of the ears, sixty and seventy hours with no sleep. . . .

And now that *is* the jukebox! Yes, no doubt about it . . . and why not? A very popular song: "Like a bridge over troubled water . . . I will lay me down . . ."

BOOM. Flashing paranoia. What kind of rat-bastard psychotic would play *that* song—right now, at this moment? Has somebody followed me here? Does the bartendress know who I am? Can she *see* me behind these mirrors?

All bartenders are treacherous, but this one is a surly middle-aged fat woman wearing a muu-muu and Iron Boy overalls . . . probably Wild Bill's woman.

Jesus, bad waves of paranoia, madness, fear and loathing— intolerable vibrations in this place. Get out. Flee . . . and suddenly it occurs to me, some final flash of lunatic shrewdness before the darkness closes in, that my legal/hotel checkout time is not until *noon* . . . which gives me at least two hours of legitimate high-speed driving to get out of this goddamn state before I become a fugitive in the eyes of the law.

Wonderful luck. By the time the alarm goes off, I can be running full bore somewhere between Needles and Death Valley—jamming the accelerator through the floorboard and shaking my fist up at Efrem Zimbalist, Jr., swooping down on me in his FBI/Screaming Eagle helicopter.

*YOU CAN RUN, BUT YOU CAN'T HIDE**

Fuck you, Efrem, that wisdom cuts both ways.

As far as you and the Mint people know, I am still up there in 1850—legally and spiritually if not in the actual flesh— with a "Do Not Disturb" sign hung out to ward off disturbance. The maids won't come near that room as long as that

(* . . . warning to smack dealers seen on a bulletin board in Boulder, Colo.)

sign is on the doorknob. My attorney saw to that—along with 600 bars of Neutrogena soap that I still have to deliver to Malibu. What will the FBI make of that? This Great Red Shark full of Neutrogena soap bars? All completely legal. The maids *gave* us that soap. They'll swear to it . . . Or will they?

Of course not. Those goddamn treacherous maids will swear they were menaced by two heavily-armed crazies who threatened them with a Vincent Black Shadow unless they gave up all their soap.

Jesus Creeping God! Is there a priest in this tavern? I want to confess! I'm a fucking *sinner!* Venal, mortal, carnal, major, minor—however you want to call it, Lord . . . I'm guilty.

But do me this one last favor: just give me five more high-speed hours before you bring the hammer down; just let me get rid of this goddamn car and off of this horrible desert.

Which is not really a hell of a lot to ask, Lord, because the final incredible truth is that I am not guilty. All I did was take your gibberish *seriously* . . . and you see where it got me? My primitive Christian instincts have made me a criminal.

Creeping through the casino at six in the morning with a suitcase full of grapefruit and "Mint 400" T-shirts, I remember telling myself, over and over again, "You are not guilty." This is merely a necessary expedient, to avoid a nasty scene. After all, I made no binding agreements; this is an *institutional debt*—nothing personal. This whole goddamn nightmare is the fault of that stinking, irresponsible *magazine*. Some fool in New York did this to me. It was *his* idea, Lord, not mine.

And now look at me: half-crazy with fear, driving 120 miles an hour across Death Valley in some car I never even wanted. You evil bastard! This is *your* work! You'd better take care of me, Lord . . . because if you don't you're going to have me *on your hands*.

12.
Hellish Speed . . .
Grappling with the
California
Highway Patrol . . . Mano
a Mano
on Highway 61

Tuesday, 12:30 P.M. . . . . Baker, California . . . Into the Ballantine Ale now, zombie drunk and nervous. I recognize this feeling: three or four days of booze, drugs, sun, no sleep and burned out adrenalin reserves—a giddy, quavering sort of high that means the crash is coming. But when? How much longer? This tension is part of the high. The possibility of physical and mental collapse is very real now. . . .

. . . but collapse is out of the question; as a solution or even a cheap alternative, it is *unacceptable*. Indeed. This is the moment of truth, that fine and fateful line between control and disaster—which is also the difference between staying loose and weird on the streets, or spending the next five years of summer mornings playing basketball in the yard at Carson City.

No sympathy for the devil; keep that in mind. Buy the ticket, take the ride . . . and if it occasionally gets a little heavier than what you had in mind, well . . . maybe chalk it off to forced *consciousness expansion:* Tune in, freak out, get beaten. It's all in Kesey's Bible. . . . The Far Side of Reality.

And so much for bad gibberish; not even Kesey can help me now. I have just had two very bad emotional experiences—one with the California Highway Patrol and another with a phantom hitchhiker who may or may not have been who I thought it was—and now, feeling right on the verge of a bad psychotic episode, I am hunkered down with my tape machine in a "beer bar" that is actually the back room of a huge Hardware Barn—all kinds of plows and harnesses and piled-up fertilizer bags, and wondering how it all happened.

About five miles back I had a brush with the CHP. Not stopped or pulled over: nothing routine. I always drive properly. A bit fast, perhaps, but always with consummate skill and a natural feel for the road that even cops recognize. No cop was ever born who isn't a sucker for a finely-executed hi-speed Controlled Drift *all the way around* one of those cloverleaf freeway interchanges.

Few people understand the psychology of dealing with a highway traffic cop. Your normal speeder will panic and immediately pull over to the side when he sees the big red light behind him . . . and then we will start apologizing, begging for mercy.

This is wrong. It arouses contempt in the cop-heart. The thing to do—when you're running along about a hundred or so and you suddenly find a red-flashing CHP-tracker on your trail—what you want to do then is *accelerate*. Never pull over with the first siren-howl. Mash it down and make the bastard chase you at speeds up to 120 all the way to the next exit. He will follow. But he won't know what to make of your blinker-signal that says you're about to turn right.

This is to let him know you're looking for a proper place to pull off and talk . . . keep signaling and hope for an off-ramp, one of those uphill side-loops with a sign saying "Max Speed 25" . . . and the trick, at this point, is to suddenly leave the freeway and take him into the chute at no less than a hundred miles an hour.

He will lock his brakes about the same time you lock yours, but it will take him a moment to realize that he's about to make a 180-degree turn at this speed . . . but you will be *ready* for it, braced for the Gs and the fast heel-toe work, and with any luck at all you will have come to a complete stop off the road at the top of the turn and be standing beside your automobile by the time he catches up.

He will not be reasonable at first . . . but no matter. Let him calm down. He will want the first word. Let him have it. His brain will be in a turmoil: he may begin jabbering, or even pull his gun. Let him unwind; keep smiling. The idea is to show him that you were always in total control of yourself and your vehicle—while *he* lost control of everything.

It helps to have a police/press badge in your wallet when he calms down enough to ask for your license. I had one of these—but I also had a can of Budweiser in my hand. Until that moment, I was unaware that I was holding it. I had felt totally on top of the situation . . . but when I looked down and saw that little red/silver evidence-bomb in my hand, I knew I was fucked. . . .

Speeding is one thing, but Drunk Driving is quite another. The cop seemed to grasp this—that I'd blown my whole performance by forgetting the beer can. His face relaxed, he actually smiled. And so did I. Because we both understood, in that moment, that my Thunder Road, moonshine-bomber act had been totally wasted: We had both scared the piss out of ourselves for nothing at all—because the fact of this beer can in my hand made any argument about "speeding" beside the point.

He accepted my open wallet with his left hand, then extended his right toward the beer can. "Could I have that?" he asked.

"Why not?" I said.

He took it, then held it up between us and poured the beer out on the road.

I smiled, no longer caring. "It was getting warm, anyway," I said. Just behind me, on the back seat of the Shark, I could see about ten cans of hot Budweiser and a dozen or so grapefruits. I'd forgotten all about them, but now they were too obvious for either of us to ignore. My guilt was so gross and overwhelming that explanations were useless.

The cop understood this. "You realize," he said, "that it's a crime to . . ."

"Yeah," I said. "I know. I'm guilty. I understand that. I knew it was a crime, but I did it anyway." I shrugged. "Shit, why argue? I'm a fucking criminal."

"That's a strange attitude," he said.

I stared at him, seeing for the first time that I was dealing with a bright-eyed young sport, around thirty, who was apparently enjoying his work.

"You know," he said, "I get the feeling you could use a nap." He nodded. "There's a rest area up ahead. Why don't you pull over and sleep a few hours?"

I instantly understood what he was telling me, but for some insane reason I shook my head. "A nap won't help," I said. "I've been awake for too long—three or four nights; I can't even remember. If I go to sleep now, I'm dead for twenty hours."

Good God, I thought. What have I said? This bastard is trying to be human; he could take me straight to jail, but he's telling me to take a fucking nap. For Christ sake, *agree* with him: Yes, officer, *of course* I'll take advantage of that rest area. And I can't tell you how *grateful* I am for this break you want to give me. . . .

But no . . . here I was insisting that if he turned me loose I would boom straight ahead for L.A. which was true, but why *say* it? Why *push* him? This is not the right time for a showdown. This is Death Valley . . . get a grip on yourself.

Of course. Get a grip. "Look," I said. "I've been out in Las Vegas covering the Mint 400." I pointed to the "VIP Parking" sticker on the windshield. "Incredible," I said. "All those bikes and dune buggies crashing around the desert for two days. Have you seen it?"

He smiled, shaking his head with a sort of melancholy understanding. I could see him thinking. Was I dangerous? Was he ready for the vicious, time-consuming scene that was bound to come if he took me under arrest? How many off-duty hours would he have to spend hanging around the courthouse, waiting to testify against me? And what kind of monster lawyer would I bring in to work out on him?

I knew, but how could he?

"OK," he said. "Here's how it is. What goes into my book, as of noon, is that I apprehended you . . . for driving too fast for conditions, and advised you . . . with this written warning"—he handed it to me—"to proceed no further than the next rest area . . . your stated destination, right? Where you plan to take a long nap . . ." He hung his ticket-pad back on his belt. "Do I make myself clear?" he asked as he turned away.

I shrugged. "How far is Baker? I was hoping to stop there for lunch."

"That's not in my jurisdiction," he said. "The city limits are two-point-two miles beyond the rest area. Can you make it that far?" He grinned heavily.

"I'll try," I said. "I've been wanting to go to Baker for a long time. I've heard a lot about it."

"Excellent seafood," he said. "With a mind like yours, you'll probably want the land-crab. Try the Majestic Diner."

I shook my head and got back in the car, feeling raped. The pig had done me on all fronts, and now he was going off to chuckle about it—on the west edge of town, waiting for me to make a run for L.A.

I got back on the freeway and drove past the rest area to the intersection where I had to turn right into Baker. As I approached the turn I saw . . . Great Jesus, it's him, the hitchhiker, the same kid we'd picked up and terrified on the way out to Vegas. Our eyes met as I slowed down to make the corner. I was tempted to wave, but when I saw him drop his thumb I thought, no, this is not the time . . . God only knows what that kid said about us when he finally got back to town.

Acceleration. Get out of sight at once. How could I be sure he'd recognized me? But the car was hard to miss. And why else would he back away from the road?

Suddenly I had two *personal* enemies in this godforsaken town. The CHP cop would bust me for sure if I tried to go on through to L.A., and this goddamn rotten kid/hitchhiker would have me hunted down like a beast if I stayed. (Holy Jesus, Sam! There he is! That guy the kid *told* us about! He's back!)

Either way, it was horrible—and if these righteous outback predators ever got their stories together . . . and they would; it was inevitable in a town this small . . . that would cash my check all around. I'd be lucky to leave town alive. A ball of tar and feathers dragged onto the prison bus by angry natives. . . .

This was it: The crisis. I raced through town and found a telephone booth on the northern outskirts, between a Sinclair station and . . . yes . . . the Majestic Diner. I placed an emergency collect call to my attorney in Malibu. He answered at once.

"They've nailed me!" I shouted. "I'm trapped in some stinking desert crossroads called Baker. I don't have much time. The fuckers are closing in."

"Who?" he said. "You sound a little paranoid."

"You bastard!" I screamed. "First I got run down by the CHP, then that *kid* spotted me! I need a lawyer *immediately!*"

"What are you doing in Baker?" he said. "Didn't you get my telegram?"

"What? Fuck telegrams. I'm in *trouble*."

"You're supposed to be in Vegas," he said. "We have a suite at the Flamingo. I was just about to leave for the airport. . . ."

I slumped in the booth. It was too horrible. Here I was calling my attorney in a moment of terrible crisis and the fool was deranged on drugs—a goddamn vegetable! "You worthless bastard," I groaned. "I'll cripple your ass for this! All that shit in the car is *yours!* You understand that? When I finish testifying out here, you'll be *disbarred!*"

"You brainless scumbag!" he shouted. "I sent you a telegram! You're supposed to be covering the National District Attorneys' Conference! I made all the reservations . . .

rented a white Cadillac convertible . . . the whole thing is *arranged!* What the hell are you doing out there in the middle of the fucking desert?"

Suddenly I remembered. Yes. The telegram. It was all very clear. My mind became calm. I saw the whole thing in a flash. "Never mind," I said. "It's all a big joke. I'm actually sitting beside the pool at the Flamingo. I'm talking from a portable phone. Some dwarf brought it out from the casino. I have total credit! Can you grasp that?" I was breathing heavily, feeling crazy, sweating into the phone.

"Don't come anywhere near this place!" I shouted. "Foreigners aren't welcome here."

I hung up and strolled out to the car. Well, I thought. This is how the world works. All energy flows according to the whims of the Great Magnet. What a fool I was to defy him. He knew. He knew all along. It was He who sacked me in Baker. I had run far enough, so He nailed me . . . closing off all my escape routes, hassling me first with the CHP and then with this filthy phantom hitchhiker . . . plunging me into fear and confusion.

Never cross the Great Magnet. I understood this now . . . and with understanding came a sense of almost terminal relief. Yes, I would go back to Vegas. Slip the Kid and confound the CHP by moving *East* again, instead of West. This would be the shrewdest move of my life. Back to Vegas and sign up for the Drugs and Narcotics conference; me and a thousand pigs. Why not? Move confidently into their midst. Register at the Flamingo and have the White Caddy sent over at once. Do it right; remember Horatio Alger. . . .

I looked across the road and saw a huge red sign that said BEER. Wonderful. I left the Shark by the phone booth and reeled across the highway into the Hardware Barn. A Jew loomed up from behind a pile of sprockets and asked me what I wanted.

"Ballantine Ale," I said . . . a very mystic long shot, unknown between Newark and San Francisco.

He served it up, ice-cold.

I relaxed. Suddenly everything was going right; I was finally getting the breaks.

The bartender approached me with a smile. "Where ya headin', young man?"

"Las Vegas," I said.

He smiled. "A great town, that Vegas. You'll have good luck there; you're the type."

"I know," I said. "I'm a Triple Scorpio."

He seemed pleased. "That's a fine combination," he said. "You can't lose."

I laughed. "Don't worry," I said. "I'm actually the district attorney from Ignoto county. Just another good American like yourself."

His smile disappeared. Did he understand? I couldn't be sure. But that hardly mattered now. I was going back to Vegas. I had no choice.

PART TWO

Ralph STEADman

About 20 miles east of Baker I stopped to check the drug bag. The sun was hot and I felt like killing something. Anything. Even a big lizard. Drill the fucker. I got my attorney's .357 Magnum out of the trunk and spun the cylinder. It was loaded all the way around: Long, nasty little slugs—158 grains with a fine flat trajectory and painted aztec gold on the tips. I blew the horn a few times, hoping to call up an iguana. Get the buggers moving. They were out there, I knew, in that goddamn sea of cactus—hunkered down, barely breathing, and every one of the stinking little bastards was loaded with deadly poison.

Three fast explosions knocked me off balance. Three deafening, double-action blasts from the .357 in my right hand. Jesus! Firing at nothing, for no reason at all. Bad craziness. I tossed the gun into the front seat of the Shark and stared nervously at the highway. No cars either way; the road was empty for two or three miles in both directions.

Fine luck. It would not *do* to be found in the desert under these circumstances: firing wildly into the cactus from a car full of drugs. And especially not now, on the lam from the Highway Patrol.

Awkward questions would arise: "Well now, Mister . . . ah . . . Duke; you understand, of course, that it *is* illegal to discharge a firearm of any kind while standing on a federal highway?"

"What? Even in self-defense? This goddamn gun has a *hair trigger*, officer. The truth is I only meant to fire *once*—just to scare the little bastards."

A heavy stare, then speaking very slowly: "Are you saying, Mister Duke . . . that you were *attacked* out here?"

"Well . . . no . . . not literally attacked, officer, but seriously *menaced*. I stopped to piss, and the minute I stepped out of the car these filthy little bags of poison were all around me. They moved like *greased lightning!*"

Would this story hold up?

No. They would place me under arrest, then routinely search the car—and when that happened all kinds of savage hell would break loose. They would never believe all these drugs were necessary to my work; that in truth I was a professional journalist on my way to Las Vegas to cover the National District Attorneys' Conference on Narcotics and Dangerous Drugs.

"Just samples, officer. I got this stuff off a road man for the Neo-American Church back in Barstow. He started acting funny, so I worked him over."

Would they buy this?

No. They would lock me in some hellhole of a jail and beat me on the kidneys with big branches—causing me to piss blood for years to come. . . .

Luckily, nobody bothered me while I ran a quick inventory on the kit-bag. The stash was a hopeless mess, all churned together and half-crushed. Some of the mescaline pellets had disintegrated into a reddish-brown powder, but I counted about thirty-five or forty still intact. My attorney had eaten all the reds, but there was quite a bit of speed left . . . no more grass, the coke bottle was empty, one acid blotter, a nice brown lump of opium hash and six loose amyls . . . Not enough for anything serious, but a careful rationing of the mescaline would probably get us through the four-day Drug Conference.

On the outskirts of Vegas I stopped at a neighborhood pharmacy and bought two quarts of Gold tequila, two fifths of Chivas Regal and a pint of ether. I was tempted to ask for some amyls. My angina pectoris was starting to act up. But the druggist had the eyes of a mean Baptist hysteric. I told him I needed the ether to get the tape off my legs, but by that time he'd already rung the stuff up and bagged it. He didn't give a fuck about ether.

I wondered what he would say if I asked him for $22 worth of Romilar and a tank of nitrous oxide. Probably he would have sold it to me. Why not? Free enterprise. . . . Give the public what it needs—especially this bad-sweaty, nervous-talkin' fella with tape all over his legs and this terrible cough, along with angina pectoris and these godawful Aneuristic flashes every time he gets in the sun. *I mean this fella was in bad shape, officer. How the hell was I to know he'd walk straight out to his car and start abusing those drugs?*

How indeed? I lingered a moment at the magazine rack, then got a grip on myself and hurried outside to the car. The idea of going completely crazy on laughing gas in the middle of a DAs' drug conference had a definite warped appeal. But not on the *first day*, I thought. Save that for later. No point getting busted and committed before the conference even starts.

I stole a Review-Journal from a rack in the parking lot, but I threw it away after reading a story on page one:

Surgery Uncertain
After Eyes Removed

BALTIMORE (UPI)—Doctors said Friday they were uncertain whether surgery would succeed in restoring the eyesight of a young man who pulled out his eyes while suffering the effects of a drug overdose in a jail cell.

Charles Innes, Jr., 25, underwent surgery late Thursday at Maryland General Hospital but doctors said it may be weeks before they could determine the outcome.

A statement issued by the hospital reported that Innes "had no light perception in either eye prior to surgery and the possibility he will ever have light perception is extremely poor."

Innes, son of a prominent Massachusetts Republican, was found in a jail cell Thursday by a turnkey who said Innes had pulled out his eyeballs.

Innes was arrested Wednesday night while walking nude through a neighborhood near where he lived. He was examined at Mercy Hospital and then placed in a jail cell. Police and one of Innes' friends said he had taken an overdose of animal tranquilizer.

Police reported the drug was PCP, a Parke-Davis product not sold for human medical purposes since 1963. However, a spokesman for Parke-Davis said he thought the drug might be available on the black market.

Taken alone, the spokesman said PCP effects would not last more than 12 to 14 hours. However, the effects of PCP combined with an hallucinogen such as LSD were not known.

Innes told a neighbor last Saturday, the day after he first took the drug, that his eyes were bothering him and that he could not read.

Wednesday night police said Innes seemed to be in a deeply depressed state and so impervious to pain that he did not scream when he pulled out his eyes.

2.
Another Day, Another Convertible... & Another Hotel Full of Cops

The first order of business was to get rid of the Red Shark. It was too obvious. Too many people might recognize it, especially the Vegas police; although as far as they knew, the thing was already back home in L.A. It was last seen running at top speed across Death Valley on Interstate 15. Stopped and warned in Baker by the CHP . . . then suddenly disappeared. . . .

The last place they would look for it, I felt, was in a rental-car lot at the airport. I had to go out there anyway, to meet my attorney. He would be arriving from L.A. in the late afternoon.

I drove very quietly on the freeway, gripping my normal instinct for bursts of acceleration and sudden lane changes— trying to remain inconspicuous—and when I got there I parked the Shark between two old Air Force buses in a "utility lot" about half a mile from the terminal. Very tall buses. Make it hard as possible for the fuckers. A little walking never hurt anybody.

By the time I got to the terminal I was pouring sweat. But nothing abnormal. I tend to sweat heavily in warm climates. My clothes are soaking wet from dawn to dusk. This worried me at first, but when I went to a doctor and described my normal daily intake of booze, drugs and poison he told me to come back when the sweating *stopped*. That would be the danger point, he said—a sign that my body's desperately overworked flushing mechanism had broken down completely. "I have great faith in the natural processes," he said. "But in your case . . . well . . . I find no precedent. We'll just have to wait and see, then work with what's left."

I spent about two hours in the bar, drinking Bloody Marys for the V-8 nutritional content and watching the flights from L.A. I'd eaten nothing but grapefruit for about twenty hours and my head was adrift from its moorings.

You better watch yourself, I thought. There *are* limits to what the human body can endure. You don't want to break down and start bleeding from the ears right here in the terminal. Not in this town. In Las Vegas they *kill* the weak and deranged.

I realized this, and kept quiet even when I felt symptoms of a terminal blood-sweat coming on. But this passed. I saw the cocktail waitress getting nervous, so I forced myself to get up and walk stiffly out of the bar. No sign of my attorney.

Down to the VIP car-rental booth, where I traded the Red Shark in for a White Cadillac Convertible. "This goddamn Chevy has caused me a lot of trouble," I told them. "I get the feeling that people are putting me down—especially in gas stations, when I have to get out and open the hood *manually.*"

"Well . . . of *course*," said the man behind the desk. "What you need, I think, is one of our Mercedes 600 Towne-Cruiser Specials, with air-conditioning. You can even carry your own fuel, if you want; we make that available. . . ."

"Do I look like a goddamn Nazi?" I said. "I'll have a natural *American* car, or nothing at all!"

They called up the white Coupe de Ville at once. Everything was automatic. I could sit in the red-leather driver's seat and make every inch of the car *jump*, by touching the proper buttons. It was a wonderful machine: Ten grand worth of gimmicks and high-priced Special Effects. The rear-windows leaped up with a touch, like frogs in a dynamite pond. The white canvas top ran up and down like a roller-coaster. The dashboard was full of esoteric lights & dials & meters that I would never understand—but there was no doubt in my mind that I was into a *superior machine*.

The Caddy wouldn't get off the line quite as fast as the Red Shark, but once it got rolling—around eighty—it was pure smooth hell . . . all that elegant, upholstered weight lashing across the desert was like rolling through midnight on the old California Zephyr.

I handled the whole transaction with a credit card that I later learned was "canceled"—completely bogus. But the Big Computer hadn't mixed me yet, so I was still a fat gold credit risk.

Later, looking back on this transaction, I *knew* the conversation that had almost certainly ensued:

"Hello. This is VIP car-rentals in Las Vegas. We're calling to check on Number 875-045-616-B. Just a routine credit check, nothing urgent. . . ."

(Long pause at the other end. Then:) "Holy shit!"

"What?"

"Pardon me. . . . Yes, we have that number. It's been placed on emergency redline status. Call the police at once and don't let him out of your sight!"

(Another long pause) "Well . . . ah . . . you see, that number is not on *our* current Red List, and . . . ah . . . Number 875-045-616-B just left our lot in a new Cadillac convertible."

"No!"

"Yes. He's long gone; totally insured."

"Where?"

"I think he said St. Louis. Yes, that's what the card says. Raoul Duke, leftfielder & batting champion of the St. Louis Browns. Five days at $25 per, plus twenty-five cents a mile. His card was valid, so of course we had no choice. . . ."

This is true. The car rental agency had no legal reason to hassle me, since my card was technically valid. During the next four days I drove that car all over Las Vegas—even passing the VIP agency's main office on Paradise Boulevard several times—and at no time was I bothered by any show of rudeness.

This is one of the hallmarks of Vegas hospitality. The only

bedrock rule is Don't Burn the Locals. Beyond that, nobody cares. They would rather not know. If Charlie Manson checked into the Sahara tomorrow morning, nobody would hassle him as long as he tipped big.

I drove straight to the hotel after renting the car. There was still no sign of my attorney, so I decided to check in on my own—if only to get off the street and avoid a public breakdown. I left the Whale in a VIP parking slot and shambled self-consciously into the lobby with one small leather bag—a hand-crafted, custom-built satchel that had just been made for me by a leathersmith friend in Boulder.

Our room was at the Flamingo, in the nerve-center of the Strip: right across the street from Caesar's Palace and the Dunes—site of the Drug Conference. The bulk of the conferees were staying at the Dunes, but those of us who signed up fashionably late were assigned to the Flamingo.

The place was full of cops. I saw this at a glance. Most of them were just standing around trying to look casual, all dressed exactly alike in their cut-rate Vegas casuals: plaid bermuda shorts, Arnie Palmer golf shirts and hairless white legs tapering down to rubberized "beach sandals." It was a terrifying scene to walk into—a super stakeout of some kind. If I hadn't known about the conference my mind might have snapped. You got the impression that somebody was going to be gunned down in a blazing crossfire at any moment— maybe the entire Manson Family.

My arrival was badly timed. Most of the national DAs and other cop-types had already checked in. These were the people who now stood around the lobby and stared grimly at newcomers. What appeared to be the Final Stakeout was only about two hundred vacationing cops with nothing better to do. They didn't even notice each other.

I waded up to the desk and got in line. The man in front of me was a Police Chief from some small town in Michigan. His Agnew-style wife was standing about three feet off to his right while he argued with the desk clerk: "Look, fella—I *told* you I have a postcard here that says I have *reservations* in this hotel. Hell, I'm with the District Attorneys' Conference! I've already *paid* for my room."

"Sorry, sir. You're on the 'late list.' Your reservations were transferred to the . . . ah . . . Moonlight Motel, which is out on Paradise Boulevard and actually a very fine place of lodging and only sixteen blocks from here, with its own pool and. . . ."

"You dirty little faggot! Call the manager! I'm tired of listening to this dogshit!"

The manager appeared and offered to call a cab. This was obviously the second or maybe even the third act in a cruel drama that had begun long before I showed up. The police chief's wife was crying; the gaggle of friends that he'd mustered for support were too embarrassed to back him up—even now, in this showdown at the desk, with this angry little cop firing his best and final shot. They knew he was beaten; he was going against the RULES, and the people hired to enforce those rules said "no vacancy."

After ten minutes of standing in line behind this noisy little asshole and his friends, I felt the bile rising. Where did this *cop*—of all people—get the nerve to argue with anybody in terms of Right & Reason? I had *been there* with these fuzzy little shitheads—and so, I sensed, had the desk clerk. He had the air of a man who'd been fucked around, in his time, by a fairly good cross-section of mean-tempered rule-crazy cops. . . .

So now he was just giving their argument back to them: It doesn't matter who's right or wrong, man . . . or who's paid his bill & who hasn't . . . what matters right now is that for the first time in my life I can work out on a pig: "Fuck you, *officer*, I'm in charge here, and I'm telling you we don't have room for you."

I was enjoying this whipsong, but after a while I felt dizzy, bad nervous, and my impatience got the better of my amusement. So I stepped around the Pig and spoke directly to the desk clerk. "Say," I said, "I hate to interrupt, but I have a reservation and I wonder if maybe I could just sort of slide through and get out of your way." I smiled, letting him know I'd been digging his snake-bully act on the cop party that was now standing there, psychologically off-balance and staring at me like I was some kind of water-rat crawling up to the desk.

I looked pretty bad: wearing old Levis and white Chuck Taylor All-Star basketball sneakers . . . and my ten-peso Acapulco shirt had long since come apart at the shoulder seams from all that road-wind. My beard was about three days old, bordering on standard wino trim, and my eyes were totally hidden by Sandy Bull's Saigon-mirror shades.

But my voice had the tone of a man who *knows* he has a reservation. I was gambling on my attorney's foresight . . . but I couldn't pass a chance to put the horn into a cop:

. . . and I was right. The reservation was in my attorney's name. The desk-clerk hit his bell to summon the bag-boy. "This is all I have with me, right now," I said. "The rest is out there in that white Cadillac convertible." I pointed to the car that we could all see parked just outside the front door. "Can you have somebody drive it around to the room?"

The desk-clerk was friendly. "Don't worry about a thing, sir. Just enjoy your stay here—and if there's anything you need, just call the desk."

I nodded and smiled, half-watching the stunned reaction of the cop-crowd right next to me. They were stupid with shock. Here they were arguing with every piece of leverage they could command, for a room they'd already *paid for*—and suddenly their whole act gets side-swiped by some crusty drifter who looks like something out of an upper-Michigan hobo jungle. And he checks in with a handful of *credit cards!* Jesus! What's happening in this world?

3.
Savage Lucy...
'Teeth Like Baseballs,
Eyes Like Jellied Fire'

I gave my bag to the boy who scurried up, and told him to bring a quart of Wild Turkey and two fifths of Bacardi Anejo with a night's worth of ice.

Our room was in one of the farthest wings of the Flamingo. The place is far more than a hotel: It is a sort of huge underfinanced Playboy Club in the middle of the desert. Something like nine separate wings, with interconnecting causeways and pools—a vast complex, sliced up by a maze of car-ramps and driveways. It took me about twenty minutes to wander from the desk to the distant wing we'd been assigned to.

My idea was to get into the room, accept the booze and baggage delivery, then smoke my last big chunk of Singapore Grey while watching Walter Cronkite and waiting for my attorney to arrive. I needed this break, this moment of peace and refuge, before we did the Drug Conference. It was going to be quite a different thing from the Mint 400. That had been an *observer* gig, but this one would need *participation*—and a very special stance: At the Mint 400 we were dealing with an essentially simpatico crowd, and if our behavior was gross and outrageous . . . well, it was only a matter of degree.

But this time our very *presence* would be an outrage. We would be attending the conference under false pretenses and dealing, from the start, with a crowd that was convened for the stated purpose of putting people like us in jail. We *were* the Menace—not in disguise, but stone-obvious drug abusers, with a flagrantly cranked-up act that we intended to push all the way to the limit . . . not to prove any final, sociological point, and not even as a conscious mockery: It was mainly a matter of life-style, a sense of obligation and even duty. If the Pigs were gathering in Vegas for a top-level Drug Conference, we felt the drug culture should be represented.

Beyond that, I'd been out of my head for so long now, that a gig like this seemed perfectly logical. Considering the circumstances, I felt totally meshed with my karma.

Or at least I was feeling this way until I got to the big grey door that opened into Mini-Suite 1150 in the Far Wing. I rammed my key into the knob-lock and swung the door open, thinking, "Ah, home at last!" . . . but the door *hit* something, which I recognized at once as a human form: a girl of indeterminate age with the face and form of a Pit Bull. She was wearing a shapeless blue smock and her eyes were angry . . .

Somehow I knew that I had the right room. I wanted to think otherwise, but the vibes were hopelessly right . . . and she seemed to know, too, because she made no move to stop me when I moved past her and into the suite. I tossed my leather satchel on one of the beds and looked around for what I knew I would see . . . my attorney . . . stark naked, standing in the bathroom door with a drug-addled grin on his face.

"You degenerate pig," I muttered.

"It can't be helped," he said, nodding at the bulldog girl. "This is Lucy." He laughed distractedly. "You know—like Lucy in the sky with diamonds . . ."

I nodded to Lucy, who was eyeing me with definite venom. I was clearly some kind of enemy, some ugly intrusion on her scene . . . and it was clear from the way she moved around the room, very quick and tense on her feet, that she was sizing me up. She was ready for violence, there was not much doubt about that. Even my attorney picked up on it.

"Lucy!" he snapped. "Lucy! Be cool, goddamnit! Remember what happened at the airport . . . no more of that, OK?" He smiled nervously at her. She had the look of a beast that had just been tossed into a sawdust pit to fight for its life . . .

"Lucy . . . this is my *client;* this is Mister Duke, the famous journalist. He's *paying* for this suite, Lucy. He's on *our* side."

She said nothing. I could see that she was not entirely in control of herself. Huge shoulders on the woman, and a chin like Oscar Bonavena. I sat down on the bed and casually reached into my satchel for the Mace can . . . and when I felt my tumb on the Shoot button I was tempted to jerk the thing out and soak her down on general principles, I desperately needed *peace*, rest, sanctuary. The last thing I wanted was a fight to the finish, in my own hotel room, with some kind of drug-crazed hormone monster.

My attorney seemed to understand this; he knew why my hand was in the satchel.

"No!" he shouted. "Not here! We'll have to move out!"

I shrugged. He was twisted. I could see that. And so was Lucy. Her eyes were feverish and crazy. She was staring at me like I was something that would have to be rendered helpless before life could get back to whatever she considered normal.

My attorney idled over and put his arm around her shoulders. "Mister Duke is my *friend*," he said gently. "He loves artists. Let's show him your paintings."

For the first time, I noticed that the room was full of artwork—maybe forty or fifty portraits, some in oil, some charcoal, all more or less the same size and all the same face. They were propped up on every flat surface. The face was vaguely familiar, but I couldn't get a fix on it. It was a girl with a broad mouth, a big nose and extremely glittering eyes—a demoniacally sensual face; the kind of over-stated, embarrassingly dramatic renderings that you find in the bedrooms of young female art students who get hung up on horses.

"Lucy paints portraits of Barbra Streisand," my attorney explained. "She's an artist up in Montana . . ." He turned to the girl. "What's that town where you live?"

She stared at him, then at me, then back at my attorney again. Then finally she said, "Kalispel. Way up north. I drew these from TV."

My attorney nodded eagerly. "Fantastic," he said. "She came all the way down here just to give all these portraits to Barbra. We're going over to the Americana Hotel tonight, and meet her backstage."

Lucy smiled bashfully. There was no more hostility in her. I dropped the Mace can and stood up. We obviously had a serious case on our hands. I hadn't counted on this: Finding my attorney whacked on acid and locked into some kind of preternatural courtship.

"Well," I said, "I guess they've brought the car around by now. Let's get the stuff out of the trunk."

He nodded eagerly. "Absolutely, let's get the stuff." He smiled at Lucy. "We'll be right back. Don't answer the phone if it rings."

She grinned and made the one-finger Jesus freak sign. "God bless," she said.

My attorney pulled on a pair of elephant-leg pants and a glaze-black shirt, then we hurried out of the room. I could see he was having trouble getting oriented, but I refused to humor him.

"Well . . ." I said. "What are your plans?"

"Plans?"

We were waiting for the elevator.

"Lucy," I said.

He shook his head, struggling to focus on the question. "Shit," he said finally. "I met her on the plane and I had all that acid." He shrugged. "You know, those little blue barrels. Jesus, she's a *religious* freak. She's running away from home for something like the fifth time in six months. It's terrible. I gave her that cap before I realized . . . shit, she's never even had a *drink!*"

"Well," I said, "it'll probably work out. We can keep her loaded and peddle her ass at the drug convention."

He stared at me.

"She's perfect for this gig," I said. "These cops will go fifty bucks a head to beat her into submission and then gang-fuck her. We can set her up in one of these back-street motels, hang pictures of Jesus all over the room, then turn these pigs loose on her . . . Hell, she's strong; she'll hold her own."

His face was twitching badly. We were in the elevator now, descending into the lobby. "Jesus Christ," he muttered. "I knew you were sick, but I never expected to hear you actually *say* that kind of stuff."

He seemed stunned.

I laughed. "It's straight economics. This girl is a *god-send!*" I fixed him with a natural Bogart smile, all teeth . . . "Shit, we're almost broke! And suddenly you pick up some muscle-bound loony who can make us a grand a day."

"No!" he shouted. "Stop *talking* like that!" The elevator door opened and we walked toward the parking lot.

"I figure she can do about four at a time," I said. "Christ, if we keep her full of acid that's more like *two grand* a day; maybe *three*."

"You filthy bastard!" he sputtered. "I should cave your fucking head in!" He was squinting at me, shielding his eyes from the sun. I spotted the Whale about fifty feet from the door. "There it is," I said. "Not a bad looking car, for a pimp . . ."

He groaned. His face reflected the struggle that I knew he was having, in his brain, with sporadic acid rushes: Bad waves of painful intensity, followed by total confusion. When I opened the trunk of the Whale to get the bags, he got angry. "What the hell are you *doing?*" he snapped. "This isn't Lucy's car."

"I know," I said. "It's mine. This is *my* luggage."

"The fuck it is!" he shouted. "Just because I'm a goddamn lawyer doesn't mean you can walk around stealing stuff right in front of me!" He backed away. "What the hell is *wrong* with you? We'll never beat a rap like this."

After much difficulty, we got back to the room and tried to have a serious talk with Lucy. I felt like a Nazi, but it had to be done. She was not *right* for us—not in this fragile situation. It was bad enough if she were only what she appeared to be—a strange young girl in the throes of a bad psychotic episode—but what worried me far more than that was the likelihood that she would probably be just sane enough, in a few hours, to work herself into a towering Jesus-based rage at the hazy recollection of being picked up and seduced in the Los Angeles International Airport by some kind of cruel Samoan who fed her liquor and LSD, then dragged her to a Vegas hotel room and savagely penetrated every orifice in her body with his throbbing, uncircumcised member.

I had a terrible vision of Lucy crashing into Barbra Streisand's dressing room at the Americana and laying this brutal story on her. That would finish us. They would track us down and probably castrate us both, prior to booking . . .

I explained this to my attorney, who was now in tears at the idea of sending Lucy away. She was still powerfully twisted, and I felt the only solution was to get her as far as possible from the Flamingo before she got straight enough to remember where she'd been and what happened to her.

Lucy, while we argued, was lying on the patio, doing a charcoal sketch of Barbra Streisand. From memory this time. It was a full-faced rendering, with teeth like baseballs and eyes like jellied fire.

The sheer intensity of the thing made me nervous. This girl was a walking bomb. God only knows what she might be doing with all that mis-wired energy right now if she didn't have her sketch pad. And what was she going to do when she got straight enough to read *The Vegas Visitor*, as I just had, and learn that Streisand wasn't due at the Americana for another three weeks?

My attorney finally agreed that Lucy would have to go. The possibility of a Mann Act conviction, resulting in disbarment proceedings and total loss of his livelihood, was a key factor in his decision. A nasty federal rap. Especially for a monster Samoan facing a typical white middle-class jury in Southern California.

"They might even call it kidnapping," I said. "Straight to the gas chamber, like Chessman. And even if you manage to beat *that*, they'll send you back to Nevada for Rape and Consensual Sodomy."

"No!" he shouted. "I felt *sorry* for the girl, I wanted to *help* her!"

I smiled. "That's what Fatty Arbuckle said, and you know what they did to him."

"Who?"

"Never mind," I said. "Just picture yourself telling a jury that you tried to help this poor girl by giving her LSD and then taking her out to Vegas for one of your special stark-naked back rubs."

He shook his head sadly. "You're right. They'd probably burn me at the goddamn stake . . . set me on fire right there in the dock. Shit, it doesn't pay to try to help somebody these days . . ."

We coaxed Lucy down to the car, telling her that we thought it was about time to "go meet Barbra." We had no trouble convincing her that she should take all her artwork, but she couldn't understand why my attorney wanted to bring her suitcase along. "I don't want to embarrass her," she protested. "She'll think I'm trying to move in with her, or something."

"No she won't," I said quickly . . . but that was all I could think of to say. I felt like Martin Bormann. What would happen to this poor wretch when we cut her loose? Jail? White slavery? What would Dr. Darwin do under these circumstances? (Survival of the . . . *fittest?* Was that the proper word? Had Darwin ever considered the idea of *temporary* unfitness? Like "temporary insanity." Could the Doctor have made room in his theory for a thing like LSD?)

All this was academic, of course. Lucy was a potentially fatal millstone on both our necks. There was absolutely no choice but to cut her adrift and hope her memory was fucked. But some acid victims—especially nervous mongoloids—have a strange kind of *idiot-savant* capacity for remembering odd details and nothing else. It was possible that Lucy might spend two more days in the grip of total amnesia, then snap out of it with no memory of anything but our room number at the Flamingo. . . .

I thought about this . . . but the only alternative was to take her out to the desert and feed her remains to the lizards. I wasn't ready for this; it seemed a bit heavy for the thing we were trying to protect: My attorney. It came down to that. So the problem was to work out a balance, to aim Lucy in a direction that wouldn't snap her mind and provoke a disastrous backlash.

She had money. My attorney had ascertained that. "At least $200," he'd said. "And we can always call the cops up there in Montana, where she lives, and turn her in."

I was reluctant to do this. The only thing worse than turning her loose in Vegas, I felt, was turning her over to "the authorities" . . . and that was clearly out of the question, anyway. Not now. "What kind of goddamn monster *are* you?" I said. "First you kidnap the girl, then you rape her, and now you want to have her locked up!"

He shrugged. "It just occurred to me," he said, "that she has *no witnesses.* Anything she says about us is completely worthless."

"Us?" I said.

He stared at me. I could see that his head was clearing. The acid was almost gone. This meant that Lucy was probably coming down, too. It was time to cut the cord.

Lucy was waiting for us in the car, listening to the radio with a twisted smile on her face. We were standing about ten yards off. Anybody watching us from a distance might have thought we were having some kind of vicious, showdown argument about who had "rights to the girl." It was a standard scene for a Vegas parking lot.

We finally decided to make her a reservation at the Americana. My attorney ambled over to the car and got her last name under some pretense, then I hurried inside and called the hotel—saying that I was her uncle and that I wanted her to be "treated very gently," because she was an artist and might seem a trifle high-strung. The room clerk assured me they'd give her every courtesy.

Then we drove her out to the airport, saying we were going to trade the White Whale in for a Mercedes 600, and my attorney took her into the lobby with all her gear. She was still unhinged and babbling when he led her away. I drove around a corner and waited for him.

Ten minutes later he shuffled up to the car and got in. "Take off slowly," he said. "Don't attract any attention."

When we got out on Las Vegas Boulevard he explained that he'd given one of the airport cab-hasslers a $10 bill to see that his "drunk girlfriend" got to the Americana, where she had a reservation. "I told him to make sure she got there," he said.

"You think she will?"

He nodded. "The guy said he'd pay the fare with the extra five bucks I gave him, and tell the cabbie to humor her. I told him I had some business to take care of, but I'd be there myself in an hour—and if the girl wasn't already checked in, I'd come back out here and rip his lungs out."

"That's good," I said. "You can't be subtle in this town."

He grinned. "As your attorney, I advise you to tell me where you put the goddamn mescaline."

I pulled over. The kit-bag was in the trunk. He fetched out two pellets and we each ate one. The sun was going down behind the scrub hills northwest of the city. A good Kristofferson tune was croaking out of the radio. We cruised back to town through the warm dusk, relaxed on the red leather seats of our electric white Coupe de Ville.

"Maybe we should take it easy tonight," I said as we flashed past the Tropicana.

"Right," he said. "Let's find a good seafood restaurant and eat some red salmon. I feel a powerful lust for red salmon."

I agreed. "But first we should go back to the hotel and settle in. Maybe have a quick swim and some rum."

He nodded, leaning back on the seat and staring up at the sky. Night was coming down slowly.

4.
No Refuge for Degenerates... Reflections on a Murderous Junkie

We drove through the parking lot of the Flamingo and around the back, through the labyrinth, to our wing. No problem with parking, no problem with the elevator, and the suite was dead quiet when we entered: half-dark and peacefully elegant, with big sliding walls opening out on the lawn and the pool.

The only thing moving in the room was the red-blinking message light on the telephone. "Probably room service," I said. "I ordered some ice and booze. I guess it came while we were gone."

My attorney shrugged. "We have plenty," he said. "But we might as well get more. Hell yes, tell them to send it up."

I picked up the phone and dialed the desk. "What's the message?" I asked. "My light is blinking."

The clerk seemed to hesitate. I could hear papers shuffling. "Ah yes," he said finally. "Mister Duke? Yes, you have two messages. One says, 'Welcome to Las Vegas, from the National District Attorneys' Association.'"

"Wonderful," I said.

". . . and the other," he continued, "says, 'Call Lucy at the Americana, room 1600.'"

"What?"

He repeated the message. There was no mistake.

"Holy shit!" I muttered.

"Excuse me?" said the clerk.

I hung up.

. . . .

My attorney was doing the Big Spit, again, in the bathroom. I walked out on the balcony and stared at the pool, this kidney-shaped bag of bright water that shimmered outside our suite. I felt like Othello. Here I'd only been in town a few hours, and we'd already laid the groundwork for a classic tragedy. The hero was doomed; he had already sown the seed of his own downfall. . . .

But who was the Hero of this filthy drama? I turned away from the pool and confronted my attorney, now emerging from the bathroom and wiping his mouth with a towel. His eyes were glazed and limpid. "This goddamn mescaline," he muttered. "Why the fuck can't they make it a little less pure? Maybe mix it up with Rollaids, or something?"

"Othello used Dramamine," I said.

He nodded, hanging the towel around his neck as he reached out to flip on the TV set. "Yeah, I heard about those remedies. Your man Fatty Arbuckle used olive oil."

"Lucy called," I said.

"What?" He sagged visibly—like an animal taking a bullet.

"I just got the message from the desk. She's at the Americana, room 1600 . . . and she wants us to call."

He stared at me . . . and just then the phone rang.

I shrugged and picked it up. There was no point trying to hide. She had found us, and that was enough.

"Hello," I said.

It was the room clerk again.

"Mister Duke?"

"Yes."

"Hello, Mister Duke. I'm sorry we were cut off a moment ago . . . but I thought I should call again, because I was wondering . . ."

"*What?*" I sensed things closing down on us. This fucker was about to spring something on me. What had that crazy bitch *said* to him? I tried to stay calm. "We're watching the goddamn news!" I screamed. "What the fuck are you interrupting me for?"

Silence.

"What do you *want?* Where's the goddamn ice I ordered? Where's the booze? There's a war on, man! People are being killed!"

"Killed?" He almost whispered the word.

"In Vietnam!" I yelled. "On the goddamn television!"

"Oh . . . yes . . . yes," he said. "This terrible war. When will it end?"

"Tell me," I said quietly. "What do you *want?*"

"Of course," he said, snapping back to his desk-clerk tone. "I thought I should tell you . . . because I know you're here with the Police Convention . . . that the woman who left that message for you sounded very *disturbed.*"

He hesitated, but I said nothing.

"I thought you should know this," he said finally.

"What did you *say* to her?" I asked.

"*Nothing.* Nothing at all, Mister Duke. I merely took the message." He paused. "But it wasn't that easy, talking to that woman. She was . . . well . . . extremely nervous. I think she was crying."

"Crying?" My brain had locked up. I couldn't think. The drug was taking over. "Why was she crying?"

"Well . . . ah . . . she didn't say, Mister Duke. But since I knew the nature of your work I thought—"

"I know," I said quickly. "Look, you want to be gentle with that woman if she ever calls again. She's our *case study.* We're watching her very carefully." I felt my head unwinding now; the words came easily: "She's perfectly harmless, of course . . . there'll be no trouble . . . this woman has been into laudanum, it's a controlled experiment, but I suspect we'll need your cooperation before this thing is over."

"Well . . . *certainly,*" he said. "We're always happy to cooperate with the police . . . just as long as there won't be any trouble . . . for us, I mean."

"Don't worry," I said. "You're protected. Just treat this poor woman like you'd treat any other human being in trouble."

"What?" He seemed to be stuttering. "Ah . . . yes, yes, I

see what you mean . . . yes . . . so *you'll* be responsible then?"

"Of course," I said. "And now I have to get back to the news."

"Thank you," he muttered.

"Send the ice," I said, and hung up.

My attorney was smiling peacefully at the TV set. "Good work," he said. "They'll treat us like goddamn lepers, after that."

I nodded, filling a tall glass with Chivas Regal.

"There hasn't been any *news* on the tube for three hours," he said absently. "That poor fool probably thinks we're plugged into some kind of special cop channel. You should call back and ask him to send up a 3000 watt sensing capacitator, along with the ice. Tell him ours just burned out . . ."

"You forgot about Lucy," I said. "She's looking for you."

He laughed. "No, she's looking for *you*."

"Me?"

"Yeah. She really flipped over you. The only way I could get rid of her, out there in the airport, was by saying you were taking me out to the desert for a showdown—that you wanted me out of the way so you could have her all to yourself." He shrugged. "Shit, I had to tell her *something*. I said she should go to the Americana and wait to see which one of us came back." He laughed again. "I guess she figures you won. That phone message wasn't for *me*, was it?"

I nodded. It made no sense at all, but I knew it was true. Drug reasoning. The rhythms were brutally clear—and, to him, they made excellent sense.

He was slumped in the chair, concentrating on *Mission Impossible*.

I thought for a while, then stood up and began stuffing things into my suitcase.

"What are you doing?" he asked.

"Never mind," I said. The zipper stuck momentarily, but I yanked it shut. Then I put on my shoes.

"Wait a minute," he said. "Jesus, you're not *leaving*?"

I nodded. "You're goddamn right, I'm leaving. But don't worry. I'll stop at the desk on my way out. You'll be taken care of."

He stood up quickly, kicking his drink over. "OK, goddamnit, this is *serious!* Where's my .357?"

I shrugged, not looking at him as I crammed the Chivas Regal bottles into my hand-satchel. "I sold it in Baker," I said. "I owe you 35 bucks."

"Jesus Christ!" he shouted. "That thing cost me a hundred and ninety goddamn dollars!"

I smiled. "You *told* me where you got that gun," I said. "Remember?"

He hesitated, pretending to think. "Oh yeah," he said finally. "Yeah . . . that punk out in Pasadena . . ." Then he flared again. "So it cost me a goddamn *grand*. That asshole shot a narc. He was looking at *life!* . . . shit, three weeks in court, and all I got was a fucking six-shooter."

"You're stupid," I said. "I warned you about dealing with junkies on credit—especially when they're *guilty*. You're lucky the bastard didn't pay you off with a bullet in the stomach."

My attorney sagged. "He was my *cousin*. The jury found him *innocent*."

"Shit!" I snapped. "How many people has that junkie bastard shot since we've known him? Six? Eight? That evil little fuck is so guilty that I should probably kill him myself, on general principles. He shot that narc just as sure as he killed that girl at the Holiday Inn . . . and that guy in Ventura!"

He eyed me coldly. "You better be careful, man. You're into some heavy *slander*."

I laughed, tossing my luggage together in a lump at the foot of the bed while I sat down to finish my drink. I actually intended to leave. I didn't really want to, but I figured that nothing I could possibly do with this gig was worth the risk of getting tangled up with Lucy . . . No doubt she was a beautiful person, if she ever got straight . . . very sensitive, with a secret reserve of fine karma underneath her Pit Bull act; a great talent with fine instincts . . . Just a heavy little gal who unfortunately went stone crazy somewhere prior to her eighteenth birthday.

I had nothing personal against her. But I knew she was perfectly capable—under these circumstances—of sending us both to prison for at least twenty years, on the strength of some heinous story we would probably never even hear until she took the stand:

"Yessir, those two men over there in the dock are the ones who gave me the LSD and took me to the hotel . . ."

"And what did they do then, Lucy?"

"Well, sir, I can't rightly remember . . ."

"Indeed? Well, perhaps this document from the District Attorney's files will refresh your memory, Lucy . . . Thïs is the statement you made to Officer Squane shortly after you were found wandering naked in the desert near Lake Mead."

"I don't know for sure what they done to me, but I remember it was horrible. One guy picked me up in the Los Angeles airport; he's the one who gave me the pill . . . and the other one met us at the hotel; he was sweating real bad and he talked so fast that I couldn't understand what he wanted . . . No sir, I don't recall *exactly* what they did to me at that point, because I was still under the influence of that drug . . . yessir, the LSD they gave me . . . and I think I was naked for a long time, maybe the whole time they had me there. I think it was evening, because I remember they had the news on. Yessir, Walter Cronkite, I remember his face all through it . . ."

No, I was not ready for this. No jury would doubt her testimony, especially when it came stuttering out through a fog of tears and obscene acid flashbacks. And the fact that she couldn't recall precisely what we had done to her would make it impossible to deny. The jury would *know* what we'd done. They would have read about people like us in the $2.95 paperbacks: *Up to the Hilt* and *Only Skin Deep* . . . and seen our type in the $5 fuck-flicks.

And of course we couldn't possibly risk taking the stand in

our own defense—not after they'd cleaned out the trunk of the Whale: "And I'd like to point out, Your Honor, that our Prosecution Exhibits A through Y are available to the jury—yes, this incredible collection of illegal drugs and narcotics which the defendants had in their possession at the time of their arrests and forcible seizure by no less than *nine* officers, six of whom are still hospitalized . . . and also Exhibit Z, sworn testimony by three professional narcotics experts selected by the president of the National District Attorneys' Conference—which was seriously embarrassed by the defendants' attempts to infiltrate, disrupt and pervert their annual convention . . . these experts have testified that the drug cache in the possession of these defendants at the time of the arrests was enough to *kill* an entire platoon of United States Marines . . . and gentlemen, I use the word kill with all due respect for the fear and loathing I'm sure it provokes in every one of you when you reflect that these *degenerate* rapists used this galaxy of narcotics to *completely destroy* the mind and morals of this once-innocent teenager, this *ruined* and degraded young girl who now sits before you in shame . . . yes, they fed this girl enough drugs to scramble her brains so horribly that she can no longer even *recall* the filthy details of that orgy she was forced to endure . . . and then they *used* her, ladies and gentlemen of the jury, for their own unspeakable ends!"

5.
A Terrible Experience with Extremely Dangerous Drugs

There was no way to cope with it. I stood up and gathered my luggage. It was important, I felt, to get out of town immediately.

My attorney seemed to finally grasp this. "Wait!" he shouted. "You can't leave me alone in this snake pit! This room is in my *name*."

I shrugged.

"OK, goddamnit," he said, moving toward the phone. "Look, I'll *call* her. I'll get her off our backs." He nodded. "You're right. She's my problem."

I shook my head. "No, it's gone too far."

"You'd make a piss-poor lawyer," he replied. "Relax. I'll handle this."

He dialed the Americana and asked for 1600. "Hi, Lucy," he said. "Yeah, it's me. I got your message . . . what? Hell no, I taught the bastard a lesson he'll never forget . . . what? . . . No, not dead, but he won't be bothering anybody for a while . . . yeah, I left him out there; I stomped him, then pulled all his teeth out . . ."

Jesus, I thought. What a terrible thing to lay on somebody with a head full of acid.

"But here's the problem," he was saying. "I have to leave here right away. That bastard cashed a bad check downstairs and gave *you* as a reference, so they'll be looking for both of you . . . yeah, I know, but you can't judge a book by its cover, Lucy; some people are just basically rotten . . . anyway, the

129

last thing in the world you want to do is call this hotel again; they'll trace the call and put you straight behind bars . . . no, I'm moving to the Tropicana right away; I'll call you from there when I know my room number . . . yeah, probably two hours; I have to act casual, or they'll capture *me* too . . . I think I'll probably use a different name, but I'll let you know what it is . . . sure, just as soon as I check in . . . what? . . . of course; we'll go to the Circus-Circus and catch the polar bear act; it'll freak you right out . . ."

He was nervously shifting the phone from ear to ear while he talked: "No . . . listen, I have to get off; they probably have the phone tapped . . . yeah, I know, it was horrible, but it's all over now . . . O MY GOD! THEY'RE KICKING THE DOOR DOWN!" He hurled the phone down and began shouting: "No! Get away from me! I'm innocent! It was Duke! I swear to God!" He kicked the phone against the wall, then leaned down to it and began yelling again: "No, I don't know *where* she is! I think she went back to Montana. You'll never catch Lucy! She's gone!" He kicked the receiver again, then picked it up and held it about a foot away from his mouth as he uttered a long, quavering groan. "No! No! Don't put that *thing* on me!" he screamed. Then he slammed the phone down.

"Well," he said quietly. "That's that. She's probably stuffing herself down the incinerator about now." He smiled. "Yeah, I think that's the last we'll be hearing from Lucy."

I slumped on the bed. His performance had given me a bad jolt. For a moment I thought his mind had snapped—that he actually believed he was being attacked by invisible enemies.

But the room was quiet again. He was back in his chair, watching *Mission Impossible* and fumbling idly with the hash pipe. It was empty. "Where's that opium?" he asked.

I tossed him the kit-bag. "Be careful," I muttered. "There's not much left."

He chuckled. "As your attorney," he said, "I advise you not worry." He nodded toward the bathroom. "Take a hit out of that little brown bottle in my shaving kit."

"What is it?"

"Adrenochrome," he said. "You won't need much. Just a little *tiny* taste."

I got the bottle and dipped the head of a paper match into it.

"That's about right," he said. "That stuff makes pure mescaline seem like ginger beer. You'll go completely crazy if you take too much."

I licked the end of the match. "Where'd you get *this?*" I asked. "You can't buy it."

"Never mind," he said. "It's absolutely pure."

I shook my head sadly. "Jesus! What kind of monster client have you picked up *this* time? There's only one source for this stuff . . ."

He nodded.

AS YOUR ATTORNEY I ADVISE YOU TO SLOW DOWN — I CANT KEEP UP MAN!

"The adrenaline glands from a *living* human body," I said. "It's no good if you get it out of a corpse."

"I know," he replied. "But the guy didn't have any cash. He's one of these Satanism freaks. He offered me human blood—said it would make me higher than I'd ever been in my life," he laughed. "I thought he was kidding, so I told him I'd just as soon have an ounce or so of pure adrenochrome—or maybe just a fresh adrenalin gland to chew on."

I could already feel the stuff working on me. The first wave felt like a combination of mescaline and methedrine. Maybe I should take a swim, I thought.

"Yeah," my attorney was saying. "They nailed this guy for child molesting, but he swears he didn't do it. 'Why should I fuck with *children?*' he says; 'They're too *small!*' " He shrugged. "Christ, what could I say? Even a goddamn were-wolf is entitled to legal counsel . . . I didn't *dare* turn the creep down. He might have picked up a letter opener and gone after my pineal gland."

"Why not?" I said. "He could probably get Melvin Belli for that." I nodded, barely able to talk now. My body felt like I'd just been wired into a 220 volt socket. "Shit, we should get us some of that stuff." I muttered finally. "Just eat a big handful and see what happens."

"Some of what?"

"Extract of pineal."

He stared at me. "Sure," he said. "That's a *good* idea. One *whiff* of that shit would turn you into something out of a god-damn medical encyclopedia! Man, your head would swell up like a watermelon, you'd probably gain about a hundred pounds in two hours . . . claws, bleeding warts, then you'd notice about six huge hairy tits swelling up on your back . . ." He shook his head emphatically. "Man, I'll try just about anything; but I'd never in hell touch a pineal gland.

"Last Christmas somebody gave me a whole Jimson weed—the root must have weighed two pounds; enough for a *year*—but I ate the whole goddamn thing in about twenty minutes!"

I was leaning toward him, following his words intently.

The slightest hesitation made me want to grab him by the throat and force him to talk faster. "Right!" I said eagerly. "Jimson weed! What happened?"

"Luckily, I vomited most of it right back up," he said. "But even so, I went blind for three days. Christ I couldn't even walk! My whole body turned to wax. I was such a mess that they had to haul me back to the ranch house in a wheelbarrow . . . they said I was trying to talk, but I sounded like a raccoon."

"Fantastic," I said. But I could barely hear him. I was so wired that my hands were clawing uncontrollably at the bedspread, jerking it right out from under me while he talked. My heels were dug into the mattress, with both knees locked . . . I could feel my eyeballs swelling, about to pop out of the sockets.

"Finish the fucking story!" I snarled. "What *happened?* What about the *glands?*"

He backed away, keeping an eye on me as he edged across the room. "Maybe you need another drink," he said nervously. "Jesus, that stuff got right on *top* of you, didn't it?"

I tried to smile. "Well . . . nothing worse . . . no, this *is* worse . . ." It was hard to move my jaws; my tongue felt like burning magnesium. "No . . . nothing to worry about," I hissed. "Maybe if you could just . . . shove me into the pool, or something . . ."

"Goddamnit," he said. "You took too *much.* You're about to explode. Jesus, look at your *face!*"

I couldn't move. Total paralysis now. Every muscle in my body was contracted. I couldn't even move my eyeballs, much less turn my head or talk.

"It won't last long," he said. "The first rush is the worst. Just ride the bastard out. If I put you in the pool right now, you'd sink like a goddamn stone."

Death. I was sure of it. Not even my lungs seemed to be functioning. I needed artificial respiration, but I couldn't open my mouth to say so. I was going to *die.* Just sitting there on the bed, unable to move . . . well at least there's no pain.

Probably, I'll black out in a few seconds, and after that it won't matter.

My attorney had gone back to watching television. The news was on again. Nixon's face filled the screen, but his speech was hopelessly garbled. The only word I could make out was "sacrifice." Over and over again: "Sacrifice . . . sacrifice . . . sacrifice. . . ."

I could hear myself breathing heavily. My attorney seemed to notice. "Just stay relaxed," he said over his shoulder, without looking at me. "Don't try to fight it, or you'll start getting brain bubbles . . . strokes, aneurisms . . . you'll just wither up and die." His hand snaked out to change channels.

It was after midnight when I finally was able to talk and move around . . . but I was still not free of the drug; the voltage had merely been cranked down from 220 to 110. I was a babbling nervous wreck, flapping around the room like a wild animal, pouring sweat and unable to concentrate on any one thought for more than two or three seconds at a time.

My attorney put down the phone after making several calls. "There's only one place where we can get fresh salmon," he said, "and it's closed on Sunday."

"Of course," I snapped. "These goddamn Jesus freaks! They're multiplying like rats!"

He eyed me curiously.

"What about the Process?" I said. "Don't they have a place here? Maybe a delicatessen or something? With a few tables in back? They have a fantastic menu in London. I ate there once; incredible food . . ."

"Get a grip on yourself," he said. "You don't want to even *mention* the Process in this town."

"You're right," I said. "Call Inspector Bloor. He knows about food. I think he has a *list*."

"Better to call room service," he said. "We can get the crab looey and a quart of Christian Brothers muscatel for about twenty bucks."

"No!" I said. "We *must* get out of this place. I need air.

Let's drive up to Reno and get a big tuna fish salad . . . hell, it won't take long. Only about four hundred miles; no traffic out there on the desert . . ."

"Forget it," he said. "That's *Army territory*. Bomb tests, nerve gas—we'd never make it."

We wound up at a place called The Big Flip about halfway downtown. I had a "New York steak" for $1.88. My attorney ordered the "Coyote Bush Basket" for $2.09 . . . and after that we drank off a pot of watery "Golden West" coffee and watched four boozed-up cowboy types kick a faggot half to death between the pinball machines.

"The action never stops in this town," said my attorney as we shuffled out to the car. "A man with the right contacts could probably pick up all the fresh adrenochrome he wanted, if he hung around here for a while."

I agreed, but I wasn't quite up to it, right then. I hadn't slept for something like eighty hours, and that fearful ordeal with the drug had left me completely exhausted . . . tomorrow we would have to get serious. The drug conference was scheduled to kick off at noon . . . and we were still not sure how to handle it. So we drove back to the hotel and watched a British horror film on the late show.

6.
Getting Down to Business...
Opening Day at the Drug Convention

"On behalf of the prosecuting attorneys of this county, I welcome you."

We sat in the rear fringe of a crowd of about 1500 in the main ballroom of the Dunes Hotel. Far up in front of the room, barely visible from the rear, the executive director of the National District Attorneys' Association—a middle-aged, well-groomed, successful GOP businessman type named Patrick Healy—was opening their Third National Institute on Narcotics and Dangerous Drugs. His remarks reached us by way of a big, low-fidelity speaker mounted on a steel pole in our corner. Perhaps a dozen others were spotted around the room, all facing the rear and looming over the crowd . . . so that no matter where you sat or even tried to hide, you were always looking down the muzzle of a big speaker.

This produced an odd effect. People in each section of the ballroom tended to stare at the nearest voice-box, instead of watching the distant figure of whoever was actually talking far up front, on the podium. This 1935 style of speaker placement totally depersonalized the room. There was something ominous and authoritarian about it. Whoever set up that sound system was probably some kind of Sheriff's auxiliary technician on leave from a drive-in theater in Muskogee, Oklahoma, where the management couldn't afford individual car speakers and relied on ten huge horns, mounted on telephone poles in the parking area.

A year or so earlier I had been to the Sky River Rock Festival in rural Washington, where a dozen stone-broke freaks from the Seattle Liberation Front had assembled a sound system that carried every small note of an acoustic guitar—even a cough or the sound of a boot dropping on the stage—to half-deaf acid victims huddled under bushes a half mile away.

But the best technicians available to the National DAs' convention in Vegas apparently couldn't handle it. Their sound system looked like something Ulysses S. Grant might have triggered up to address his troops during the Seige of Vicksburg. The voices from up front crackled with a fuzzy, high-pitched urgency, and the delay was just enough to keep the words disconcertingly out of phase with the speaker's gestures.

"We must come to terms with the Drug Culture in this country! . . . country . . . country . . ." These echoes drifted back to the rear in confused waves. "The reefer butt is called a 'roach' because it resembles a cockroach . . .cockroach . . . cockroach . . ."

"What the fuck are these people talking about?" my attorney whispered. "You'd have to be crazy on acid to think a joint looked like a goddamn cockroach!"

I shrugged. It was clear that we'd stumbled into a prehistoric gathering. The voice of a "drug expert" named Bloomquist crackled out of the nearby speakers: ". . . about these flashbacks, the patient never knows; he thinks it's all over and he gets himself straightened out for six months . . . and then, darn it, the whole trip comes back on him."

Gosh darn that fiendish LSD! Dr. E. R. Bloomquist, MD, was the keynote speaker, one of the big stars of the conference. He is the author of a paperback book titled *Marijuana*, which—according to the cover—"tells it like it is." (He is also the inventor of the roach/cockroach theory . . .)

According to the book jacket, he is an "Associate Clinical Professor of Surgery (Anesthesiology) at the University of Southern California School of Medicine" . . . and also "a well known authority on the abuse of dangerous drugs." Dr. Bloomquist "has appeared on national network television panels, has served as a consultant for government agencies, was a member of the Committee on Narcotics Addiction and Alcoholism of the Council on Mental Health of the American Medical Association." His wisdom is massively reprinted and distributed, says the publisher. He is clearly one of the heavies on that circuit of second-rate academic hustlers who get paid anywhere from $500 to $1000 a hit for lecturing to cop-crowds.

Dr. Bloomquist's book is a compendium of state bullshit. On page 49 he explains, the "four states of being" in the cannabis society: "Cool, Groovy, Hip & Square"—in that descending order. "The square is seldom if ever cool," says Bloomquist. "He is 'not with it,' that is, he doesn't know 'what's happening.' But if he manages to figure it out, he moves up a notch to 'hip.' And if he can bring himself to approve of what's happening, he becomes 'groovy.' And after that, with much luck and perseverence, he can rise to the rank of 'cool.' "

Bloomquist writes like somebody who once bearded Tim Leary in a campus cocktail lounge and paid for all the drinks. And it was probably somebody like Leary who told him, with a straight face, that sunglasses are known in the drug culture as "tea shades."

This is the kind of dangerous gibberish that used to be posted, in the form of mimeographed bulletins, in Police Department locker rooms.

Indeed: *KNOW YOUR DOPE FIEND. YOUR LIFE MAY DEPEND ON IT! You will not be able to see his eyes because of Tea-Shades, but his knuckles will be white from inner tension and his pants will be crusted with semen from constantly jacking off when he can't find a rape victim. He will stagger and babble when questioned. He will not respect your badge. The Dope Fiend fears nothing. He will attack, for no reason, with every weapon at his command—including yours. BEWARE. Any officer apprehending a suspected marijuana addict should use all necessary force immediately. One stitch in time (on him) will usually save nine on you. Good luck.*

The Chief

Indeed. Luck is always important, especially in Las Vegas
. . . and ours was getting worse. It was clear at a glance that
this Drug Conference was not what we'd planned on. It was
far too *open*, too mixed. About a third of the crowd looked
like they'd just stopped by, for the show, en route to a Fra-
zier-Ali rematch at the Vegas Convention Center across
town. Or maybe a benefit bout, for Old Smack Dealers, between Liston and Marshal Ky.

The room fairly bristled with beards, mustaches and super-
Mod dress. The DAs' conference had obviously drawn a
goodly contingent of undercover narcs and other twilight
types. An assistant DA from Chicago wore a light-tan sleeveless knit suit: His lady was the star of the Dunes casino; she
flashed through the place like Grace Slick at a Finch College
class reunion. They were a classic couple; stone swingers.

Just because you're a cop, these days, doesn't mean you
can't be With It. And this conference attracted some real peacocks. But my own costume—$40 FBI wingtips and a Pat
Boone madras sportcoat—was just about right for the mass-
median; because for every urban-hipster, there were about
twenty crude-looking rednecks who could have passed for assistant football coaches at Mississippi State.

These were the people who made my attorney nervous.
Like most Californians, he was shocked to actually *see* these
people from The Outback. Here was the cop-cream from Middle America . . . and, Jesus, they looked and talked like a
gang of drunken pig farmers!

I tried to console him. "They're actually nice people," I said,
"once you get to know them."

He smiled: *"Know them?* Are you kidding? Man, I know
these people in my goddamn *blood!"*

"Don't *mention* that word around here," I said. "You'll get
them excited."

He nodded. "You're right. I saw these bastards in *Easy
Rider,* but I didn't believe they were real. Not like *this.* Not
hundreds of them!"

My attorney was wearing a double-breasted blue pinstripe

suit, a far more stylish outfit than my own . . . but it made him exceedingly nervous. Because to be stylishly dressed in this crowd meant that you were probably an undercover cop, and my attorney makes his living with people who are very sensitive in that area. "This is a fucking *nightmare!*" he kept muttering. "Here I am infiltrating a goddamn Pig conference, but sure as hell there's some dope-dealing bomb freak in this town who's going to recognize me and put the word out that I'm out here partying with a thousand *cops!*"

We all wore name tags. They came with the $100 "registration fee." Mine said I was a "private investigator" from L.A. —which was true, in a sense; and my attorney's name-tag identified him as an expert in "Criminal Drug Analysis." Which was also true, in a sense.

But nobody seemed to care who was what, or why. Security was too loose for that kind of gritty paranoia. But we were also a bit tense because we'd given the registrar a bad check for our dual registration fee. It was a check from one of my attorney's pimp/drug underworld clients that he assumed, from long experience, was absolutely worthless.

7.
If You Don't Know, Come to Learn . . . If You Know, Come to Teach

*—motto on invitations to
National DAs' Convention
in Vegas, April 25–29, 1971*

The first session—the opening remarks—lasted most of the afternoon. We sat patiently through the first two hours, although it was clear from the start that we weren't going to Learn anything and it was equally clear that we'd be crazy to try any Teaching. It was easy enough to sit there with a head full of mescaline and listen to hour after hour of irrelevant gibberish. . . . There was certainly no risk involved. These poor bastards didn't know mescaline from macaroni.

I suspect we could have done the whole thing on acid . . . except for some of the people; there were faces and bodies in that group who would have been absolutely unendurable on acid. The sight of a 344-pound police chief from Waco, Texas, necking openly with his 290-pound wife (or whatever woman he had with him) when the lights were turned off for a Dope Film was just barely tolerable on mescaline—which is mainly a sensual/surface drug that exaggerates reality, instead of altering it—but with a head full of acid, the sight of two fantastically obese human beings far gone in a public grope while a thousand cops all around them watched a movie about the "dangers of marijuana" would not be emotionally acceptable. The brain would reject it: The medulla would attempt to close itself off from the signals it was getting from the fron-

143

tal lobes . . . and the middle-brain, meanwhile, would be trying desperately to put a different interpretation on the scene, before passing it back to the medulla and the risk of physical action.

Acid is a relatively *complex* drug, in its effects, while mescaline is pretty simple and straightforward—but in a scene like this, the difference was academic. There was simply no call, at this conference, for anything but a massive consumption of Downers: Reds, Grass and Booze, because the whole program had apparently been set up by people who had been in a Seconal stupor since 1964.

Here were more than a thousand top-level cops telling each other "we *must* come to terms with the drug culture," but they had no idea where to start. They couldn't even *find* the goddamn thing. There were rumors in the hallways that maybe the Mafia was behind it. Or perhaps the Beatles. At one point somebody in the audience asked Bloomquist if he thought Margaret Mead's "strange behavior," of late, might possibly be explained by a private marijuana addiction.

"I really don't know," Bloomquist replied. "But at her age, if she did smoke grass, she'd have one hell of a trip."

The audience roared with laughter at this remark.

My attorney leaned over to whisper that he was leaving. "I'll be down in the casino," he said. "I know a hell of a lot better ways to waste my time than listening to *this* bullshit." He stood up, knocking his ashtray off the arm of his chair, and plunged down the aisle toward the door.

The seats were not arranged for random movement. People tried to make a path for him, but there was no room to move.

"Watch yourself!" somebody shouted as he bulled over them.

"Fuck you!" he snarled.

"Down in front!" somebody else yelled.

By now he was almost to the door. "I have to get *out!*" he shouted. "I don't *belong* here!"

"Good riddance," said a voice.

He paused, looking around—then he seemed to think better of it, and kept moving. By the time he got to the exit the whole rear of the room was in turmoil. Even Bloomquist, far up front on the stage, seemed aware of a distant trouble. He stopped talking and peered nervously in the direction of the noise. Probably he thought a brawl had erupted—maybe a racial conflict of some kind, something that couldn't be helped.

I stood up and plunged toward the door. It seemed like as good a time as any to flee. "Pardon me, I feel sick," I said to the first leg I stepped on. It jerked back, and I said it again: "Sorry, I'm about to be sick . . . sorry, sick . . . beg pardon, yes, feeling sick. . . ."

This time a path opened very nicely. Not a word of protest. Hands actually helped me along. They feared I was about to vomit, and nobody wanted it—at least not on them. I made it to the door in about forty-five seconds.

My attorney was downstairs at the bar, talking to a sporty-looking cop about forty whose plastic name-tag said he was the DA from someplace in Georgia. "I'm a whiskey man, myself," he was saying. "We don't have much problem with drugs down where I come from."

"You will," said my attorney. "One of these nights you'll wake up and find a junkie tearing your bedroom apart."

"Naw!" said the Georgia man. "Not down in *my* parts."

I joined them and ordered a tall glass of rum, with ice.

"You're another one of these California boys," he said. "Your friend here's been tellin' me about dope fiends."

"They're everywhere," I said. "Nobody's safe. And sure as hell not in the South. They like the warm weather."

"They work in pairs," said my attorney. "Sometimes in gangs. They'll climb right into your bedroom and sit on your chest, with big Bowie knives." He nodded solemnly. "They might even sit on your *wife's chest*—put the blade right down on her throat."

"Jesus God almighty," said the southerner. "What the hell's *goin' on* in this country?"

"You'd never believe it," said my attorney. "In L.A. it's out of control. First it was drugs, now it's witchcraft."

"Witchcraft? Shit, you can't mean it!"

"Read the newspapers," I said. "Man, you don't know trouble until you have to face down a bunch of these addicts gone crazy for human sacrifice!"

"Naw!" he said. "That's science fiction stuff!"

"Not where *we* operate," said my attorney. "Hell, in Malibu alone, these goddamn Satan-worshippers kill six or eight people *every day*." He paused to sip his drink. "And all they want is the blood," he continued. "They'll take people right off the street if they have to." He nodded. "Hell, yes. Just the other day we had a case where they grabbed a girl right out of a McDonald's hamburger stand. She was a waitress. About sixteen years old . . . with a lot of people watching, too!"

"What happened?" said our friend. "What did they *do* to her?" He seemed very agitated by what he was hearing.

"Do?" said my attorney. "Jesus Christ man. They chopped her goddamn head off right there in the parking lot! Then they cut all kinds of holes in her and sucked out the blood!"

"God *almighty!*" The Georgia man exclaimed . . . "And nobody *did* anything?"

"What *could* they do?" I said. "The guy that took the head was about six-seven and maybe three hundred pounds. He was packing two Lugers, and the others had M-16s. They were all veterans. . . ."

"The big guy used to be a major in the Marines," said my attorney. "We know where he lives, but we can't get near the house."

"Naw!" our friend shouted. "Not a major!"

"He wanted the pineal gland," I said. "That's how he got so big. When he quit the Marines he was just a *little guy.*"

"O my god!" said our friend. "That's horrible!"

"It happens every day," said my attorney. "Usually it's whole families. During the night. Most of them don't even wake up until they feel their heads going—and then, of course, it's too late."

The bartender had stopped to listen. I'd been watching him. His expression was not calm.

"Three more rums," I said. "With plenty of ice, and maybe

a handful of lime chunks."

He nodded, but I could see that his mind was not on his work. He was staring at our name-tags. "Are you guys with that police convention upstairs?" he said finally.

"We sure are, my friend," said the Georgia man with a big smile.

The bartender shook his head sadly. "I thought so," he said. "I never heard that kind of talk at this bar before. Jesus Christ! How do you guys *stand* that kind of work?"

My attorney smiled at him. "We *like* it," he said. "It's groovy."

The bartender drew back; his face was a mask of repugnance.

"What's wrong with you?" I said. "Hell, *somebody* has to do it."

He stared at me for a moment, then turned away.

"Hurry up with those drinks," said my attorney. "We're thirsty." He laughed and rolled his eyes as the bartender glanced back at him. "Only *two* rums," he said. "Make mine a Bloody Mary."

The bartender seemed to stiffen, but our Georgia friend didn't notice. His mind was somewhere else. "Hell, I really hate to hear this," he said quietly. "Because everything that happens in California seems to get down our way, sooner or later. Mostly Atlanta, but I guess that was back when the goddamn bastards were *peaceful*. It used to be that all we had to do was keep 'em under surveillance. They didn't roam around much. . . ." He shrugged. "But now, Jesus, *nobody's* safe. They could turn up anywhere."

"You're right," said my attorney. "We learned that in California. You remember where Manson turned up, don't you? Right out in the middle of Death Valley. He had a whole *army* of sex fiends out there. We only got our hands on a few. Most of the crew got away; just ran off across the sand dunes, like big lizards . . . and every one of them stark naked, except for the weapons."

"They'll turn up somewhere, pretty soon," I said. "And let's hope we'll be ready for them."

The Georgia man whacked his fist on the bar. "But we can't just lock ourselves in the house and be prisoners!" he exclaimed. "We don't even know who these people are! How do you *recognize* them?

"You can't," my attorney replied. "The only way to do it is to take the bull by the horns—go to the mat with this scum!"

"What do you mean by that?" he asked.

"You *know* what I mean," said my attorney. "We've done it before, and we can damn well do it again."

"Cut their goddamn heads off," I said. "Every one of them. That's what we're doing in California."

"What?"

"Sure," said my attorney. "It's all on the Q.T., but everybody who *matters* is with us all the way down the line."

"God! I had no idea it was that bad out there!" said our friend.

"We keep it quiet," I said. "It's not the kind of thing you'd want to talk about upstairs, for instance. Not with the press around."

Our man agreed. "Hell no!" he said. "We'd never hear the goddamn end of it."

"Dobermans don't talk," I said.

"What?"

"Sometimes it's easier to just rip out the backstraps," said my attorney. "They'll fight like hell if you try to take the head without dogs."

"God almighty!"

We left him at the bar, swirling the ice in his drink and not smiling. He was worried about whether or not to tell his wife about it. "She'd never understand," he muttered. "You know how women are."

I nodded. My attorney was already gone, scurrying through a maze of slot machines toward the front door. I said goodbye to our friend, warning him not to say anything about what we'd told him.

8.
Back Door Beauty...
& Finally a Bit
of Serious Drag
Racing on the Strip

Sometime around midnight my attorney wanted coffee. He had been vomiting fairly regularly as we drove around the Strip, and the right flank of the Whale was badly streaked. We were idling at a stoplight in front of the Silver Slipper beside a big blue Ford with Oklahoma plates . . . two hoggish-looking couples in the car, probably cops from Muskogee using the Drug Conference to give their wives a look at Vegas. They looked like they'd just beaten Caesar's Palace for about $33 at the blackjack tables, and now they were headed for the Circus-Circus to whoop it up. . . .

. . . but suddenly, they found themselves next to a white Cadillac convertible all covered with vomit and a 300-pound Samoan in a yellow fishnet T-shirt yelling at them:

"Hey there! You folks want to buy some heroin?"

No reply. No sign of recognition. They'd been warned about this kind of crap: Just ignore it. . . .

"Hey, honkies!" my attorney screamed. "Goddamnit, I'm serious! I want to sell you some pure fuckin' *smack!*" He was leaning out of the car, very close to them. But still nobody answered. I glanced over, very briefly, and saw four middle-American faces frozen with shock, staring straight ahead.

We were in the middle lane. A quick left turn would be illegal. We would have to go straight ahead when the light changed, then escape at the next corner. I waited, tapping the accelerator nervously. . . .

My attorney was losing control: "Cheap heroin!" he was shouting. "This is the real stuff! You won't get hooked! Goddamnit, I *know* what I have here!" He whacked on the side of the car, as if to get their attention . . . but they wanted no part of us.

"You folks never talked to a *vet* before?" said my attorney. "I just got back from Veet Naam. This is *scag*, folks! Pure scag!"

Suddenly the light changed and the Ford bolted off like a rocket. I stomped on the accelerator and stayed right next to them for about two hundred yards, watching for cops in the mirror while my attorney kept screaming at them: "Shoot! Fuck! Scag! Blood! Heroin! Rape! Cheap! Communist! Jab it right into your fucking eyeballs!"

We were approaching the Circus-Circus at high speed and the Oklahoma car was veering left, trying to muscle into the turn lane. I stomped the Whale into passing gear and we ran fender to fender for a moment. He wasn't up to hitting me; there was horror in his eyes. . . .

The man in the back seat lost control of himself . . . lunging across his wife and snarling wildly: "You dirty bastards! Pull over and I'll kill you! God damn you! You bastards!" He seemed ready to leap out the window and into our car, crazy with rage. Luckily the Ford was a two-door. He couldn't get out.

We were coming up to the next stoplight and the Ford was still trying to move left. We were both running full bore. I glanced over my shoulder and saw that we'd left the other traffic far behind; there was a big opening to the right. So I mashed on the brake, hurling my attorney against the dashboard, and in the instant the Ford surged ahead I cut across his tail and zoomed into a side-street. A sharp right turn across three lanes of traffic. But it worked. We left the Ford stalled in the middle of the intersection, hung in the middle of a screeching left turn. With a little luck, he'd be arrested for reckless driving.

My attorney was laughing as we careened in low gear, with the lights out, through a dusty tangle of back streets behind the Desert Inn. "Jesus Christ," he said. "Those Okies were getting excited. That guy in the back seat was trying to *bite* me! Shit, he was frothing at the mouth." He nodded solemnly. "I should have maced the fucker . . . a criminal psychotic, total breakdown . . . you never know when they're likely to explode."

I swung the Whale into a turn that seemed to lead out of the maze—but instead of skidding, the bastard almost rolled.

"Holy shit!" my attorney screamed. "Turn on the fucking lights!" He was clinging to the top of the windshield . . . and suddenly he was doing the Big Spit again, leaning over the side.

I refused to slow down until I was sure nobody was following us—especially that Oklahoma Ford: those people were definitely dangerous, at least until they calmed down. Would they report that terrible quick encounter to the police? Probably not. It had happened too fast, with no witnesses, and the odds were pretty good that nobody would believe them anyway. The idea that two heroin pushers in a white Cadillac convertible would be dragging up and down the Strip, abusing total strangers at stoplights, was prima facie absurd. Not even Sonny Liston ever got that far out of control.

We made another turn and almost rolled again. The Coupe de Ville is not your ideal machine for high speed cornering in residential neighborhoods. The handling is very mushy . . . unlike the Red Shark, which had responded very nicely to situations requiring the quick four-wheel drift. But the Whale —instead of cutting loose at the critical moment—had a tendency to *dig in*, which accounted for that sickening "here we go" sensation.

At first I thought it was only because the tires were soft, so I took it into the Texaco station next to the Flamingo and had the tires pumped up to fifty pounds each—which alarmed the attendant, until I explained that these were "experimental" tires.

But fifty pounds each didn't help the cornering, so I went back a few hours later and told him I wanted to try seventy-five. He shook his head nervously. "Not me," he said, handing me the air hose. "Here. They're your tires. *You* do it."

"What's wrong?" I asked. "You think they can't *take* seventy-five?"

He nodded, moving away as I stooped to deal with the left front. "You're damn right," he said. "Those tires want twenty-eight in the front and thirty-two in the rear. Hell, fifty's *dangerous*, but seventy-five is *crazy*. They'll explode!"

I shook my head and kept filling the left front. "I told you," I said. "Sandoz laboratories designed these tires. They're special. I could load them up to a hundred.

"God almighty!" he groaned. "Don't do that here."

"Not today," I replied. "I want to see how they corner with seventy-five."

He chuckled. "You won't even *get* to the corner, Mister."

"We'll see," I said, moving around to the rear with the airhose. In truth, I was nervous. The two front ones were tighter than snare drums; they felt like teak wood when I tapped on them with the rod. But what the hell? I thought. If they explode, so what? It's not often that a man gets a chance to run terminal experiments on a virgin Cadillac and four brand-new $80 tires. For all I knew, the thing might start cornering like a Lotus Elan. If not, all I had to do was call the VIP agency and have another one delivered . . . maybe threaten them with a lawsuit because all four tires had exploded on me, while driving in heavy traffic. Demand an Eldorado, next time, with four Michelin Xs. And put it all on the card . . . charge it to the St. Louis Browns.

As it turned out, the Whale behaved very nicely with the altered tire pressures. The ride was a trifle rough; I could feel every pebble on the highway, like being on roller skates in a gravel pit . . . but the thing began cornering in a very stylish manner, very much like driving a motorcycle at top speed in a hard rain: one slip and ZANG, over the high side, cartwheeling across the landscape with your head in your hands.

.   .   .

About thirty minutes after our brush with the Okies we pulled into an all-night diner on the Tonopah highway, on the outskirts of a mean/scag ghetto called "North Las Vegas." Which is actually outside the city limits of Vegas proper. North Vegas is where you go when you've fucked up once too often on the Strip, and when you're not even welcome in the cut-rate downtown places around Casino Center.

This is Nevada's answer to East St. Louis—a slum and a graveyard, last stop before permanent exile to Ely or Winnemuca. North Vegas is where you go if you're a hooker turning forty and the syndicate men on the Strip decide you're no longer much good for business out there with the high rollers . . . or if you're a pimp with bad credit at the Sands . . . or what they still call, in Vegas, "a hophead." This can mean almost anything from a mean drunk to a junkie, but in terms of commercial acceptability, it means you're finished in all the right places.

The big hotels and casinos pay a lot of muscle to make sure the high rollers don't have even momentary hassles with "undesirables." Security in a place like Caesar's Palace is super tense and strict. Probably a third of the people on the floor at any given time are either shills or watchdogs. Public drunks and known pickpockets are dealt with instantly—hustled out to the parking lot by Secret Service-type thugs and given a quick, impersonal lecture about the cost of dental work and the difficulties of trying to make a living with two broken arms.

The "high side" of Vegas is probably the most closed society west of Sicily—and it makes no difference, in terms of the day to day life-style of the place, whether the Man at the Top is Lucky Luciano or Howard Hughes. In an economy where Tom Jones can make $75,000 a week for two shows a night at Caesar's, the palace guard is indispensable, and they don't care who signs their paychecks. A gold mine like Vegas breeds its own army, like any other gold mine. Hired muscle tends to accumulate in fast layers around money/power poles

. . . and big money, in Vegas, is synonymous with the Power to protect it.

So once you get blacklisted on the Strip, for any reason at all, you either get out of town or retire to nurse your act along, on the cheap, in the shoddy limbo of North Vegas . . . out there with the gunsels, the hustlers, the drug cripples and all the other losers. North Vegas, for instance, is where you go if you need to score smack before midnight with no references.

But if you're looking for cocaine, and you're ready up front with some bills and the proper code words, you want to stay on the Strip and get next to a well-connected hooker, which will take at least one bill for starters.

And so much for all that. We didn't fit the mold. There is no formula for finding yourself in Vegas with a white Cadillac full of drugs and nothing to mix with properly. The Fillmore style never quite caught on here. People like Sinatra and Dean Martin are still considered "far out" in Vegas. The "underground newspaper" here—the Las Vegas *Free Press*—is a cautious echo of *The People's World*, or maybe the *National Guardian*.

A week in Vegas is like stumbling into a Time Warp, a regression to the late fifties. Which is wholly understandable when you see the people who come here, the Big Spenders from places like Denver and Dallas. Along with National Elks Club conventions (no niggers allowed) and the All-West Volunteer Sheepherders' Rally. These are people who go absolutely crazy at the sight of an old hooker stripping down to her pasties and prancing out on the runway to the big-beat sound of a dozen 50-year-old junkies kicking out the jams on "September Song."

It was some time around three when we pulled into the parking lot of the North Vegas diner. I was looking for a copy of the Los Angeles *Times*, for news of the outside world, but a quick glance at the newspaper racks made a bad joke of that notion. They don't need the *Times* in North Vegas. No news is good news.

"Fuck newspapers," said my attorney. "What we need right now is coffee."

I agreed, but I stole a copy of the Vegas *Sun* anyway. It was yesterday's edition, but I didn't care. The idea of entering a coffee shop without a newspaper in my hands made me nervous. There was always the Sports Section; get wired on the baseball scores and pro-football rumors: "Bart Starr Beaten by Thugs in Chicago Tavern; Packers Seek Trade" . . . "Namath Quits Jets to be Governor of Alabama" . . . and a speculative piece on page 46 about a rookie sensation named Harrison Fire, out of Grambling: runs the hundred in nine flat, 344 pounds and still growing.

"This man Fire has definite promise," says the coach. "Yesterday, before practice, he destroyed a Greyhound Bus with his bare hands, and last night he killed a subway. He's a natural for color TV. I'm not one to play favorites, but it looks like we'll have to make room for him."

Indeed. There is always room on TV for a man who can beat people to jelly in nine flat . . . But not many of these were gathered, on this night, in the North Star Coffee Lounge. We had the place to ourselves—which proved to be fortunate, because we'd eaten two more pellets of mescaline on the way over, and the effects were beginning to manifest.

My attorney was no longer vomiting, or even acting sick. He ordered coffee with the authority of a man long accustomed to quick service. The waitress had the appearance of a very old hooker who had finally found her place in life. She was definitely *in charge* here, and she eyed us with obvious disapproval as we settled onto our stools.

I wasn't paying much attention. The North Star Coffee Lounge seemed like a fairly safe haven from our storms. There are some you go into—in this line of work—that you know will be heavy. The details don't matter. All you know, for sure, is that your brain starts humming with brutal vibes as you approach the front door. Something wild and evil is about to happen; and it's going to involve *you*.

But there was nothing in the atmosphere of the North Star to put me on my guard. The waitress was passively hostile, but I was accustomed to that. She was a big woman. Not fat, but large in every way, long sinewy arms and a brawler's jawbone. A burned-out caricature of Jane Russell: big head of dark hair, face slashed with lipstick and a 48 Double-E chest that was probably spectacular about twenty years ago when she might have been a Mama for the Hell's Angels chapter in Berdoo . . . but now she was strapped up in a giant pink elastic brassiere that showed like a bandage through the sweaty white rayon of her uniform.

Probably she was married to somebody, but I didn't feel like speculating. All I wanted from her, tonight, was a cup of black coffee and a 29¢ hamburger with pickles and onions. No hassles, no talk—just a place to rest and re-group. I wasn't even hungry.

My attorney had no newspaper or anything else to compel his attention. So he focused, out of boredom, on the waitress. She was taking our orders like a robot when he punched through her crust with a demand for "two glasses of ice water—with ice."

My attorney drank his in one long gulp, then asked for another. I noticed that the waitress seemed tense.

Fuck it, I thought. I was reading the funnies.

About ten minutes later, when she brought the hamburgers, I saw my attorney hand her a napkin with something printed on it. He did it very casually, with no expression at all on his face. But I knew, from the vibes, that our peace was about to be shattered.

"What was that?" I asked him.

He shrugged, smiling vaguely at the waitress who was standing about ten feet away, at the end of the counter, keeping her back to us while she pondered the napkin. Finally she turned and stared . . . then she stepped resolutely forward and tossed the napkin at my attorney.

"What *is* this?" she snapped.

"A napkin," said my attorney.

There was a moment of nasty silence, then she began screaming: "Don't give me that bullshit! I *know* what it means! You goddamn fat pimp bastard!"

My attorney picked up the napkin, looked at what he'd written, then dropped it back on the counter. "That's the name of a horse I used to own," he said calmly. "What's *wrong* with you?"

"You sonofabitch!" she screamed. "I take a lot of shit in this place, but I sure as hell don't have to take it off a *spic pimp!*"

Jesus! I thought. What's happening? I was watching the woman's hands, hoping she wouldn't pick up anything sharp or heavy. I picked up the napkin and read what the bastard had printed on it, in careful red letters: "Back Door Beauty?" The question mark was emphasized.

The woman was screaming again: "Pay your bill and get the hell out! You want me to call the cops?"

I reached for my wallet, but my attorney was already on his feet, never taking his eyes off the woman . . . then he reached under his shirt, not into his pocket, coming up suddenly with the Gerber Mini-Magnum, a nasty silver blade which the waitress seemed to understand instantly.

She froze: her eyes fixed wildly on the blade. My attorney, still watching her, moved about six feet down the aisle and lifted the receiver off the hook of the pay phone. He sliced it off, then brought the receiver back to his stool and sat down.

The waitress didn't move. I was stupid with shock, not knowing whether to run or start laughing.

"How much is that lemon meringue pie?" my attorney asked. His voice was casual, as if he had just wandered into the place and was debating what to order.

"Thirty-five cents!" the woman blurted. Her eyes were turgid with fear, but her brain was apparently functioning on some basic motor survival level.

My attorney laughed. "I mean the *whole* pie," he said.

She moaned.

My attorney put a bill on the counter. "Let's say it's five dollars," he said. "OK?"

She nodded, still frozen, watching my attorney as he walked around the counter and got the pie out of the display case. I prepared to leave.

The waitress was clearly in shock. The sight of the blade, jerked out in the heat of an argument, had apparently triggered bad memories. The glazed look in her eyes said her throat had been cut. She was still in the grip of paralysis when we left.

9.
Breakdown on Paradise Blvd.

EDITOR'S NOTE:

At this point in the chronology, Dr. Duke appears to have broken down completely; the original manuscript is so splintered that we were forced to seek out the original tape recording and transcribe it verbatim. We made no attempt to edit this section, and Dr. Duke refused even to read it. There was no way to reach him. The only address/contact we had, during this period, was a mobile phone unit somewhere on Highway 61—and all efforts to reach Duke at that number proved futile.

In the interests of journalistic purity, we are publishing the following section just as it came off the tape—one of many that Dr. Duke submitted for purposes of verification—along with his manuscript. According to the tape, this section follows an episode involving Duke, his attorney and a waitress at an all-night diner in North Vegas. The rationale for the following transaction appears to be based on a feeling—shared by both Duke and his attorney—that the American Dream would have to be sought out somewhere far beyond the dreary confines of the District Attorneys' Conference on Narcotics and Dangerous Drugs.

The transcription begins somewhere on the Northeast outskirts of Las Vegas—zooming along Paradise Road in the White Whale. . . .

Att'y: Boulder City is to the right. Is that a town?

Duke: Yeah.

Att'y: Let's go to Boulder City.

Duke: All right. Let's get some coffee somewhere . . .

161

Att'y: Right up here, Terry's Taco Stand, USA. I could go for a taco. Five for a buck.

Duke: Sounds horrible. I'd rather go somewhere where's there's one for 50¢.

Att'y: No . . . this might be the last chance we get for tacos.

Duke: . . . I need some coffee.

Att'y: I want tacos . . .

Duke: Five for a buck, that's like . . . *five hamburgers* for a buck.

Att'y: No . . . don't judge a taco by its price.

Duke: You think you might make a deal?

Att'y: I might. There's a hamburger for 29¢. Tacos are 29¢. It's just a cheap place, that's all.

Duke: Go bargain with them. . . .

[*Only garbled sounds here.—Ed.*]

Att'y: . . . Hello.

Waitress: May I help you?

Att'y: Yeah, you have tacos here? Are they Mexican tacos or just regular tacos? I mean, do you have chili in them and things like that?

Waitress: We have cheese and lettuce, and we have sauce, you know, put on them.

Att'y: I mean do you guarantee that they are authentic Mexican tacos?

Waitress: . . . I don't know. Hey Lou, do we have authentic Mexican tacos?

Woman's voice from kitchen: What?

Waitress: Authentic Mexican tacos.

Lou: We have tacos. I don't know how Mexican they are.

Att'y: Yeah, well, I just want to make sure I get what I'm paying for. 'Cause they're five for a dollar? I'll take five of them.

Duke: Taco burger, what's that?

[*Sounds of diesel engine trucks.—Ed.*]

Att'y: That's a hamburger with a taco in the middle.

Waitress: . . . instead of a shell.

Duke: A taco on a bun.

Att'y: I betcha your tacos are just hamburgers with a shell instead of a bun.

Waitress: I don't know . . .

Att'y: You just started working here?

Waitress: Today.

Att'y: I thought so, I've never saw you here before. You go to school around here?

Waitress: No, I don't go to school.

Att'y: Oh? Why not? Are you sick?

Duke: Never mind that. We came here for tacos.

[*Pause.*]

Att'y: As your attorney I advise you to get the chiliburger. It's a hamburger with chili on it.

Duke: That's too heavy for me.

Att'y: Then I advise you to get a taco burger, try that one.

Duke: . . . the taco has meat in it. I'll try that one. And some coffee now. Right now. So I can drink it while I'm waiting.

Waitress: That's all you want, one taco burger?

Duke: Well, I'll try it, I might want two.

Att'y: Are your eyes blue or green?

Waitress: Pardon?

Att'y: Blue or green?

Waitress: They change.

Att'y: Like a lizard?

Waitress: Like a cat.

Att'y: Oh, the lizard changes the color of his skin . . .

Waitress: Want anything to drink?

Att'y: Beer. And I have beer in the car. Tons of it. The whole back seat's full of it.

Duke: I don't like mixing coconuts up with beer and hamburgers.

Att'y: Well, let's smash the bastards . . . right in the middle of the highway . . . Is Boulder City somewhere around here?

Waitress: Boulder City? Do you want sugar?

Duke: Yeah.

Att'y: We're *in* Boulder City, huh? Or very close to it?

Duke: I don't know.

Waitress: There it is. That sign says Boulder City, OK. Aren't you from Nevada?

Att'y: No. We've never been here before. Just traveling through.

Waitress: You just go straight up this road here.

Att'y: Any action up there in Boulder City?

Waitress: Don't ask me. I don't . . .

Att'y: Any gambling there?

Waitress: I don't know, it's just a little town.

Duke: Where is the casino?

Waitress: I don't know.

Att'y: Wait a minute, where are you from?

Waitress: New York.

Att'y: And you've just been here a day.

Waitress: No, I've been here for a while.

Att'y: Where do you go around here? Say you wanted to go swimming or something like that?

Waitress: In my backyard.

Att'y: What's the address?

Waitress: Um, go to the . . . ah . . . the pool's not open yet.

Att'y: Let me explain it to you, let me run it down just briefly if I can. We're looking for the American Dream, and we were told it was somewhere in this area. . . . Well, we're here looking for it, 'cause they sent us out here all the way from San Francisco to look for it. That's why they gave us this white Cadillac, they figure that we could catch up with it in that . . .

Waitress: Hey Lou, you know where the American Dream is?

Att'y (to Duke): She's asking the cook if he knows where the American Dream is.

Waitress: Five tacos, one taco burger. Do you know where the American Dream is?

Lou: What's that? What is it?

Att'y: Well, we don't know, we were sent out here from San Francisco to look for the American Dream, by a magazine, to cover it.

Lou: Oh, you mean a place.

Att'y: A place called the American Dream.

Lou: Is that the old Psychiatrist's Club?

Waitress: I think so.

Att'y: The old Psychiatrist's Club?

Lou: Old Psychiatrist's Club, it's on Paradise . . . Are you guys serious?

Att'y: Oh, no honest, look at that car, I mean, do I look like I'd own a car like that?

Lou: Could that be the old Psychiatrist's Club? It was a discotheque place . . .

Att'y: Maybe that's it.

Waitress: It's on Paradise and what?

Lou: Ross Allen had the old Psychiatrist's Club. Is he the owner now?

Duke: I don't know.

Att'y: All we were told was, go till you find the American Dream. Take this white Cadillac and go find the American Dream. It's somewhere in the Las Vegas area.

Lou: That has to be the old . . .

Att'y: . . . and it's a silly story to do, but you know, that's what we get paid for.

Lou: Are you taking pictures of it, or . . .

Att'y: No, no—no pictures.

Lou: . . . or did somebody just send you on a goose chase?

Att'y: It's sort of a wild goose chase, more or less, but personally, we're dead serious.

Lou: That has to be the old Psychiatrist's Club, but the only people who hang out there is a bunch of pushers, peddlers, uppers and downers, and all that stuff.

Att'y: Maybe that's it. Is it a night-time place or is it an all day . . .

Lou: Oh, honey, this *never stops*. But it's not a casino.

Duke: What kind of place is it?

Lou: It's on Paradise, uh, the old Psychiatrist's Club's on Paradise.

Att'y: Is that what it's called, the old Psychiatrist's Club?

Lou: No, that is what it used to be, but someone bought it . . . but I didn't hear about it as the American Dream, it was something like, associated with, uh . . . it's a mental joint, where all the dopers hang out.

Att'y: A mental joint? You mean like a mental hospital?

Lou: No, honey, where all the dope peddlers and all the pushers, everybody hangs out. It's a place where all the kids are potted when they go in, and everything . . . but it's not called what you said, the American Dream.

Att'y: Do you have any idea what it might be called? Or more or less where it might be located?

Lou: Right off of Paradise and Eastern.

Waitress: But Paradise and Eastern are parallel.

Lou: Yeah, but I know I come off of Eastern, and then I go to Paradise . . .

Waitress: Yeah I know it, but then that would make it off Paradise around the Flamingo, straight up here. I think somebody's handed you a . . .

Att'y: We're staying at the Flamingo. I think this place you're talking about and the way you're describing it, I think that maybe that's it.

Lou: It's not a tourist joint.

Att'y: Well, that's why they sent me. He's the writer: I'm the bodyguard. 'Cause I figure it will be . . .

Lou: These guys are nuts . . . these kids are nuts.

Att'y: That's OK.

Waitress: Yeah, they got new laws.

Duke: Twenty-four-hour-a-day violence? Is that what we're saying?

Lou: Exactly. Now here's the Flamingo . . . Oh, I can't show you this; I can tell you better my way. Right up here at the first gas station is Tropicana, take a right.

Att'y: Tropicana to the right.

Lou: The first gas station is Tropicana. Take a right on

Tropicana and take this way . . . right on Tropicana, right on Paradise, you'll see a big black building, it's all painted black and real weird looking.

Att'y: Right on Tropicana, right on Paradise, black building . . .

Lou: And there's a sign on the side of the building that says Psychiatrist's Club, but they're completely remodeling it and everything.

Att'y: All right, that's close enough . . .

Lou: If there's anything I can do for ya, honey . . . I don't know if that's even it or not. But it sounds like it is. I think you boys are on the right track.

Att'y: Right. That's the best lead we've had for two days, we've been asking people all around.

Lou: . . . I could make a couple calls and sure as hell find out.

Att'y: Could you?

Lou: Sure I'll call Allen and ask him.

Att'y: Gee, I'd appreciate that if you could.

Waitress: When you go down to Tropicana, it's not the first gas station, the second.

Lou: There's a big sign right down the street here, it says Tropicana Avenue. Make a right, and when you get to Paradise make another right.

Att'y: OK. Big black building, right on Paradise: twenty-four-hour-a-day violence, drugs . . .

Waitress: See, here's Tropicana, and this is Boulder Highway that goes clear down like that.

Duke: Well, that's pretty far into town then.

Waitress: Well, here's Paradise split up somewhere around there. There's Paradise. Yeah, we're down in here. See, this is Boulder Highway . . . and Tropicana.

Lou: Well, that's not it, that bartender in there is a pothead too . . .

Att'y: Yeah, well, it's a lead.

Lou: You gonna be glad you stopped here, boys.

Duke: Only if we find it.

Att'y: Only if we write the article and get it in.

Waitress: Well, why don't you come inside and sit down?

Duke: We're trying to get as much sun as we can.

Att'y: She's going to make a phone call to find out where it is.

Duke: Oh. OK, well, let's go inside.

EDITOR'S NOTE (cont.):

Tape cassettes for the next sequence were impossible to transcribe due to some viscous liquid encrusted behind the heads. There is a certain consistency in the garbled sounds however, indicating that almost two hours later Dr. Duke and his attorney finally located what was left of the "Old Psychiatrist's Club"—a huge slab of cracked, scorched concrete in a vacant lot full of tall weeds. The owner of a gas station across the road said the place had "burned down about three years ago."

10.
Heavy Duty
at the Airport...
Ugly Peruvian Flashback...
'No! It's Too Late!
Don't Try It!'

My attorney left at dawn. We almost missed the first flight to L.A. because I couldn't find the airport. It was less than thirty minutes from the hotel. I was sure of that. So we left the Flamingo at exactly seven-thirty . . . but for some reason we failed to make the turnoff at the stoplight in front of the Tropicana. We kept going straight ahead on the freeway, which parallels the main airport runway, but on the *opposite* side from the terminal . . . and there is no way to get across legally.

"Goddamnit! We're lost!" my attorney was shouting. "What are we *doing* out here on this godforsaken road? The airport is right over there!" He pointed hysterically across the tundra.

"Don't worry," I said. "I've never missed a plane yet." I smiled as the memory came back. "Except once in Peru," I added. "I was already checked out of the country, through customs, but I went back to the bar to chat with this Bolivian cocaine dealer . . . and all of a sudden I heard those big 707 engines starting up, so I ran out to the runway and tried to get aboard, but the door was right behind the engines and they'd already rolled the ladder away. Shit, those afterburners would have fried me like bacon . . . but I was completely out of my head: I was desperate to get aboard.

"The airport cops saw me coming, and they gathered into a knot at the gate. I was running like a bastard, straight at them. The guy with me was screaming: 'No! It's too late! Don't try it!'

"I saw the cops waiting for me, so I slowed down like maybe I'd changed my mind . . . but when I saw them *relax*, I did a quick change of pace and tried to run right *over* the bastards." I laughed. "Jesus, it was like running full bore into a closet full of gila monsters. The fuckers almost killed me. All I remember is seeing five or six billyclubs coming down on me at the same time, and a lot of voices screaming: 'No! No! It's suicide! Stop the crazy gringo!'

"I woke up about two hours later in a bar in downtown Lima. They'd stretched me out in one of those half-moon leather booths. My luggage was all stacked beside me. Nobody had opened it . . . so I went back to sleep and caught the first flight out, the next morning."

My attorney was only half listening. "Look," he said, "I'd really like to hear more about your adventures in Peru, but not *now*. Right now all I care about is getting across that goddamn runway."

We were flashing along at good speed. I was looking for an opening, some kind of access road, some lane across the runway to the terminal. We were five miles past the last stoplight and there wasn't enough time to turn around and go back to it.

There was only one way to make it on time. I hit the brakes and eased the Whale down into the grassy moat between the two freeway lanes. The ditch was too deep for a head-on run, so I took it at an angle. The Whale almost rolled, but I kept the wheels churning and we careened up the opposite bank and into the oncoming lane. Fortunately, it was empty. We came out of the moat with the nose of the car up in the air like a hydroplane . . . then bounced on the freeway and kept right on going into the cactus field on the other side. I recall running over a fence of some kind and dragging it a few hundred yards, but by the time we got to the runway we were fully under control . . . screaming along about 60 miles an hour in low gear, and it looked like a wide-open run all the way to the terminal.

My only worry was the chance of getting crushed like a roach by an incoming DC-8, which we probably wouldn't see until it was right on top of us. I wondered if they could see us from the tower. Probably so, but why worry? I kept the thing floored. There was no point in turning back now.

My attorney was hanging onto the dashboard with both hands. I glanced over and saw fear in his eyes. His face appeared to be grey, and I sensed he was not happy with this move, but we were going so fast across the runway—then cactus, then runway again—that I knew he understood our position: We were past the point of debating the wisdom of this move; it was already done, and our only hope was to get to the other side.

I looked at my skeleton-face Accutron and saw that we had three minutes and fifteen seconds before takeoff. "Plenty of time," I said. "Get your stuff together. I'll drop you right next to the plane." I could see the big red and silver Western jetliner about 1000 yards ahead of us . . . and by this time we were skimming across smooth asphalt, past the incoming runway.

"No!" he shouted. "I can't get out! They'll crucify me. I'll have to take the blame!"

"Ridiculous," I said. "Just say you were hitchhiking to the airport and I picked you up. You never saw me before. Shit, this town is full of white Cadillac convertibles . . . and I plan to go through there so fast that nobody will even glimpse the goddamn license plate."

We were approaching the plane. I could see passengers boarding, but so far nobody had noticed us . . . approaching from this unlikely direction. "Are you ready?" I said.

He groaned. "Why not? But for Christ's sake, let's do it fast!" He was scanning the loading area, then he pointed: "Over there!" he said. "Drop me behind that big van. Just pull in behind it and I'll jump out where they can't see me, then you can make a run for it."

I nodded. So far, we had all the room we needed. No sign of alarm or pursuit. I wondered if maybe this kind of thing happened all the time in Vegas—cars full of late-arriving passengers screeching desperately across the runway, dropping off wild-eyed Samoans clutching mysterious canvas bags who would sprint onto planes at the last possible second and then roar off into the sunrise.

Maybe so, I thought. Maybe this kind of thing is standard procedure in this town . . .

I swung in behind the van and hit the brakes just long enough for my attorney to jump out. "Don't take any guff from these swine," I yelled. "Remember, if you have any trouble you can always send a telegram to the Right People."

He grinned. "Yeah . . . Explaining my Position," he said. "Some asshole wrote a poem about that once. It's probably good advice, if you have shit for brains." He waved me off.

"Right," I said, moving out. I'd already spotted a break in the big hurricane fence—and now, with the Whale in low gear, I went for it. Nobody seemed to be chasing me. I couldn't understand it. I glanced in the mirror and saw my attorney climbing into the plane, no sign of a struggle . . . and then I was through the gate and out into the early morning traffic on Paradise Road.

I took a fast right on Russell, then a left onto Maryland Parkway . . . and suddenly I was cruising in warm anonymity past the campus of the University of Las Vegas . . . no tension on these faces; I stopped at a red light and got lost, for a moment, in a sunburst of flesh in the cross-walk: fine sinewy thighs, pink mini-skirts, ripe young nipples, sleeveless blouses, long sweeps of blonde hair, pink lips and blue eyes— all the hallmarks of a dangerously innocent culture.

I was tempted to pull over and start mumbling obscene entreaties. "Hey, Sweetie, let's you and me get weird. Jump into this hotdog Caddy and we'll flash over to my suite at the Flamingo, load up on ether and behave like wild animals in my private, kidney-shaped pool . . ."

Sure we will, I thought. But by this time I was far down the parkway, easing into the turn lane for a left at Flamingo Road. Back to the hotel, to take stock. There was every reason to believe I was heading for trouble, that I'd pushed my luck a bit far. I'd abused every rule Vegas lived by—burning the locals, abusing the tourists, terrifying the help.

The only hope now, I felt, was the possibility that we'd gone to such excess, with our gig, that nobody in a position to bring the hammer down on us could possibly *believe* it. Particularly not since we'd signed in with the Police Conference. When you bring an act into this town, you want to bring it in heavy. Don't waste any time with cheap shucks and misdemeanors. Go straight for the jugular. Get right into felonies.

The mentality of Las Vegas is so grossly atavistic that a really massive crime often slips by unrecognized. One of my neighbors recently spent a week in the Vegas jail for "vagrancy." He's about twenty years old: Long hair, Levi jacket, knapsack—an out-front *drifter*, a straight Road Person. Totally harmless; he just wanders around the country looking for whatever it was that we all thought we'd nailed down in the Sixties—sort of an early Bob Zimmerman trip.

On a trip from Chicago to L.A., he got curious about Vegas and decided to have a look at it. Just passing through, strolling along and digging the sights on the Strip . . . no hurry, why rush? He was standing on a street-corner near the Circus-Circus, watching the multi-colored fountain, when the cop-cruiser pulled up.

Wham. Straight to jail. No phone call, no lawyer, no charge. "They put me in the car and took me down to the station," he said. "They took me into a big room full of people and told me to take off all my clothes before they booked me. I was standing in front of a big desk, about six feet tall, with a cop sitting behind it and looking down at me like some kind of medieval judge.

"The room was full of people. Maybe a dozen prisoners; twice that many cops, and about ten policewomen. You had to walk out in the middle of the room, then take everything out of your pockets and put it up on the desk and then strip naked—with everybody watching you.

"I only had about twenty bucks, and the fine for vagrancy was twenty-five, so they put me over on a bench with the people who were going to jail. Nobody hassled me. It was like an assembly line.

"The two guys right behind me were longhairs. Acid people. They'd been picked up for vagrancy, too. But when they started emptying their pockets, the whole room freaked. Between them, they had $130,000, mostly in big bills. The cops couldn't believe it. These guys just kept pulling out wads of money and dumping it up there on the desk—both of them naked and kind of hunched over, not saying anything.

"The cops went crazy when they saw all that money. They started whispering to each other; shit, there was no way they could hold these guys for 'vagrancy.' " He laughed. "So they charged them with 'suspicion of evasion of income taxes.'

"They took us all to jail, and these two guys were just about nuts. They were dealers, of course, and they had their stash back in their hotel room—so they had to get out before the cops found out where they were staying.

"They offered one of the guards a hundred bucks to go out and get the best lawyer in town . . . and about twenty minutes later there he was, yelling about *habeas corpus* and that kind of shit . . . hell, I tried to talk to him myself, but this guy had a one-track mind. I told him I could make bail and even pay him something if they'd let me call my father in Chicago, but he was too busy hustling for these other guys.

"About two hours later he came back with a guard and said 'Let's go.' They were out. One of the guys had told me, while they were waiting, that it was going to cost them $30,000 . . . and I guess it did, but what the hell? That's cheap, compared to what would have happened if they hadn't got themselves sprung.

"They finally let me send a telegram to my old man and he wired me 125 bucks . . . but it took seven or eight days; I'm

not sure how long I was in there, because the place didn't
have any windows and they fed us every twelve hours . . .
you lose track of time when you can't see the sun.

"They had seventy-five guys in each cell—big rooms with a
toilet bowl out in the middle. They gave you a pallet when
you came in, and you slept wherever you wanted. The guy
next to me had been in there for thirty years, for robbing a
gas station.

"When I finally got out, the cop on the desk took another
twenty-five bucks out of what my father sent me, on top of
what I owed for the vagrancy fine. What could I say? He just
took it. Then he gave me the other $75 and said they had a
taxi waiting for me outside, for the ride to the airport . . .
and when I got in the cab the driver said, 'We're not making
any stops, fella, and you'd better not *move* until we get to the
terminal.'

"I didn't move a goddamn muscle. He'd have shot me. I'm
sure of that. I went straight to the plane and I didn't say a
word to anybody until I knew we were out of Nevada. Man,
that's one place I'll *never* go back to."

11.
Fraud?
Larceny?
Rape?...
A Brutal Connection
with the Alice from
Linen Service

I was brooding on this tale as I eased the White Whale into
the Flamingo parking lot. Fifty bucks and a week in jail for
just standing on a corner and acting curious . . . Jesus, what
kind of incredible penalties would they spew out on *me?* I
checked off the various charges—but in skeleton, legal-lan-
guage form they didn't seem so bad:

Rape? We could surely beat that one. I'd never even cov-
eted the goddamn girl, much less put my hands on her flesh.
Fraud? Larceny? I could always offer to "settle." Pay it off.
Say I was sent out here by *Sports Illustrated* and then drag
the Time, Inc. lawyers into a nightmare lawsuit. Tie them up
for years with a blizzard of writs and appeals. Attach all their
assets in places like Juneau and Houston, then constantly file
motions for change of venue to Quito, Nome and Aruba . . .
Keep the thing moving, run them in circles, force them into
conflict with the accounting department:

TIME SHEET FOR ABNER H. DODGE,
CHIEF COUNSEL

*Item: $44,066.12 . . . Special outlay, to wit: We pursued the
defendant, R. Duke, throughout the Western Hemisphere and
finally brought him to bay in a village on the north shore of an
island known as Culebra in the Caribbean, where his attorneys obtained a ruling that all further proceedings should be*

conducted in the language of the Carib tribe. We sent three men to Berlitz for this purpose, but nineteen hours before the date scheduled for opening arguments, the defendant fled to Colombia, where he established residence in a fishing village called Guajira near the Venezuelan border, where the official language of jurisprudence is an obscure dialect known as "Guajiro." After many months we were able to establish jurisdiction in this place, but by that time the defendant had moved his residence to a virtually inaccessible port at the headwaters of the Amazon River, where he cultivated powerful connections with a tribe of headhunters called "Jibaros." Our stringer in Manaus was dispatched upriver, to locate and hire a native attorney conversant in Jibaro, but the search has been hampered by serious communications problems. There is in fact grave concern, in our Rio office, that the widow of the aforementioned Manaus stringer might obtain a ruinous judgment—due to bias in local courts—far larger than anything a jury in our own country would consider reasonable or even sane.

Indeed. But what is sane? Especially here in "our own country"—in this doomstruck era of Nixon. We are all wired into a *survival* trip now. No more of the speed that fueled the Sixties. Uppers are going out of style. This was the fatal flaw in Tim Leary's trip. He crashed around America selling "consciousness expansion" without ever giving a thought to the grim meat-hook realities that were lying in wait for all the people who took him too seriously. After West Point and the Priesthood, LSD must have seemed entirely logical to him . . . but there is not much satisfaction in knowing that he blew it very badly for himself, because he took too many others down with him.

Not that they didn't deserve it: No doubt they all Got What Was Coming To Them. All those pathetically eager acid freaks who thought they could buy Peace and Understanding for three bucks a hit. But their loss and failure is ours, too. What Leary took down with him was the central illusion of a whole life-style that he helped to create . . . a generation of permanent cripples, failed seekers, who never understood the essential old-mystic fallacy of the Acid Culture: the desperate assumption that somebody—or at least some *force*—is tending that Light at the end of the tunnel.

This is the same cruel and paradoxically benevolent bullshit that has kept the Catholic Church going for so many centuries. It is also the military ethic . . . a blind faith in some higher and wiser "authority." The Pope, The General, The Prime Minister . . . all the way up to "God."

One of the crucial moments of the Sixties came on that day when the Beatles cast their lot with the Maharishi. It was like Dylan going to the Vatican to kiss the Pope's ring.

First "gurus." Then, when that didn't work, back to Jesus. And now, following Manson's primitive/instinct lead, a whole new wave of clan-type commune Gods like Mel Lyman, ruler of Avatar, and What's His Name who runs "Spirit and Flesh."

Sonny Barger never quite got the hang of it, but he'll never know how close he was to a king-hell breakthrough. The Angels blew it in 1965, at the Oakland-Berkeley line, when they acted on Barger's hardhat, con-boss instincts and attacked the front ranks of an anti-war march. This proved to be an historic schism in the then Rising Tide of the Youth Movement of the Sixties. It was the first open break between the Greasers and the Longhairs, and the importance of that break can be read in the history of SDS, which eventually destroyed itself in the doomed effort to reconcile the interests of the lower/working class biker/dropout types and the upper/middle, Berkeley/student activists.

Nobody involved in that scene, at the time, could possibly have foreseen the Implications of the Ginsberg/Kesey failure to persuade the Hell's Angels to join forces with the radical Left from Berkeley. The final split came at Altamont, four years later, but by that time it had long been clear to everybody except a handful of rock industry dopers and the national press. The orgy of violence at Altamont merely *drama-*

tized the problem. The realities were already fixed; the illness
was understood to be terminal, and the energies of The Movement were long since aggressively dissipated by the rush to
self-preservation.

Ah; this terrible gibberish. Grim memories and bad flashbacks, looming up through the time/fog of Stanyan Street
. . . no solace for refugees, no point in looking back. The
question, as always, is *now* . . . ?

I was slumped on my bed in the Flamingo, feeling dangerously out of phase with my surroundings. Something ugly
was about to happen. I was sure of it. The room looked like
the site of some disastrous zoological experiment involving

whiskey and gorillas. The ten-foot mirror was shattered, but still hanging together—bad evidence of that afternoon when my attorney ran amok with the coconut hammer, smashing the mirror and all the lightbulbs.

We'd replaced the lights with a package of red and blue Christmas tree lights from Safeway, but there was no hope of replacing the mirror. My attorney's bed looked like a burned-out rat's nest. Fire had consumed the top half, and the rest was a mass of wire and charred stuffing. Luckily, the maids hadn't come near the room since that awful confrontation on Tuesday.

I had been asleep when the maid came in that morning. We'd forgotten to hang out the "Do Not Disturb" sign . . . so she wandered into the room and startled my attorney, who was kneeling, stark naked, in the closet, vomiting into his shoes . . . thinking he was actually in the bathroom, and then suddenly looking up to see a woman with a face like Mickey Rooney staring down at him, unable to speak, trembling with fear and confusion.

"She was holding that mop like an axe-handle," he said later. "So I came out of the closet in a kind of running crouch, still vomiting, and hit her right at the knees . . . it was pure instinct; I thought she was ready to kill me . . . and then, when she screamed, that's when I put the icebag on her mouth."

Yes. I remembered that scream . . . one of the most terrifying sounds I'd ever heard. I woke up and saw my attorney grappling desperately on the floor right next to my bed with what appeared to be an *old woman*. The room was full of powerful electric noise. The TV set, hissing at top volume on a nonexistent channel. I could barely hear the woman's muffled cries as she struggled to get the icebag away from her face . . . but she was no match for my attorney's naked bulk, and he finally managed to pin her in a corner behind the TV set, clamping his hands on her throat while she babbled pitifully: "Please . . . please . . . I'm only the maid, I didn't *mean* nothin' . . ."

I was out of bed in a flash, grabbing my wallet and waving the gold Policemen's Benevolent Assn. press badge in front of her face.

"You're under arrest!" I shouted.

"No!" she groaned. "I just wanted to clean up!"

My attorney got to his feet, breathing heavily. "She must have used a pass key," he said. "I was polishing my shoes in the closet when I noticed her sneaking in—so I *took her.*" He was trembling, drooling vomit off his chin, and I could see at a glance that he understood the gravity of this situation. Our behavior, this time, had gone far past the boundaries of private kinkiness. Here we were, both naked, staring down at a terrified old woman—a hotel *employee*—stretched out on the floor of our suite in a paroxysm of fear and hysteria. She would have to be dealt with.

"What made you do it?" I asked her. "Who paid you off?"

"Nobody!" she wailed. "I'm the *maid!*"

"You're lying!" shouted my attorney. "You were after the evidence! Who put you up to this—the manager?"

"I work for the *hotel,*" she said. "All I do is clean up the rooms."

I turned to my attorney. "This means they know what we *have,*" I said. "So they sent this poor old woman up here to steal it."

"No!" she yelled. "I don't know what you're talking about!"

"Bullshit!" said my attorney. "You're just as much a part of it as they are."

"Part of *what?*"

"The dope ring," I said. "You *must* know what's going on in this hotel. Why do you think we're here?"

She stared at us, trying to speak but only blubbering. "I *know* you're cops," she said finally. "But I thought you were just here for that convention. I *swear!* All I wanted to do was clean up your room. I don't know anything about *dope!*"

My attorney laughed. "Come on, baby. Don't try to tell us you never heard of the Grange Gorman."

"No!" she yelled. "No! I swear to Jesus I never heard of that stuff!"

My attorney seemed to think for a moment, then he leaned down to help the old lady to her feet. "Maybe she's telling the truth," he said to me. "Maybe she's *not part* of it."

"No! I swear I'm not!" she howled.

"Well . . ." I said. "In that case, maybe we won't have to put her away . . . maybe she can *help*."

"Yes!" she said eagerly. "I'll help you all you need! I *hate* dope!"

"So do we, lady," I said.

"I think we should put her on the payroll," said my attorney. "Have her checked out, then line her up for a Big One each month, depending on what she comes up with."

The old woman's face had changed markedly. She no longer seemed disturbed to find herself chatting with two naked men, one of whom had tried to strangle her just a few moments earlier.

"Do you think you could handle it?" I asked her.

"What?"

"One phone call every day," said my attorney. "Just tell us what you've seen." He patted her on the shoulder. "Don't worry if it doesn't add up. That's our problem."

She grinned. "You'd *pay* me for that?"

"You're damn right," I said. "But the first time you say anything about this, to *anybody*—you'll go straight to prison for the rest of your life."

She nodded. "I'll help any way that I can," she said. "But who should I call?"

"Don't worry," said my attorney. "What's your name?"

"Alice," she said. "Just ring Linen Service and ask for Alice."

"You'll be contacted," I said. "It'll take about a week. But meanwhile, just keep your eyes open and try to act normal. Can you do that?"

"Oh yes sir!" she said. "Will I see you gentlemen again?"

She grinned sheepishly. "After *this*, I mean . . . ."

"No," said my attorney. "They sent us down from Carson City. You'll be contacted by Inspector Rock. Arthur Rock. He'll be posing as a politician, but you won't have any trouble recognizing him."

She seemed to be shuffling nervously.

"What's wrong?" I said. "Is there something you haven't *told* us?"

"Oh no!" she said quickly. "I was just wondering—who's going to *pay* me?"

"Inspector Rock will take care of that," I said. "It'll all be in cash: a thousand dollars on the ninth of every month."

"Oh Lord!" she exclaimed. "I'd do just about anything for that!"

"You and a lot of other people," said my attorney. "You'd be surprised who we have on the payroll—right here in this same hotel."

She looked stricken. "Would I *know* them?"

"Probably," I said. "But they're all undercover. The only way you'll ever know is if something really serious happens and one of them has to contact you in public, with the password."

"What *is* it?" she asked.

" 'One Hand Washes the Other,' " I said. "The minute you hear that, you say: 'I fear nothing.' That way, they'll *know* you."

She nodded, repeating the code several times, while we listened to make sure she had it right.

"OK," said my attorney. "That's it for now. We probably won't be seeing you again until the hammer comes down. You'll be better off ignoring us until we leave. Don't bother to make up the room. Just leave a pile of towels and soap outside the door, exactly at midnight." He smiled. "That way, we won't have to risk another one of these little incidents, will we?"

She moved toward the door. "Whatever you say, gentlemen. I can't tell you how sorry I am about what happened

. . . but it was only because I didn't *realize*."

My attorney ushered her out. "We understand," he said gently. "But it's all over now. Thank God for the *decent* people."

She smiled as she closed the door behind her.

12.
Return to the
Circus-Circus...
Looking for the Ape...
to Hell with the
American Dream

Almost seventy-two hours had passed since that strange encounter, and no maid had set foot in the room. I wondered what Alice had told them. We had seen her once, trundling a laundry cart across the parking area as we rolled up in the Whale, but we offered no sign of recognition and she seemed to understand.

But it couldn't last much longer. The room was full of used towels; they were hanging everywhere. The bathroom floor was about six inches deep with soap bars, vomit, and grapefruit rinds, mixed with broken glass. I had to put my boots on every time I went in there to piss. The nap of the mottled grey rug was so thick with marijuana seeds that it appeared to be turning green.

The general back-alley ambience of the suite was so rotten, so incredibly foul, that I figured I could probably get away with claiming it was some kind of "Life-slice exhibit" that we'd brought down from Haight Street, to show cops from other parts of the country how deep into filth and degeneracy the drug people will sink, if left to their own devices.

But what kind of addict would need all these coconut husks and crushed honeydew rinds? Would the presence of junkies account for all these uneaten french fries? These puddles of glazed catsup on the bureau?

Maybe so. But then why all this *booze?* And these crude pornographic photos, ripped out of pulp magazines like *Whores of Sweden* and *Orgies in the Casbah*, that were plastered on the broken mirror with smears of mustard that had dried to a hard yellow crust. . . . and all these signs of violence, these strange red and blue bulbs and shards of broken glass embedded in the wall plaster . . .

No; these were not the hoofprints of your normal, godfearing junkie. It was far too savage, too aggressive. There was evidence, in his room, of excessive consumption of almost every type of drug known to civilized man since 1544 A.D. It could only be explained as a *montage*, a sort of exaggerated medical exhibit, put together very carefully to show what might happen if twenty-two serious drug felons—each with a *different* addiction—were penned up together in the same room for five days and nights, without relief.

Indeed. But of course that would never happen in Real Life, gentlemen. We just put this thing together for *demonstration* purposes . . .

Suddenly the phone was ringing, jerking me out of my fantasy stupor. I looked at it. Riiiinnnnnggggggg . . . Jesus, what now? Is this *it?* I could almost hear the shrill voice of the Manager, Mr. Heem, saying the police were on their way up to my room and would I please not shoot through the door when they began kicking it down.

Riinnnngggg . . . No, they wouldn't call first. Once they decided to take me, they would probably set an ambush in the elevator: first Mace, then a gang-swarm. It would come with no warning.

So I picked up the phone. It was my friend Bruce Innes, calling from the Circus-Circus. He had located the man who wanted to sell the ape I'd been inquiring about. The price was $750.

"What kind of a greedhead are we dealing with?" I said. "Last night it was four hundred."

"He claims he just found out it was housebroken," said Bruce. "He let it sleep in the trailer last night, and the thing actually shit in the shower stall."

"That doesn't mean anything," I said. "Apes are attracted to water. Next time it'll shit in the sink."

"Maybe you should come down and argue with the guy," said Bruce. "He's here in the bar with me. I told him you really wanted the ape and that you could give it a fine home. I think he'll negotiate. He's really *attached* to the stinking thing. It's here in the bar with us, sitting up on a goddamn stool, slobbering into a beer schooner."

"Okay," I said. "I'll be there in ten minutes. Don't let the bastard get drunk. I want to meet him under natural conditions."

When I got to the Circus-Circus they were loading an old man into an ambulance outside the main door. "What happened?" I asked the car-keeper.

"I'm not sure," he said. "Somebody said he had a stroke. But I noticed the back of his head was all cut up." He slid into the Whale and handed me a stub. "You want me to save your drink for you?" he asked, holding up a big glass of tequila that was on the seat of the car. "I can put it in the cooler if you want."

I nodded. These people were familiar with my habits. I had been in and out of the place so often, with Bruce and the other band members, that the car-keepers knew me by name —although I'd never introduced myself, and nobody had ever asked me. I just assumed it was all part of the gig here; that they'd probably rifled the glove compartment and found a notebook with my name on it.

The real reason, which didn't occur to me at the time, was that I was still wearing my ID/badge from the District Attorneys' Conference. It was dangling from the pocket-flap of my multi-colored bird-shooting jacket, but I'd long since forgotten about it. No doubt they all assumed I was some kind of super-weird undercover agent . . . or maybe not; maybe they were just humoring me because they figured anybody crazy enough to pose as a cop while driving around Vegas in a white Cadillac convertible with a drink in his hand almost *had* to be Heavy, and perhaps even dangerous. In a scene where nobody with any ambition is really what he appears to be, there's not much risk in acting like a king-hell freak. The overseers will nod wisely at each other and mutter about "these goddamn no-class put-ons."

The other side of that coin is the "Goddamn! Who's *that?*" syndrome. This comes from people like doormen and floor-walkers who assume that anybody who acts crazy, but still tips big, *must* be important—which means he should be humored, or at least treated gently.

But none of this makes any difference with a head full of mescaline. You just blunder around, doing anything that seems to be right, and it usually is. Vegas is so full of natural freaks—people who are genuinely twisted—that drugs aren't really a problem, except for cops and the scag syndicate. Psychedelics are almost irrelevant in a town where you can wander into a casino any time of the day or night and witness the crucifixion of a gorilla—on a flaming neon cross that suddenly turns into a pinwheel, spinning the beast around in wild circles above the crowded gambling action.

I found Bruce at the bar, but there was no sign of the ape. "Where is it?" I demanded. "I'm ready to write a check. I want to take the bastard back home on the plane with me. I've already reserved two first-class seats—R. Duke and Son."

"Take him on the *plane?*"

"Hell yes," I said. "You think they'd *say* anything? Call attention to my son's infirmities?"

He shrugged. "Forget it," he said. "They just took him away. He attacked an old man right here at the bar. The creep started hassling the bartender about 'allowing barefoot rabble in the place' and just about then the ape let out a shriek—so the old guy threw a beer at him, and the ape went crazy, came out of his seat like a jack-in-the-box and took a big bite out of the old man's head . . . the bartender had to call an ambulance, then the cops came and took the ape away."

"Goddamnit," I said. "What's the bail? I *want* that ape."

"Get a grip on yourself," he said. "You better stay clear of that jail. That's all they'd need to put the cuffs on you. Forget that ape. You don't need him."

I gave it some thought, then decided he was probably right. There was no sense blowing everything for the sake of some violent ape I'd never even met. For all I knew, he'd take a bite out of *my* head if I tried to bail him out. It would take him a while to calm down, after the shock of being put behind bars, and I couldn't afford to wait around.

"When are you taking off?" Bruce asked.

"As soon as possible," I said. "No point hanging around this town any longer. I have all I need. Anything else would only confuse me."

He seemed surprised. "You *found* the American Dream?" he said. "In *this* town?"

I nodded. "We're sitting on the main nerve right now," I said. "You remember that story the manager told us about the owner of this place? How he always wanted to run away and join the circus when he was a kid?"

Bruce ordered two more beers. He looked over the casino for a moment, then shrugged. "Yeah, I see what you mean," he said. "Now the bastard has his *own* circus, and a license to steal, too." He nodded. "You're right—he's the model."

"Absolutely," I said. "It's pure Horatio Alger, all the way down to his attitude. I tried to have a talk with him, but some heavy-sounding dyke who claimed to be his Executive Secretary told me to fuck off. She said he hates the press worse than anything else in America."

"Him and Spiro Agnew," Bruce muttered.

"They're both right," I said. "I tried to tell the woman that I agreed with everything he stood for, but she said if I knew what was good for me I'd get the hell out of town and not even *think* about bothering the Boss. 'He really hates reporters,' she said. 'I don't mean this to sound like a warning, but if I were you I'd take it that way. . . .'"

Bruce nodded. The Boss was paying him a thousand bucks a week to work two sets a night in the Leopard Lounge, and another two grand for the group. All they had to do was make a hell of a lot of noise for two hours every night. The Boss didn't give a flying fuck what kind of songs they sang, just as long as the beat was heavy and the amps were turned up loud enough to lure people into the bar.

It was strange to sit there in Vegas and hear Bruce singing powerful stuff like "Chicago" and "Country Song." If the management had bothered to hear the lyrics, the whole band would have been tarred and feathered.

Several months later, in Aspen, Bruce sang the same songs in a club jammed with tourists and a former Astronaut* . . . and when the last set was over, —— came over to our table and began yelling all kinds of drunken, super-patriot gibberish, hitting on Bruce about "What kind of nerve does a goddamn *Canadian* have to come down here and *insult this country?*"

"Say man," I said. "I'm an *American*. I live here, and I agree with every fucking word he says."

At this point the hash-bouncers appeared, grinning inscrutably and saying: "Good evening to you gentlemen. The *I Ching* says it's time to be quiet, right? And *nobody* hassles the musicians in this place, is that clear?"

The Astronaut left, muttering darkly about using his influence to "get something done, damn quick," about the Immigration Statutes. "What's *your name?*" he asked me, as the hash-bouncers eased him away.

"Bob Zimmerman," I said. "And if there's one thing I hate in this world, it's a goddamn bonehead Polack."

"You think I'm a *Polack?*" he screamed. "You dirty *goldbricker!* You're all *shit!* You don't *represent* this country."

"Christ, let's hope to hell *you* don't," Bruce muttered.

—— was still raving as they muscled him out to the street. The next night, in another restaurant, The Astronaut was scarfing up his chow—stone sober—when a fourteen-year-old boy approached the table to ask for his autograph. —— acted

* Name deleted at insistence of publisher's lawyer.

coy for a moment, feigning embarrassment, then he scrawled his signature on the small piece of paper the boy handed him. The boy looked at it for a moment, then tore it into small pieces and dropped it in ——'s lap. "Not everybody loves you, man," he said. Then he went back and sat down at his own table, about six feet away.

The Astronaut's party was speechless. Eight or ten people —wives, managers and favored senior engineers, showing —— a good time in fabulous Aspen. Now they looked like somebody had just sprayed their table with shit-mist. Nobody said a word. They ate quickly, and left without tipping.

So much for Aspen and astronauts. —— would never have that kind of trouble in Las Vegas.

A little bit of this town goes a very long way. After five days in Vegas you feel like you've been here for five years. Some people say they like it—but then some people like Nixon, too. He would have made a perfect Mayor for this town; with John Mitchell as Sheriff and Agnew as Master of Sewers.

13.
End of the Road...
Death of the Whale...
Soaking Sweats
in the Airport

When I tried to sit down at the baccarat table the bouncers put the arm on me. "You don't belong here," one of them said quietly. "Let's go outside."

"Why not?" I said.

They took me out to the front entrance and signaled for the Whale to be brought up. "Where's your friend?" they asked, while we waited.

"What friend?"

"The big spic."

"Look," I said. "I'm a Doctor of Journalism. You'd never catch me hanging around this place with a goddamn spic."

They laughed. "Then what about *this?*" they said. And they confronted me with a big photograph of me and my attorney sitting at a table in the floating bar.

I shrugged. "That's not me," I said. "That's a guy named Thompson. He works for *Rolling Stone* . . . a really vicious, crazy kind of person. And that guy sitting next to him is a hit-man for the Mafia in Hollywood. Shit, have you *studied* this photograph? What kind of a maniac would roam around Vegas wearing *one black glove.*"

"We noticed that," they said. "Where is he *now?*"

I shrugged. "He moves around pretty fast," I said. "His orders come out of St. Louis."

They stared at me. "How do *you* know all this stuff?"

I showed them my gold PBA badge, flashing it quickly with my back to the crowd. "Act natural," I whispered. "Don't put me on the spot."

They were still standing there when I drove off in the Whale. The geek had brought it up at exactly the right moment. I gave him a five-dollar bill and hit the street with a stylish screech of rubber.

It was all over now. I drove across to the Flamingo and loaded all my luggage into the car. I tried to put the top up, for privacy, but something was wrong with the motor. The generator light had been on, fiery red, ever since I'd driven the thing into Lake Mead on a water test. A quick run along the dashboard disclosed that every circuit in the car was totally fucked. Nothing worked. Not even the headlights—and when I hit the air conditioner button I heard a nasty explosion under the hood.

The top was jammed about halfway up, but I decided to try for the airport. If this goddamn junker wouldn't run right, I could always abandon it and call a cab. To hell with this garbage from Detroit. They shouldn't be allowed to get away with it.

The sun was coming up when I got to the airport. I left the Whale in the VIP parking lot. A kid about fifteen years old checked it in, but I refused to answer his questions. He was very excited about the overall condition of the vehicle. "Holy God!" he kept shouting. "How did *this* happen?" He kept moving around the car, pointing at various dents, rips and crushed places.

"I know," I said. "They beat the shit out of it. This is a terrible goddamn town for driving around in convertibles. The worst time was right out on the Boulevard in front of the Sahara. You know that corner where all the junkies hang out? Jesus, I couldn't believe it when they all went crazy *at once*."

The kid was none too bright. His face had gone blank early on, and now he seemed in a state of mute fear.

"Don't worry," I said. "I'm insured." I showed him the contract, pointing to the small-print clause where it said I was insured against *all damages*, for only two dollars a day.

The kid was still nodding when I fled. I felt a bit guilty about leaving him to deal with the car. There was no way to explain the massive damage. It was finished, a wreck, totaled out. Under normal circumstances I would have been seized and arrested when I tried to turn it in . . . but not at this hour of the morning, with only this kid to deal with. I was, after all, a "VIP." Otherwise, they would never have chartered the car to me in the first place. . . .

Let the chickens come home to roost, I thought as I hurried into the airport. It was still too early to act normal, so I hunkered down in the coffee shop behind the L.A. *Times*. Somewhere down the corridor a jukebox was playing "One Toke Over the Line." I listened for a moment, but my nerve ends were no longer receptive. The only song I might have been able to relate to, at that point, was "Mister Tambourine Man." Or maybe "Memphis Blues Again. . . ."

"Awww, mama . . . can this really . . . be the end . . . ?"

My plane left at eight, which meant I had two hours to kill. Feeling desperately visible. There was no doubt in my mind that they were looking for me; the net was closing down . . . it was only a matter of time before they ran me down like some kind of rabid animal.

I checked all my luggage through the chute. All but the leather satchel, which was full of drugs. And the .357. Did they have the goddamn metal detector system in this airport? I strolled around to the boarding gate and tried to look casual while I cased the area for black boxes. None were visible. I decided to take the chance—just zip through the gate with a big smile on my face, mumbling distractedly about "a bad slump in the hardware market. . . ."

Just another failed salesman checking out. Blame it all on that bastard Nixon. Indeed. I decided it might look more natural if I found somebody to chat with—a routine line of small talk, between passengers:

"Hy're yew, fella! I guess you're probably wonderin' what makes me sweat like this? Yeah! Well, god *damn*, man! Have you read the newspapers today? . . . You'd never believe what those dirty bastards have done *this* time!"

I figured that would cover it . . . but I couldn't find anybody who looked safe enough to talk to. The whole airport was full of people who looked like they might go for my floating rib if I made a false move. I felt very paranoid . . . like some kind of criminal skullsucker on the lam from Scotland Yard.

Everywhere I looked I saw Pigs . . . because on that morning the Las Vegas airport *was* full of cops: the mass exodus after the climax of the District Attorneys' Conference. When I finally put this together I felt much better about the health of my own brain . . .

VERYTHING seems to be ready. Are you Ready? Ready?

Well, why not? This is a heavy day in Vegas. A thousand cops are checking out of town, scurrying through the airport in groups of three and six. They are heading back home. The drug conference is finished. The Airport Lounge is humming with mean talk and bodies. Short beers and Bloody Marys, here and there a victim of chest rash rubbing Mexsana under the armpit straps of a thick shoulder holster. No point hiding this business any longer. Let it all hang out . . . or at least get some air to it.

Yes, thank you kindly . . . I think I busted a button on my trousers. I hope they don't fall down. You don't want my trousers to fall down now, do you?

Fuck no. Not today. Not right here in the middle of the Las Vegas airport, on this sweaty-hard morning at the tail end of this mass meeting on Narcotics and Dangerous Drugs.

"When the train . . . come in the station . . . I looked her in the eye . . ."

Grim music in this airport.

"Yes, it's hard to tell it's hard to tell, when all your love's in Vain. . . ."

Every now and then you run up on one of those days when *everything's* in vain . . . a stone bummer from start to finish; and if you know what's good for you, on days like these you sort of hunker down in a safe corner and *watch*. Maybe think a bit. Lay back on a cheap wooden chair, screened off from the traffic, and shrewdly rip the poptops out of five or eight Budweisers . . . smoke off a pack of King Marlboros, eat a peanut-butter sandwich, and finally toward evening gobble up a wad of good mescaline . . . then drive out, later on, to the beach. Get out in the surf, in the fog, and slosh along on numb-frozen feet about ten yards out from the tideline . . . stomping through tribes of wild sandpeckers . . . riderunners, whorehoppers, stupid little birds and crabs and saltsuckers, with here and there a big pervert or woolly reject gimping off in the distance, wandering alone by themselves behind the dunes and driftwood. . . .

These are the ones you will never be properly introduced to—at least not if your luck holds. But the beach is less complicated than a boiling fast morning in the Las Vegas airport.

I felt very obvious. Amphetamine psychosis? Paranoid dementia?—What *is* it? My Argentine luggage? This crippled, loping walk that once made me a reject from the Naval ROTC?

Indeed. *This man will never be able to walk straight, Captain! Because one leg is longer than the other. . . .* Not much. Three eighths of an inch or so, which counted out to about two-eighths more than the Captain could tolerate.

So we parted company. He accepted a command in the South China Sea, and I became a Doctor of Gonzo Journalism . . . and many years later, killing time in the Las Vegas airport this terrible morning, I picked up a newspaper and saw where the Captain had fucked up very badly:

SHIP COMMANDER BUTCHERED
BY NATIVES AFTER
"ACCIDENTAL" ASSAULT
ON GUAM

(AOP)—*Aboard the U.S.S. Crazy Horse: Somewhere in the Pacific* (Sept. 25)—The entire 3465-man crew of this newest American aircraft carrier is in violent mourning today, after five crewmen including the Captain were diced up like pineapple meat in a brawl with the Heroin Police at the neutral port of Hong See. Dr. Bloor, the ship's chaplain, presided over tense funeral services at dawn on the flight deck. The 4th Fleet Service Choir sang "Tom Thumb's Blues" . . . and then, while the ship's bells tolled frantically, the remains of the five were set afire in a gourd and hurled into the Pacific by a hooded officer known only as "The Commander."

Shortly after the services ended, the crewmen fell to fighting among themselves and all communications with the ship were severed for an indefinite period. Official spokesmen at 4th Fleet Headquarters on Guam said the Navy had "no comment" on the situation, pending the results of a top-level investigation by a team of civilian specialists headed by former New Orleans district attorney James Garrison.

. . . Why bother with newspapers, if this is all they offer? Agnew was right. The press is a gang of cruel faggots. Journalism is not a profession or a trade. It is a cheap catch-all for fuckoffs and misfits—a false doorway to the backside of life, a filthy piss-ridden little hole nailed off by the building inspector, but just deep enough for a wino to curl up from the sidewalk and masturbate like a chimp in a zoo-cage.

14.
Farewell to Vegas...
'God's Mercy
on You Swine!'

As I skulked around the airport, I realized that I was still wearing my police identification badge. It was a flat orange rectangle, sealed in clear plastic, that said: "Raoul Duke, Special Investigator, Los Angeles." I saw it in the mirror above the urinal.

Get rid of this thing, I thought. Tear it off. The gig is finished . . . and it proved nothing. At least not to me. And certainly not to my attorney—who also had a badge—but now he was back in Malibu, nursing his paranoid sores.

It had been a waste of time, a lame fuckaround that was only—in clear retrospect—a cheap excuse for a thousand cops to spend a few days in Las Vegas and lay the bill on the taxpayers. Nobody had *learned* anything—or at least nothing new. Except maybe me . . . and all I learned was that the National District Attorneys' Association is about ten years behind the grim truth and harsh kinetic realities of what they have only just recently learned to call "the Drug Culture" in this foul year of Our Lord, 1971.

They are still burning the taxpayers for thousands of dollars to make films about "the dangers of LSD," at a time when acid is widely known—to everybody but cops—to be the Studebaker of the drug market; the popularity of psychedelics has fallen off so drastically that most volume dealers no longer even handle quality acid or mescaline except as a favor to special customers: Mainly jaded, over-thirty drug dilettantes—like me, and my attorney.

The big market, these days, is in Downers. Reds and smack
—Seconal and heroin—and a hellbroth of bad domestic grass
sprayed with everything from arsenic to horse tranquillizers.
What sells, today, is whatever Fucks You Up—whatever
short-circuits your brain and grounds it out for the longest
possible time. The ghetto market has mushroomed into subur-
bia. The Miltown man has turned, with a vengeance, to skin-
popping and even mainlining . . . and for every ex-speed
freak who drifted, for relief, into smack, there are 200 kids
who went straight to the needle off Seconal. They never even
bothered to *try* speed.

Uppers are no longer stylish. Methedrine is almost as rare,
on the 1971 market, as pure acid or DMT. "Consciousness Expansion" went out with LBJ . . . and it is worth noting, his-
torically, that downers came in with Nixon.

I limped onto the plane with no problem except a wave of
ugly vibrations from the other passengers . . . but my head
was so burned out, by then, that I wouldn't have cared if I'd
had to climb aboard stark naked and covered with oozing
chancres. It would have taken extreme physical force to keep
me off that plane. I was so far beyond simple fatigue that I
was beginning to feel nicely adjusted to the idea of permanent hysteria. I felt like the slightest misunderstanding with
the stewardess would cause me to either cry or go mad . . .
and the woman seemed to sense this, because she treated me
very gently.

When I wanted more ice cubes for my Bloody Mary, she
brought them quickly . . . and when I ran out of cigarettes,
she gave me a pack from her own purse. The only time she
seemed nervous was when I pulled a grapefruit out of my
satchel and began slicing it up with a hunting knife. I noticed
her watching me closely, so I tried to smile. "I never go anywhere without grapefruit," I said. "It's hard to get a really
good one—unless you're rich."

She nodded.

I flashed her the grimace/smile again, but it was hard to know what she was thinking. It was entirely possible, I knew, that she'd already decided to have me taken off the plane in a cage when we got to Denver. I stared fixedly into her eyes for a time, but she kept herself under control.

I was asleep when our plane hit the runway, but the jolt brought me instantly awake. I looked out the window and saw the Rocky Mountains. What the fuck was I doing *here?* I wondered. It made no sense at all. I decided to call my attorney as soon as possible. Have him wire me some money to buy a huge albino Doberman. Denver is a national clearing house for stolen Dobermans; they come from all parts of the country.

Since I was already here, I thought I might as well pick up a vicious dog. But first, something for my nerves. Immediately after the plane landed I rushed up the corridor to the airport drugstore and asked the clerk for a box of amyls.

She began to fidget and shake her head. "Oh, no," she said finally. "I can't sell *those* things except by prescription."

"I know," I said. "But you see, I'm a *doctor*. I don't need a prescription."

She was still fidgeting. "Well . . . you'll have to show me some I.D.," she moaned.

"Of course." I jerked out my wallet and let her see the police badge while I flipped through the deck until I located my Ecclesiastical Discount Card—which identifies me as a Doctor of Divinity, a certified Minister of the Church of the New Truth.

She inspected it carefully, then handed it back. I sensed a new respect in her manner. Her eyes grew warm. She seemed to want to touch me. "I hope you'll forgive me, Doctor," she said with a fine smile. "But I had to ask. We get some *real freaks* in this place. All kinds of dangerous addicts. You'd never believe it."

"Don't worry," I said. "I understand perfectly. But I have a bad heart and I hope—"

"Certainly!" she exclaimed—and within seconds she was back with a dozen amyls. I paid without quibbling about the ecclesiastical discount. Then I opened the box and cracked one under my nose immediately, while she watched.

"Just be thankful your heart is young and strong," I said. "If I were you I would never . . . ah . . . holy shit! . . . what? Yes, you'll have to excuse me now; I feel it coming on." I turned away and reeled off in the general direction of the bar.

"God's mercy on you swine!" I shouted at two Marines coming out of the men's room.

They looked at me, but said nothing. By this time I was laughing crazily. But it made no difference. I was just another fucked-up cleric with a bad heart. Shit, they'll love me down at the Brown Palace. I took another big hit off the amyl, and by the time I got to the bar my heart was full of joy. I felt like a monster reincarnation of Horatio Alger . . . a Man on the Move, and just sick enough to be totally confident.

OTHER AMERICAN STORIES

Jacket Copy for <u>Fear & Loathing in Las Vegas:</u> <u>A Savage Journey to the Heart of the American Dream</u>

The book began as a 250-word caption for *Sports Illustrated*. I was down in LA, working on a very tense and depressing investigation of the allegedly accidental killing of a journalist named Ruben Salazar by the Los Angeles County Sheriff's Dept—and after a week or so on the story I was a ball of nerves & sleepless paranoia (figuring that *I* might be next) . . . and I needed some excuse to *get away* from the angry vortex of that story & try to make sense of it without people shaking butcher knives in my face all the time.

My main contact on that story was the infamous Chicano lawyer Oscar Acosta—an old friend, who was under bad pressure at the time, from his super-militant constituents, for even *talking* to a gringo/gabacho journalist. The pressure was so heavy, in fact, that I found it impossible to talk to Oscar alone. We were always in the midst of a crowd of heavy street-fighters who didn't mind letting me know that they wouldn't need much of an excuse to chop me into hamburger.

This is no way to work on a very volatile & very complex story. So one afternoon I got Oscar in my rented car and drove him over to the Beverly Hills Hotel—away from his bodyguards, etc.—and told him I was getting a bit wiggy from the pressure; it was like being on stage all the time, or maybe in the midst of a prison riot. He agreed, but the nature of his position as "leader of the militants" made it impossible for him to be openly friendly with a gabacho.

I understood this . . . and just about then, I remembered that another old friend, now working for *Sports Illustrated*, had asked me if I felt like going out to Vegas for the weekend, at their expense, and writing a few words about a motorcycle race. This seemed like a good excuse to get out of LA for a few days, and if I took Oscar along it would also give us time to talk and sort out the evil realities of the Salazar/Murder story.

So I called *Sports Illustrated*—from the patio of the Polo Lounge—and said I was ready to do the "Vegas thing." They agreed . . . and from here on in there is no point in running down details, because they're all in the book.

More or less . . . and this qualifier is the essence of what, for no particular reason, I've decided to call Gonzo Journalism. It is a style of "reporting" based on William Faulkner's idea that the best fiction is far more *true* than any kind of journalism—and the best journalists have always known this.

Which is not to say that Fiction is necessarily "more true" than Journalism—or vice versa—but that both "fiction" and "journalism" are artificial categories; and that both forms, at their best, are only two different means to the same end. This is getting pretty heavy . . . so I should cut back and explain, at this point, that *Fear & Loathing in Las Vegas* is a *failed experiment* in Gonzo Journalism. My idea was to buy a fat notebook and record the whole thing, *as it happened*, then send in the notebook for publication—without editing. That way, I felt, the eye & mind of the journalist would be functioning as a camera. The writing would be selective & necessarily interpretive—but once the image was written, the words would be final; in the same way that a Cartier-Bresson photograph is always (he says) the full-frame negative. No alterations in the darkroom, no cutting or cropping, no spotting . . . no editing.

But this is a hard thing to do, and in the end I found myself imposing an essentially fictional framework on what began as a piece of straight/crazy journalism. True Gonzo reporting needs the talents of a master journalist, the eye of an artist/photographer and the heavy balls of an actor. Because the writer *must* be a participant in the scene, while he's writing it—or at least taping it, or even sketching it. Or all three. Probably the closest analogy to the ideal would be a film director/producer who writes his own scripts, does his own camera work and somehow manages to film himself in action, as the protagonist or at least a main character.

The American print media are not ready for this kind of thing, yet. *Rolling Stone* was probably the only magazine in America where I could get the Vegas book published. I sent *Sports Illustrated* 2500 words—instead of the 250 they asked for—and my manuscript was aggressively rejected. They refused to even pay my minimum expenses . . .

But to hell with all that. I seem to be drifting away from the point—that *Fear & Loathing* is not what I thought it would be. I began writing it during a week of hard typewriter nights in a room at the Ramada Inn—in a place called Arcadia, California—up the road from Pasadena & right across the street from the Santa Anita racetrack. I was there during the first week of the Spring Racing—and the rooms all around me were jammed with people I couldn't quite believe.

Heavy track buffs, horse trainers, ranch owners, jockeys & their women . . . I was lost in that swarm, sleeping most of each day and writing all night on the Salazar article. But each night, around dawn, I would knock off the Salazar work and spend an hour or so, cooling out, by letting my head unwind and my fingers run wild on the big black Selectric . . . jotting down notes about the weird trip to Vegas. It had worked out nicely, in terms of the Salazar piece—plenty of hard straight talk about who was lying and who wasn't, and Oscar had finally relaxed enough to talk to me straight. Flashing across the desert at 110 in a big red convertible with the top down, there is not much danger of being bugged or overheard.

But we stayed in Vegas a bit longer than we'd planned to. Or at least *I* did. Oscar had to get back for a nine o'clock court appearance on Monday. So he took a plane and I was left alone out there—just me and a massive hotel bill that I knew I couldn't pay, and the treacherous reality of that scene caused me to spend about 36 straight hours in my room at the Mint Hotel . . . writing feverishly in a notebook about a nasty situation that I thought I might *not* get away from.

These notes were the genesis of *Fear & Loathing.* After my escape from Nevada and all through the tense work week that followed (spending all my afternoons on the grim streets of East LA and my nights at the typewriter in that Ramada Inn hideout) . . . my only loose & human moments would come around dawn when I could relax and fuck around with this slow-building, stone-crazy Vegas story.

By the time I got back to the Rolling Stone Hq. in San Francisco, the Salazar story was winding out at around 19,000 words, and the strange Vegas "fantasy" was running on its own spaced energy and pushing 5000 words—with no end in sight and no real reason to continue working on it, except the pure pleasure of unwinding on paper. It was sort of an exercise—like *Bolero*—and it might have stayed that way if Jann Wenner, the editor of *Rolling Stone,* hadn't liked the first 20 or so jangled pages enough to take it seriously on its own terms and tentatively schedule it for publication—which gave me the push I needed to keep working on it.

So now, six months later, the ugly bastard is finished. And I like it—despite the fact that I failed at what I was trying to do. As true Gonzo Journalism, this doesn't work at all—and even if it did, I couldn't possibly admit it. Only a goddamn lunatic would write a thing like this and then claim it was true. The week the first section of *Fear & Loathing* appeared in *Rolling Stone* I found myself applying for White House press credentials— a plastic pass that would give me the run of the White House, along with at least theoretical access to the big oval room where Nixon hangs out, pacing back & forth on those fine thick taxpayers' carpets and pondering Sunday's pointspread. (Nixon is a *serious* pro football freak. He and I are old buddies on this front: We once spent a long night together on the Thruway from Boston to Manchester, dissecting the pro & con strategy of the Oakland-Green Bay Super Bowl game. It was the only time I've ever seen the bugger relaxed—laughing, whacking me on the knee as he recalled Max McGee's one-handed catch for the back-breaking touchdown. I was *impressed*. It was like talking to Owsley about Acid.)

The trouble with Nixon is that he's a serious *politics junkie*. He's totally hooked . . . and like any other junkie, he's a bummer to have around: Especially as President.

And so much for all that . . . I have all of 1972 to fuck around with Nixon, so why hassle it here?

Anyway, the main point I want to make about *Fear & Loathing* is that although it's not what I meant it to be, it's still so *complex* in its failure that I feel I can take the risk of defending it as a first, gimped effort in a direction that what Tom Wolfe calls "The New Journalism" has been flirting with for almost a decade.

Wolfe's problem is that he's too crusty to *participate* in his stories. The people he feels comfortable with are dull as stale dogshit, and the people who seem to fascinate him as a writer are so weird that they make him nervous. The only thing new and unusual about Wolfe's journalism is that he's an abnormally *good* reporter; he has a fine sense of echo and at least a peripheral understanding of what John Keats was talking about when he said that thing about Truth & Beauty. The only reason Wolfe seems "new" is because William Randolph Hearst bent the spine of American journalism very badly when it was just getting started. All Tom Wolfe did—after he couldn't make it on the *Washington Post* and couldn't even get hired by the *National Observer*—was to figure out that there was really not much percentage in playing the old *Collier's* game, and that if he was ever going to make it in "journalism," his only hope was to make it on his own terms: By being *good* in the classical—rather than the contemporary—sense, and by being the kind of journalist that the American print media honor mainly in the breach. Or, failing that, at the funeral. Like Stephen Crane, who couldn't even get a copyboy's job on today's *New York Times*. The only difference between working for the *Times* and *Time* magazine is the difference between being a third-string All-American fullback at Yale instead of Ohio State.

And again, yes, we seem to be rambling—so perhaps I should close this off.

The only other important thing to be said about *Fear & Loathing* at this time is that it was *fun* to write, and that's rare—for me, at least, because I've always considered writing the most hateful kind of work. I suspect it's a bit like fucking, which is only fun for amateurs. Old whores don't do much giggling.

Nothing is fun when you *have to do it*—over & over, again & again—or else you'll be evicted, and that gets old. So it's a rare goddamn trip for a locked-in, rent-paying writer to get into a gig that, even in retrospect, was a kinghell, highlife fuckaround from start to finish . . . and then to actually get *paid* for writing this kind of manic gibberish seems genuinely weird; like getting paid for kicking Agnew in the balls.

So maybe there's hope. Or maybe I'm going mad. These are not easy things to be sure of, either way . . . and in the meantime we have this failed experiment in Gonzo Journalism, the certain truth of which will never be established. That much is definite. *Fear & Loathing in Las Vegas* will have to be chalked off as a frenzied experiment, a fine idea that went crazy about halfway through . . . a victim of its own conceptual schizophrenia, caught & finally crippled in that vain, academic limbo between "journalism" & "fiction." And then hoist on its own petard of multiple felonies and enough flat-out crime to put anybody who'd admit to this kind of stinking behavior in the Nevada State Prison until 1984.

So now, in closing, I want to thank everybody who helped me put this happy work of fiction together. Names are not necessary here; they know who they are—and in this foul era of Nixon, that knowledge and private laughter is probably the best we can hope for. The line between martyrdom and stupidity depends on a certain kind of tension in the body politic—but that line disappeared, in America, at the trial of the "Chicago 7/8," and there is no point in kidding ourselves, now, about Who Has the Power.

In a nation ruled by swine, all pigs are upward-mobile—and the rest of us are fucked until we can put our acts together: Not necessarily to Win, but mainly to keep from Losing Completely. We owe that to ourselves and our crippled self-image as something better than a nation of panicked sheep . . . but we owe it especially to our children, who will have to live with our loss and all its long-term consequences. I don't want my son asking me, in 1984, why his friends are calling me a "Good German."

Which gets down to a final point about *Fear & Loathing in Las Vegas*. I have called it, only half sarcastically, "a vile epitaph for the Drug Culture of the Sixties," and I think it is. This whole twisted saga is a sort of Atavistic Endeavor, a dream-trip into the past—however recent—that was only half successful. I think we both understood, all along, that we were running a hell of a risk by laying a sixties trip on Las Vegas in 1971 . . . and that neither one of us would ever pass this way again.

So we pushed it as far as we could, and we survived—which means something, I guess, but not much beyond a good story . . . and now, having done it, written it, and humping a reluctant salute to that decade that started so high and then went so brutally sour, I don't see much choice but to lash down the screws and get on with what has to be done. Either that or do nothing at all—fall back on the Good German, Panicked Sheep syndrome, and I don't think *I'm* ready for that. At least not right now.

Because it was nice to be loose and crazy with a good credit card in a time when it was *possible* to run totally wild in Las Vegas and then get paid for writing a book about it . . . and it occurs to me that I probably just made it, just under the wire and the deadline. Nobody will dare admit this kind of behavior in print if Nixon wins again in '72.

The Swine are gearing down for a serious workout this time around. Four more years of Nixon means four more years of John Mitchell—and four more years of Mitchell means another decade or more of bureaucratic fascism that will be so entrenched, by 1976, that nobody will feel up to fighting it. We will feel too old by then, too beaten, and by then even the Myth of the Road will be dead—if only for lack of exercise. There will not be any wild-eyed, dope-sucking anarchists driving around the country in fireapple red convertibles if Nixon wins again in '72.

There will not even be any convertibles, much less any dope. And all the anarchists will be locked up in rehabilitation pens. The international hotel-chain lobby will ram a bill thru congress, setting mandatory death penalties for anyone jumping a hotel bill—and death by castration & whipping if the deed is done in Vegas. The only legal high will be supervised Chinese acupuncture, in government hospitals at $200 a day—with Martha Mitchell as Secretary of Health, Education & Welfare, operating out of a luxurious penthouse on top of the Walter Reed Army Hospital.

So much, then, for The Road—and for the last possibilities of running amok in Las Vegas & living to tell the tale. But maybe we won't really miss it. Maybe Law & Order is really the best way to go, after all.

Yeah . . . maybe so, and if that's the way it happens . . . well, at least I'll know I was *there*, neck deep in the madness, before the deal went down, and I got so high and wild that I felt like a two-ton Manta Ray jumping all the way across the Bay of Bengal.

It was a good way to go, and I recommend it highly—at least for those who can stand the trip. And for those who can't, or won't, there is not much else to say. Not now, and certainly not by me, or Raoul Duke either. *Fear & Loathing in Las Vegas* marks the end of an era . . . and now, on this fantastic Indian summer morning in the Rockies, I want to leave this noisy black machine and sit naked on my porch for a while, in the sun.

Strange Rumblings in Aztlan

THE . . . MURDER . . . AND RESURRECTION OF RUBEN SALAZAR BY THE LOS ANGELES COUNTY SHERIFF'S DEPARTMENT . . . SAVAGE POLARIZATION & THE MAKING OF A MARTYR . . . BAD NEWS FOR THE MEXICAN-AMERICAN . . . WORSE NEWS FOR THE PIG . . . AND NOW THE NEW CHICANO . . . RIDING A GRIM NEW WAVE . . . THE RISE OF THE BATOS LOCOS . . . BROWN POWER AND A FISTFUL OF REDS . . . RUDE POLITICS IN THE BARRIO . . . WHICH SIDE ARE YOU ON . . . BROTHER? . . . THERE IS NO MORE MIDDLEGROUND . . . NO PLACE TO HIDE ON WHITTIER BOULEVARD . . . NO REFUGE FROM THE HELICOPTERS . . . NO HOPE IN THE COURTS . . . NO PEACE WITH THE MAN . . . NO LEVERAGE ANYWHERE . . . AND NO LIGHT AT THE END OF THIS TUNNEL . . . NADA . . .

Morning comes hard to the Hotel Ashmun; this is not a place where the guests spring eagerly out of bed to greet the fresh new day. But on this particular morning everybody in the place is awake at the crack of dawn: There is a terrible pounding and shrieking in the hallway, near room No. 267. Some junkie has ripped the doorknob off the communal bathroom, and now the others can't get in—so they are trying to kick the door down. The voice of the manager wavers hysterically above the din: "Come on now, fellas—do I have to call the sheriff?" The reply comes hard and fast: "You filthy gabacho pig! You call the fuckin sheriff and I'll cut your fuckin throat." And now the sound of

wood cracking, more screaming, the sound of running feet outside my door, No. 267.

The door is locked, thank Christ—but how can you say for
sure in a place like the Hotel Ashmun? Especially on a morning
like this with a mob of wild junkies locked out of the hall bathroom and maybe knowing that No. 267 is the only room within
lunging distance that has a private bath. It is the best in the
house, at $5.80 a night, and the lock on the door is brand new.
The old one was ripped out about 12 hours earlier, just before I
checked in.

The desk clerk had gone to a lot of trouble to get me into this
room. His key wouldn't fit the new lock. "Jesus Christ!" he kept
muttering. "This key *has* to fit! This is a brand new *Yale lock.*"
He stared balefully at the bright new key in his hand.

"Yeah," I said. "But that key is for a *Webster* lock."

"By God you're *right!*" he exclaimed. And he rushed off,
leaving us standing there in the hallway with big chunks of ice
in our hands. "What's wrong with that guy?" I asked. "He
seems out of control—all this sweating and grappling and jabbering . . ."

Benny Luna laughed. "Man, he's nervous! You think it's *normal* for him to be lettin four nasty lookin Chicanos into his best
room at three in the morning? With all of us carryin chunks of
ice and funny-lookin leather bags?" He was staggering around
the hall, convulsed with laughter. "Man, this guy is *freaked!* He
doesn't know *what's* goin on!"

"*Three* Chicanos," said Oscar. "And one hillbilly."

"You didn't tell him I was a writer, did you?" I asked. I'd noticed Oscar talking to the man, a tall sort of defeated looking
Germanic type, but I hadn't paid much attention.

"No, but he recognized *me,*" Oscar replied. "He said, 'You're
the lawyer, aren't you?' So I said 'That's right, and I want your
best room for this gabacho friend of mine.'" He grinned. "Yeah,
he knows *something's* wrong with this scene, but he doesn't
know what. These guys are scared of *everything* now. Every

merchant on Whittier Boulevard is sure he's living on borrowed time, so they go all to pieces at the first sign of anything strange going on. It's been this way ever since Salazar."

The room clerk/manager/keeper/etc. suddenly rounded the hallway corner with the right key, and let us into the room. It was a winner—a rundown echo of a place I stayed in a few years ago in the slums of Lima, Peru. I can't recall the name of that place, but I remember that all the room keys were attached to big wooden knobs about the size of grapefruits, too big to fit in a pocket. I thought about suggesting this to our man in the Hotel Ashmun, but he didn't wait around for tips or small-talk. He was gone in a flash, leaving us alone to deal with a quart of rum and God only knows what else.... We put the ice in a basin next to the bed and chopped it up with a huge rigging knife. The only music was a tape cassette of *Let It Bleed.*

What better music for a hot night on Whittier Boulevard in 1971? This has not been a peaceful street, of late. And in truth it was *never* peaceful. Whittier is to the vast Chicano *barrio* in East Los Angeles what the Sunset Strip is to Hollywood. This is where the street action lives: The bars, the hustlers, the drug market, the whores—and also the riots, the trashings, killings, gassings, the sporadic bloody clashes with the hated, common enemy: The cops, the Pigs, the Man, that blue-crusted army of fearsome gabacho troops from the East L.A. Sheriff's Department.

The Hotel Ashmun is a good place to stay if you want to get next to whatever's happening on Whittier Boulevard. The window of No. 267 is about 15 feet above the sidewalk and just a few blocks west of the Silver Dollar Cafe, a nondescript tavern that is not much different from any of the others nearby. There is a pool table in the rear, a pitcher of beer sells for a dollar, and the faded Chicano barmaid rolls dice with the patrons to keep the jukebox going. Low number pays, and nobody seems to care who selects the music.

We had been in there earlier, when not much was happening.

It was my first visit in six months, since early September when the place was still rancid with the stench of CS gas and fresh varnish. But now, six months later, the Silver Dollar had aired out nicely. No blood on the floor, no ominous holes in the ceiling. The only reminder of my other visit was a thing hanging over the cash register that we all noticed immediately. It was a black gas mask, staring blindly out at the room—and below the gas mask was a stark handprinted sign that said: "In memory of August 29, 1970."

Nothing else, no explanation. But no explanation was necessary—at least not to anybody likely to be found drinking in the Silver Dollar. The customers are locals: Chicanos and barrio people—and every one of them is acutely aware of what happened in the Silver Dollar Cafe on August 29, 1970.

That was the day that Ruben Salazar, the prominent "Mexican-American" columnist for the Los Angeles *Times* and News Director for bilingual KMEX-TV, walked into the place and sat down on a stool near the doorway to order a beer he would never drink. Because just about the time the barmaid was sliding his beer across the bar a Los Angeles County sheriff's deputy named Tom Wilson fired a tear gas bomb through the front door and blew half of Ruben Salazar's head off. All the other customers escaped out the back exit to the alley, but Salazar never emerged. He died on the floor in a cloud of CS gas—and when his body was finally carried out, hours later, his name was already launched into martyrdom. Within 24 hours, the very mention of the name "Ruben Salazar" was enough to provoke tears and fist-shaking tirades not only along Whittier Boulevard but all over East L.A.

Middle-aged housewives who had never thought of themselves as anything but lame-status "Mexican-Americans" just trying to get by in a mean Gringo world they never made suddenly found themselves shouting "Viva La Raza" *in public*. And their husbands—quiet Safeway clerks and lawn-care salesmen, the lowest and most expendable cadres in the Great

Gabacho economic machine—were volunteering to *testify;* yes, to stand up in court, or wherever, and calling themselves Chicanos. The term "Mexican-American" fell massively out of favor with all but the old and conservative—and the rich. It suddenly came to mean "Uncle Tom." Or, in the argot of East L.A.—"Tio Taco." The difference between a Mexican-American and a Chicano was the difference between a Negro and a Black.

All this has happened very suddenly. Too suddenly for most people. One of the basic laws of politics is that Action Moves Away from the Center. The middle of the road is only popular when nothing is happening. And nothing serious has been happening politically in East L.A. for longer than most people can remember. Until six months ago the whole place was a colorful tomb, a vast slum full of noise and cheap labor, a rifle shot away from the heart of downtown Los Angeles. The barrio, like Watts, is actually a part of the city core—while places like Hollywood and Santa Monica are separate entities. The Silver Dollar Cafe is a ten-minute drive from City Hall. The Sunset Strip is a 30-minute sprint on the Hollywood Freeway.

Whittier Boulevard is a hell of a long way from Hollywood, by any measure. There is no psychic connecton at all. After a week in the bowels of East L.A. I felt vaguely guilty about walking into the bar in the Beverly Hills Hotel and ordering a drink—as if I didn't quite belong there, and the waiters all knew it. I had been there before, under different circumstances, and felt totally comfortable. Or almost. There is no way to . . . well, to hell with that. The point is that this time I felt *different.* I was oriented to a completely different world—15 miles away.

MARCHA POR LA JUSTICIA

There are no police community relations in the Chicano communities. No, ever since the police riot on August 29th it has become too obvious to ignore the fact that the LAPD, the sheriffs, and the Highway Patrol

HAVE FOR YEARS BEEN SYSTEMATICALLY TRYING TO DESTROY THE TRUE SPIRIT OF OUR PEOPLE. IN THE PAST, POLICE HAVE BROKEN UP EVERY ATTEMPT OF OUR PEOPLE TO GET JUSTICE, THEY HAVE BEATEN YOUNG STUDENTS PROTESTING POOR EDUCATION, RAIDED OFFICES, ARRESTED LEADERS, CALLED US COMMUNISTS AND GANGSTERS IN THE PRESS, AND EVERYTHING ELSE ON THE STREETS WHEN THE PRESS WAS GONE.

EVEN MORE INSIDIOUS THAN THE DIRECT POLITICAL REPRESSION AGAINST LEADERS AND DEMONSTRATIONS IS THE CONTINUOUS ATTACKS ON THE EVERYDAY LIFE OF PEOPLE IN THE BARRIOS. ALMOST EVERY MONTH EACH BARRIO HAS SUFFERED THROUGH AT LEAST ONE CASE OF SEVERE BRUTALITY OR MURDER AND THEN STRUGGLED TO DEFEND FRIENDS AND WITNESSES WHO FACE BUM RAPS. ONE WEEK IT'S SAN FERNANDO, THEN LINCOLN HEIGHTS, EAST L.A., VENICE, THE HARBOR AND POMONA . . . . . . THEY HIT ONE BARRIO AT A TIME, TRYING TO BREAK OUR UNITY AND OUR SPIRIT.

ON AUGUST 29TH, THROUGH ALL OF OUR BARRIOS WERE DEMONSTRATIONS FOR PEACE AND JUSTICE AND THE POLICE RIOTED AND ATTACKED. OUT OF FEAR, THEY INSTALLED MARTIAL LAW, ARRESTING AND ABUSING HUNDREDS OF COMMUNITY PEOPLE. THEY KILLED GILBERTO DIAZ, LYNN WARD, AND RUBEN SALAZAR, THE MAN WHO COULD TELL OUR STORY TO THE NATION AND THE WORLD.

WE MUST NOT FORGET THE LESSON OF AUGUST 29TH, THAT THE MAJOR SOCIAL AND POLITICAL ISSUE WE FACE IS POLICE BRUTALITY. SINCE THE 29TH POLICE ATTACKS HAVE BEEN WORSE, EITHER THE PEOPLE CONTROL THE POLICE, OR WE ARE LIVING IN A POLICE STATE.

WE MUST NOT ALLOW THE POLICE TO BREAK OUR UNITY. WE MUST CARRY ON THE SPIRIT OF RUBEN SALAZAR AND EXPOSE THIS BRUTALITY TO THE NATION AND THE WORLD. THE CHICANO MORATORIUM COMMITTEE CALLS UPON YOU TO SUPPORT OUR NON-VIOLENT MARCH FOR JUSTICE THROUGH THE BARRIOS OF THE GREATER LOS ANGELES AREA.

CARAVANS WILL BE COMING FROM DOZENS OF CITIES AND
AROUND OUR BARRIOS. WE WILL ALL MEET AT THE E.L.A. SHER-
IFF'S SUB-STATION ON 3RD STREET BETWEEN FETTERLY AND
WOODS AT 11:00 AM JANUARY 31, 1971. JOIN YOUR LOCAL CARA-
VAN. FOR FURTHER INFORMATION CALL 268-6745.
  —Handbill from the National Chicano Moratorium Committee

My first night in the Hotel Ashmun was not restful. The others had left around five, then there was the junkie eruption at
seven . . . followed an hour later by a thundering, low-fidelity
outburst of wailing Norteno music from the jukebox in the
Boulevard Cafe across the street . . . and then, about nine-
thirty, I was jerked up again by a series of loud whistles from
the sidewalk right under my window, and a voice calling,
"Hunter! Wake-up, man! Let's get moving."

Holy jesus! I thought. Only three people in the world know
where I am right now, and they're all asleep. Who else could
have tracked me to this place? I bent the metal slats of the
venetian blind apart just enough to look down at the street and
see Rudy Sanchez, Oscar's quiet little bodyguard, looking up at
my window and waving urgently: "Come on out, man, it's time.
Oscar and Benny are up the street at the Sweetheart. That's
the bar on the corner where you see all those people in front.
We'll wait for you there, OK? You awake?"

"Sure I'm awake," I said. "I've been sitting here *waiting* for
you lazy criminal bastards. Why do Mexicans need so much
fucking sleep?"

Rudy smiled and turned away. "We'll be *waiting* for you,
man. We're gonna be drinkin a hell of a lot of bloody marys and
you know the rule we have down here."

"Never mind that," I muttered. "I need a shower."

But my room had no shower. And somebody, that night, had
managed to string a naked copper wire across the bathtub and
plug it into a socket underneath the basin outside the bathroom
door. For what reason? Demon Rum, I had no idea. Here I was

in the best room in the house, looking for the shower and finding only an electrified bathtub. And no place to righteously shave—in the best hotel on the strip. Finally I scrubbed my face with a hot towel and went across the street to the Sweetheart Lounge.

Oscar Acosta, the Chicano lawyer, was there; leaning on the bar, talking idly with some of the patrons. Of the four people around him—all in their late twenties—two were ex-cons, two were part-time dynamite freaks and known fire-bombers, and three of the four were veteran acid-eaters. Yet none of this surfaced in the conversation. The talk was political, but only in terms of the courtroom. Oscar was dealing with two hyperpolitical trials at the same time.

In one, the trial of the "Biltmore Six," he was defending six young Chicanos who'd been arrested for trying to burn down the Biltmore Hotel one night about a year ago, while Governor Ronald Reagan was delivering a speech there in the ballroom. Their guilt or innocence was immaterial at this point, because the trial had developed into a spectacular attempt to overturn the entire Grand Jury selection system. In the preceding months, Acosta had subpoenaed every Superior Court Judge in Los Angeles County and cross-examined all 109 of them at length, under oath, on the subject of their "racism." It was a wretched affront to the whole court system, and Acosta was working overtime to make it as wretched as possible. Here were these hundred and nine old men, these *judges*, compelled to take time out from whatever they were doing and go into another courtroom to take the stand and deny charges of "racism" from an attorney they all loathed.

Oscar's contention, throughout, was that all Grand Juries are racist, since all grand jurors have to be recommended by Superior Court Judges—who naturally tend to recommend people they know personally or professionally. And that therefore no ratbastard Chicano street crazy, for instance, could possibly be indicted by "a jury of his peers." The implications of a victory in this case were so obvious, so clearly menacing to the court system, that interest in the verdict had filtered all the way down to places like the Boulevard, the Silver Dollar and the Sweetheart. The level of political consciousness is not normally high in these places—especially on Saturday mornings—but Acosta's very presence, no matter where he goes or what he seems to be doing, is so grossly political that anybody who wants to talk to him has to figure out some way to deal on a meaningful political level.

"The thing is to never talk down," he says. "We're not trying to win votes out here. Hell, that trip's been done, it's over. The idea now is to make people *think*. Force them to think. And you can't do that by walking around slapping strangers on the back and buying them beers." Then grinning. "Unless you happen to be babbling drunk or stoned. Which is certainly not my style; I want to make that one thing very clear."

But today the talk was easy, with no ulterior politics. "Say, Oscar," somebody asked. "How do we stand on that Grand Jury thing? What's our chances?"

Acosta shrugged. "We'll win. Maybe not on this level, but we'll win on appeal."

"That's good, man. I hear you're really workin out on the bastards."

"Yeah, we're fuckin em over. But that one might take another year. Right now we have to think about Corky's trial. It starts Tuesday."

"Corky's in town?" The interest is obvious. Heads turn to listen. Rudy eases back a few feet so he can watch the whole bar, scanning the faces for any that might be *too* interested. Paranoia is rampant in the barrio: Informers. Narcs. Assassins—who knows? And Rudolfo "Corky" Gonzales is a definite heavy, prime target for a frame or a set-up. A scholarly, soft-spoken ex-boxer, his Denver-based "Crusade for Justice" is one of the few *viable* Chicano political organizations in the country. Gonzales is a poet, a street-fighter, a theorist, an organizer, and the most influential "Chicano leader" in the country next to Cesar Chavez.

Whenever Corky Gonzales appears in East L.A.—if only to stand trial on a misdemeanor weapons bust—the level of political tension rises noticeably. Gonzales has a very intense following in the barrio. Most of his supporters are young: Students, dropouts, artists, poets, crazies—the people who *respect* Cesar Chavez, but who can't really *relate* to churchgoing farmworkers.

"This weekend is going to be hell," Oscar had told me the night before. "Whenever Corky's in town, my apartment turns into a fucking zoo. I have to go to a motel to get any sleep. Shit, I can't stay up all night arguing radical politics when I have to be in court the next morning. These wild-eyed fuckers show up at all hours; they bring wine, joints, acid, mescaline, guns . . . Jesus, Corky wouldn't dare take that kind of risk. He's already here, but I don't know where he's staying. He's checked into some kind of goddamn Holiday Inn or something, about five miles out on Rosemeade, but he won't tell anybody where it is—not even me, his lawyer." He smiled, "And that's pretty shrewd, because if I knew where he was I might go over there some night all twisted and crazy about calling a general strike at dawn, or some other dangerous bullshit that would freak him."

He nodded, smiling lazily down at his drink. "As a matter of fact, I *have* been thinking about calling a general strike. The movement is so goddamn splintered right now that almost anything would help. Yeah, maybe I should write Corky a speech along those lines, then call a press conference for tomorrow afternoon in the Silver Dollar." He laughed bitterly and called for another bloody mary.

Acosta has been practicing law in the barrio for three years. I met him a bit earlier than that, in another era—which hardly matters here, except that it might be a trifle less than fair to run this story all the way out to the end without saying at least once, for the record, that Oscar is an old friend and occasional antagonist. I first met him, as I recall, in a bar called "The Daisy Duck" in Aspen, when he lumbered up to me and started raving about "ripping the system apart like a pile of cheap hay," or something like that . . . and I remember thinking, "Well, here's another one of those fucked-up, guilt-crazed dropout lawyers from San Francisco—some dingbat who ate one too many tacos and decided he was really Emiliano Zapata."

Which was OK, I felt, but it was a hard act to handle in Aspen in that high white summer of 1967. That was the era of Sergeant Pepper, the Surrealistic Pillow and the original Buffalo Springfield. It was a good year for everybody—or for *most* people, anyway. There were exceptions, as always. Lyndon Johnson was one, and Oscar Acosta was another. For entirely different reasons. That was not a good summer to be either the President of the United States or an angry Mexican lawyer in Aspen.

Oscar didn't hang around long. He washed dishes for a while, did a bit of construction work, bent the County Judge out of shape a few times, then took off for Mexico to "get serious." The next thing I heard, he was working for the public defender's office in L.A. That was sometime around Christmas of 1968, which was not a good year for anybody—except Richard Nixon and perhaps Oscar Acosta. Because by that time Oscar was beginning to find his own track. He was America's only "Chicano lawyer," he explained in a letter, and he liked it. His clients were all Chicanos and most were "political criminals," he said. And if they were guilty it was only because they were "doing what had to be done."

That's fine, I said. But I couldn't really get into it. I was all *for* *it*, you understand, but only on the basis of a personal friendship. *Most* of my friends are into strange things I don't totally understand—and with a few shameful exceptions I wish them all well. Who am I, after all, to tell some friend he shouldn't change his name to Oliver High, get rid of his family and join a

Satanism cult in Seattle? Or to argue with another friend who wants to buy a single-shot Remington Fireball so he can go out and shoot cops from a safe distance?

Whatever's right, I say. Never fuck with a friend's head by accident. And if their private trips get out of control now and then—well, you do what has to be done.

Which more or less explains how I suddenly found myself involved in the murder of Ruben Salazar. I was up in Portland, Oregon, at the time, trying to cover the National American Legion Convention and the Sky River Rock Festival at the same time . . . and I came back to my secret room in the Hilton one night to find an "urgent message" to call Mr. Acosta in Los Angeles.

I wondered how he had managed to track me down in Portland. But I knew, somehow, what he was calling about. I had seen the L.A. *Times* that morning, with the story of Salazar's death, and even at a distance of 2000 miles it gave off a powerful stench. The problem was not just a gimp or a hole in the story; the whole goddamn thing was wrong. It made no sense at all.

The Salazar case had a very special hook in it: Not that he was a Mexican or a Chicano, and not even Acosta's angry insistence that the cops had killed him in cold blood and that nobody was going to do anything about it. These were all proper ingredients for an outrage, but from my own point of view the most ominous aspect of Oscar's story was his charge that the police had deliberately gone out on the streets and killed a reporter who'd been giving them trouble. If this was true, it meant the ante was being upped drastically. When the cops declare open season on journalists, when they feel free to declare any scene of "unlawful protest" a free fire zone, that will be a very ugly day—and not just for journalists.

For thirteen devastated blocks, darkened stores stood gaping, show windows smashed. Traffic signs, spent shotgun shells,

*chunks of brick and concrete littered the pavement. A pair of
sofas, gutted by fire, smouldered at a curbside splashed with
blood. In the hot blaze of police flares, three Chicano youths
swaggered down the ruined street. "Hey brother," one yelled to
a black reporter, "was this better than Watts?"*

—Newsweek, *Feb. 15, '71*

Ruben Salazar is a bonafide martyr now—not only in East
L.A., but in Denver and Santa Fe and San Antonio, throughout
the Southwest. The length and breadth of Aztlan—the "con-
quered territories" that came under the yoke of Gringo occupation troops more than 100 years ago, when "vendido politicians
in Mexico City sold out to the US" in order to call off the invasion that Gringo history books refer to as the "Mexican-
American War." (Davy Crockett, Remember the Alamo, etc.)

As a result of this war, the US government was ceded about
half of what was then the Mexican nation. This territory was
eventually broken up into what is now the states of Texas, New
Mexico, Arizona and the southern half of California. This is Aztlan, more a concept than a real definition. But even as a concept
it has galvanized a whole generation of young Chicanos to a
style of political action that literally terrifies their Mexican-
American parents. Between 1968 and 1970 the "Mexican-
American Movement" went through the same drastic changes
and heavy trauma that had earlier afflicted the "Negro Civil
Rights Movement" in the early Sixties. The split was mainly
along generational lines, and the first "young radicals" were
overwhelmingly the sons and daughters of middle-class
Mexican-Americans who had learned to live with "their problem."

At this stage, the Movement was basically intellectual. The
word "Chicano" was forged as a necessary identity for the people of Aztlan—neither Mexicans nor Americans, but a con-
quered Indian/Mestizo nation sold out like slaves by its leaders
and treated like indentured servants by its conquerers. Not

even their language was definable, much less their identity. The language of East L.A. is a speedy sort of *cholo* mixture of Mexican Spanish and California English. You can sit in the Boulevard Cafe on Whittier on a Saturday morning and hear a young Chicano ex-con explaining to his friends: "This goddamn gabacho parole officer tells me I have to get the sewing machine back. I talked to that goddamn vendido and the vieja tambien, and they tell me don't worry, we won't say nothing that would send you back to the joint. But the gabacho keeps pushin me. What can I do?" And then, suddenly noticing a vagrant gringo nearby, he finishes the whole story in rapid, angry Spanish.

There are a lot of ex-cons in the Movement now, along with a whole new element—the *"Batos Locos."* And the only difference, really, is that the ex-cons are old enough to have done time for the same things the *batos locos* haven't been arrested for, yet. Another difference is that the ex-cons are old enough to frequent the action bars along Whittier, while most of the *batos locos* are still teenagers. They drink heavily, but not in the Boulevard or the Silver Dollar. On Friday night you will find them sharing quarts of sweet Key Largo in the darkness of some playground in the housing project. And along with the wine, they eat Seconal—which is massively available in the barrio, and also cheap: a buck or so for a rack of five reds, enough to fuck *anybody* up. Seconal is one of the few drugs on the market (legal or otherwise) that is flat guaranteed to turn you *mean*. Especially with wine on the side and a few "whites," bennies, for a chaser. This is the kind of diet that makes a man want to go out and stomp people . . . the only other people I've ever seen heavily into the red/white/wine diet were the Hell's Angels.

The results are about the same. The Angels would get loaded and then snarl around looking for somebody to chainwhip. The *batos locos* get loaded and start looking for their own kind of action (burning a store, rat-packing a nigger, or stealing some cars for a night of high-speed cruising on the freeways). The action is almost always illegal, usually violent—but only recently has it become "political."

Perhaps the main Movement/focus in the barrio these days is the politicalization of the *batos locos*. The term translates literally as "crazy guys," but in harsh political terms it translates as "street crazies," teenage wildmen who have nothing to lose except their hostility and a vast sense of doom and boredom with the world as they know it. "These guys aren't afraid of the pigs," a Chicano activist told me. "Hell, they *like* a fight with the pigs. They *want* it. And there's a hell of a lot of 'em, man. Maybe two hundred thousand. If we can organize these guys, man, we can move on *anybody*."

But the *batos locos* are not easily organized. For one thing, they're hopelessly ignorant about politics. They hate politicians—even Chicano politicians. They are also very young, very hostile, and when you get them excited they are likely to do almost anything—especially when they're full of wine and reds. One of the first overt attempts to bring the *batos locos* into the new Chicano politics was the mass rally against police brutality last January 31st. The organizers took great care to make sure the thing would be peaceful. The word went out all over the barrio that "this one has to be cool—no riot, no violence." A truce was arranged with the East L.A. sheriff's department; the cops agreed to "keep a low profile," but they nonetheless sand-bagged and barricaded the sheriff's substation right next to the site of the rally in Belvedere Park.

Writing in The Nation, a Chicago priest named David F. Gomez described the scene as the rally gathered steam: "Despite the tension, a fiesta atmosphere prevailed as Chicanos sat on the scarred grass of the park's soccer field and listened while barrio speakers aired grievances of police brutality and the gringo occupation of Aztlan. Oscar Acosta gave the most rousing talk of the afternoon. '*Ya es tiempo*. The time is now! There's only one issue. Not police abuse. We are going to be clubbed over the head for as long as we live because we're Chicanos! The real issue is *nuestra tierra*, our land. Some people call us rebels and revolutionaries. Don't believe it. Emiliano Zapata was a revolutionary because he fought against other Mexicans. But we are not fighting our own people but gringos! We are not trying to overturn our own government. We don't have a government! Do you think there would be police helicopters patrolling our communities day and night if anybody considered us real citizens with rights!' "

The rally *was* peaceful—all the way to the end. But then, when fighting broke out between a handful of Chicanos and jittery cops, nearly a thousand young *batos locos* reacted by making a frontal assault on the cop headquarters with rocks, bottles, clubs, bricks and everything else they could find. The cops withstood the attack for about an hour, then swarmed out of the place with a stunning show of force that included firing deadly buckshot balls out of 12-gauge shotguns straight into the crowd. The attackers fled through the backstreets to Whittier Boulevard, and trashed the street again. The cops pursued, firing shotguns and pistols at point blank range. After two hours of street warfare, the toll was one dead, 30 serious injuries and a little less than a half million dollars' worth of damage—including 78 burned and battered police cars.

The entire L.A. power structure was outraged. And the Chicano Moratorium Committee was aghast. The rally's main organizer—24-year-old Rosalio Munoz, a former president of the UCLA student body—was so shocked by the outburst that he reluctantly agreed—with the sheriff—that any further mass rallies would be too dangerous. "We will have to find a new way of expressing grievances," said a spokesman for the more moderate Congress of Mexican-American Unity. "From now on the course will be to play a low profile."

But nobody spoke for the *batos locos*—except maybe the sheriff. "This violence was not caused by outsiders," he said, "but by members of the Chicano community! They can't say we provoked them this time." This was a definite switch from the standard-brand cop-analysis of "Mexican violence." In the past they had always blamed it on "Communists and Outside Agitators." But now, it seemed, the sheriff was finally catching on. The real enemy was the same people his men had to deal with every goddamn day of the week, in all kinds of routine situations—on streetcorners, in bars, domestic brawls and car accidents. The *gente*, the street-people, the ones who *live* there. So in the end, being a sheriff's deputy in East L.A. was not much different from being a point man for the Americal Division in Vietnam. "Even the kids and old women are VC."

This is the new drift, and everybody in East L.A. who's willing to talk about it uses the term "since Salazar." In the six months since the murder and the unsettling coroner's inquest that followed it up, the Chicano community has been harshly sundered by a completely new kind of polarization, another painful amoeba-trip. But the split this time was not between the young militants and the old Tio Tacos; this time it was between student-type militants and this whole new breed of super-militant street crazies. The argument was no longer *whether* to fight—but When, and How, and with What Weapons.

Another awkward aspect of the new split was that it was no longer a simple matter of "the generation gap"—which had been painful, but essentially simple; now it was more than a conflict of life-styles and attitudes; the division this time was more along economic, or *class* lines. And this was painfully complex. The original student activists had been militant, but also reasonable—in their own eyes, if not in the eyes of the law.

But the *batos locos* never even pretended to be reasonable. They wanted to get it on, and the sooner the better. Anytime, anywhere: Just give us a reason to work out on the pig, and we're ready.

This attitude created definite problems within the movement. The street people had right instincts, said the leadership, but they were not wise. They had no program; only violence and vengeance—which was wholly understandable, of course, but how could it *work?* How could the traditionally stable

Mexican-American community gain anything, in the long run, by declaring total war on the gabacho power structure and meanwhile purging its own native *vendidos?*

AZTLAN! LOVE IT OR LEAVE IT.
—sign at Chicano rally

Ruben Salazar was killed in the wake of a Watts-style riot that erupted when hundreds of cops attacked a peaceful rally in Laguna Park, where 5000 or so liberal/student/activist type Chicanos had gathered to protest the drafting of "Aztlan citizens" to fight for the US in Vietnam. The police suddenly appeared in Laguna Park, with no warning, and "dispersed the crowd" with a blanket of tear gas, followed up by a Chicago-style mop-up with billyclubs. The crowd fled in panic and anger, inflaming hundreds of young spectators who ran the few blocks to Whittier Boulevard and began trashing every store in sight. Several buildings were burned to the ground; damage was estimated at somewhere around a million dollars. Three people were killed, 60 injured—but the central incident of that August 29th, 1970, rally was the killing of Ruben Salazar.

And six months later, when the National Chicano Moratorium Committee felt it was time for another mass rally, they called it to "carry on the spirit of Ruben Salazar."

There is irony in this, because Salazar was nobody's militant. He was a professional journalist with ten years of experience on a variety of assignments for the neo-liberal Los Angeles Times. He was a nationally known reporter, winning prizes for his work in places like Vietnam, Mexico City and the Dominican Republic. Ruben Salazar was a veteran war correspondent, but he had never shed blood under fire. He was good, and he seemed to like the work. So he must have been slightly bored when the Times called him back from the war zones, for a raise and a well-deserved rest covering "local affairs."

He focused on the huge barrio just east of city hall. This was a scene he had never really known, despite his Mexican-American heritage. But he locked into it almost instantly. Within months, he had narrowed his work for the Times down to a once-a-week column for the newspaper, and signed on as News Director for KMEX-TV—the "Mexican-American station," which he quickly transformed into an energetic, aggressively political voice for the whole Chicano community. His coverage of police activities made the East Los Angeles sheriff's department so unhappy that they soon found themselves in a sort of running private argument with this man Salazar, this Spic who refused to be reasonable. When Salazar got onto a routine story like some worthless kid named Ramirez getting beaten to death in a jail-fight, he was likely to come up with almost anything—including a series of hard-hitting news commentaries strongly suggesting that the victim had been beaten to death by the jailers. In the summer of 1970 Ruben Salazar was warned three times, by the cops, to "tone down his coverage." And each time he told them to fuck off.

This was not common knowledge in the community until after he was murdered. When he went out to cover the rally that August afternoon he was still a "Mexican-American journalist." But by the time his body was carried out of the Silver Dollar, he was a stone Chicano martyr. Salazar would have smiled at this irony, but he would not have seen much humor in the way the story of his death was handled by the cops and the politicians. Nor would he have been pleased to know that almost immediately after his death his name would become a battle cry, prodding thousands of young Chicanos who had always disdained "protest" into an undeclared war with the hated gringo police.

His paper, the L.A. Times, carried the account of its former foreign correspondent's death on its Monday front page: "Mexican-American newsman Ruben Salazar was killed by a bullet-like tear gas shell fired by a sheriff's deputy into a bar during rioting Saturday in East Los Angeles." The details were hazy, but the new, hastily revised police version was clearly constructed to show that Salazar was the victim of a Regrettable Accident which the cops were not aware of until many hours later. Sheriff's deputies had cornered an armed man in a bar, they said, and when he refused to come out—even after "loud warnings" (with a bull horn) "to evacuate"—"the tear gas shells were fired and several persons ran out the back door."

At that time, according to the sheriff's nervous mouthpiece, Lt. Norman Hamilton, a woman and two men—one carrying a 7.65 automatic pistol—were met by deputies, who questioned them. "I don't know whether the man with the gun was arrested on a weapons violation or not," Hamilton added.

Ruben Salazar was not among those persons who ran out the back door. He was lying on the floor, inside, with a huge hole in his head. But the police didn't know this, Lieutenant Hamilton explained, because, "they didn't enter the bar until approximately 8 PM, when rumors began circulating that Salazar was missing," and "an unidentified man across the street from the bar" told a deputy, "I think there's an injured man in there." "At this point," said Hamilton, "deputies knocked down the door and found the body." Two and a half hours later at 10:40 PM, the sheriff's office admitted that "the body" was Ruben Salazar.

"Hamilton could not explain," said the *Times*, "why two accounts of the incident given to the *Times* by avowed eyewitnesses differed from the sheriff's accounts."

For about 24 hours Hamilton clung grimly to his original story—a composite, he said, of firsthand police accounts. According to this version, Ruben Salazar had been "killed by errant gunfire . . . during the height of a sweep of more than 7000 people in (Laguna) Park when police ordered everyone to disperse." Local TV and radio newscasts offered sporadic variations on this theme—citing reports "still under investigation" that Salazar had been shot accidentally by careless street-snipers. It was tragic, of course, but tragedies like this are inevitable when crowds of innocent people allow themselves to be manipulated by a handful of violent, cop-hating anarchists.

By late Sunday, however, the sheriff's story had collapsed completely—in the face of sworn testimony from four men who were standing within ten feet of Ruben Salazar when he died in the Silver Dollar Cafe at 4045 Whittier Boulevard, at least a mile from Laguna Park. But the real shocker came when these men testified that Salazar had been killed—not by snipers or errant gunfire—but by a cop with a deadly tear gas bazooka.

Acosta had no trouble explaining the discrepancy. "They're lying," he said. "They *murdered* Salazar and now they're trying to cover it up. The sheriff already panicked. All he can say is, 'No comment.' He's ordered every cop in the county to *say nothing* to anybody—especially the press. They've turned the East L.A. sheriff's station into a fortress. Armed guards all around it." He laughed. "Shit, the place looks like a prison—but with all the cops *inside!*"

Sheriff Peter J. Pitchess refused to talk to me when I called. The rude aftermath of the Salazar killing had apparently unhinged him completely. On Monday he called off a scheduled press conference and instead issued a statement, saying: "There are just too many conflicting stories, some from our own officers, as to what happened. The sheriff wants an opportunity to digest them before meeting with newsmen."

Indeed. Sheriff Pitchess was not alone in his inability to digest the garbled swill that his office was doling out. The official version of the Salazar killing was so crude and illogical—even after revisions—that not even the sheriff seemed surprised when it began to fall apart even before Chicano partisans had a chance to attack it. Which they would, of course. The sheriff had already got wind of what was coming: many eyewitnesses, sworn statements, first-hand accounts—all of them hostile.

The history of Chicano complaints against cops in East L.A. is not a happy one. "The cops never lose," Acosta told me, "and they won't lose this one either. They just murdered the only guy in the community they were really afraid of, and I guarantee you no cop will ever stand trial for it. Not even for manslaughter."

I could accept that. But it was difficult, even for me, to believe that the cops had killed him deliberately. I knew they were capable of it, but I was not quite ready to believe they had actually done it . . . because once I believed that, I also had to accept the idea that they are prepared to kill anybody who seemed to be annoying them. Even me.

As for Acosta's charge of murder, I knew him well enough to understand how he could make that charge *publicly* . . . I also knew him well enough to be sure he wouldn't try to hang that kind of monstrous bullshit on me. So our phone talk naturally disturbed me . . . and I fell to brooding about it, hung on my own dark suspicions that Oscar had told me the truth.

On the plane to L.A. I tried to make some kind of a case—either pro or con—from my bundle of notes and newsclips relating to Salazar's death. By that time at least six reportedly reliable witnesses had made sworn statements that differed drastically, on several crucial points, with the original police version—which nobody believed anyway. There was something very disturbing about the sheriff's account of that accident; it wasn't even a good *lie*.

Within hours after the Times hit the streets with the news that Ruben Salazar had in fact been killed by cops—rather than street-snipers—the sheriff unleashed a furious assault on "known dissidents" who had flocked into East Los Angeles that weekend, he said, to provoke a disastrous riot in the Mexican-American community. He praised his deputies for the skillful zeal they displayed in restoring order to the area within two and a half hours, "thus averting a major holocaust of much greater proportions."

Pitchess did not identify any "known dissidents," but he insisted that they had committed "hundreds of provocative acts."

For some reason the sheriff failed to mention that his deputies had already jailed one of the most prominent Chicano militants in the nation. "Corky" Gonzales had been arrested during Saturday's riot on a variety of charges that the police never really explained. Gonzales, fleeing the combat zone on a flatbed truck with 28 others, was arrested first for a traffic violation, then on a concealed weapons charge and finally for "suspicion of robbery" when police found $300 in his pocket. Police Inspector John Kinsling said it was a "routine" booking. "Any time we stop a traffic case and find that there is a weapon in the car and that its occupants have a sizeable amount of money," he said, "we always book them for suspicion of robbery."

Gonzales ridiculed the charge, saying, "Anytime a Mexican is found with more than $100 he's charged with a felony." The police had originally claimed he was carrying a loaded pistol and more than 1000 rounds of ammunition, along with many spent cartridges—but by Wednesday all felony charges had been dropped. As for "robbery," Gonzales said, "Only a lunatic or a fool could believe that 29 people would rob a place and then jump on a flatbed truck to make their getaway." He had climbed aboard the truck with his two children, he said, to get them away from the cops who were gassing the rally, to which he'd been invited as one of the main speakers. The $300, he said, was expense money for himself and his children—for meals in L.A. and three round-trip bus tickets from Denver to L.A.

That was the extent of Corky Gonzales' involvement in the Salazar incident, and at a glance it seems hardly worth mentioning—except for a rumor on the Los Angeles lawyers' grapevine that the robbery charge was only a ruse, a necessary holding action, to set Gonzales up for a "Chicano Seven" conspiracy bust—charging that he came from Denver to Los Angeles with the intention of causing a riot.

Both Sheriff Pitchess and Los Angeles Police Chief Edward Davis were quick to seize on this theory. It was the perfect tool for this problem: not only would it frighten the local Chicanos and hamstring nationally-known militants like Gonzales, but it could also be used to create a sort of "red menace" smokescreen to obscure the nasty realities of the Ruben Salazar killing.

The sheriff fired the first salvo, which earned him a giant banner headline in Tuesday's L.A. Times and a heavy pro-police editorial in Wednesday's Herald-Examiner. Meanwhile, Chief Davis launched a second blast from his listening post in Portland, where he had gone to vent his wisdom at the American Legion convention. Davis blamed all the violence, that Saturday, on a "hard core group of subversives who infiltrated the antiwar rally and turned it into a mob," which soon ran wild in a frenzy of burning and looting. "Ten months ago," he explained, "the Communist Party in California said it was giving up on the blacks to concentrate on the Mexican-Americans."

Nowhere in the Herald editorial—and nowhere in either statement by the sheriff and the police chief—was there any mention of the name Ruben Salazar. The Herald, in fact, had been trying to ignore the Salazar story from the very beginning. Even in Sunday's first story on the riot—long before any "complications" developed—the classic Hearst mentality was evident in the paper's full-page headline: "East Los Angeles Peace Rally Explodes in Bloody Violence . . . Man Shot to Death; Buildings Looted, Burned." Salazar's name appeared briefly, in a statement by a spokesman for the L.A. County sheriff's department—a calm and confident assertion that the "veteran reporter" had been shot in Laguna Park, by persons unknown, in the midst of a bloody clash between police and militants. So much for Ruben Salazar.

And so much for the Los Angeles Herald-Examiner—a genuinely rotten newspaper that claims the largest circulation of any afternoon daily in America. As one of the few remaining Hearst organs, it serves a perverted purpose in its role as a monument to everything cheap, corrupt and vicious in the realm of journalistic possibility. It is hard to understand, in fact, how the shriveled Hearst management can still find enough gimps, bigots and deranged Papists to staff a rotten paper like the Herald. But they manage, somehow . . . and they also manage to sell a lot of advertising in the monster. Which means the thing is actually being read, and perhaps taken seriously, by hundreds of thousands of people in America's second largest city. At the top of Wednesday's editorial page—right next to the Red Menace warning—was a large cartoon titled "At the Bottom of it All." It showed a flaming Molotov cocktail crashing through a window, and on the bottom (*bottom*, get it?) of the bottle is a hammer and sickle emblem. The editorial itself was a faithful echo of the Davis-Pitchess charges: "Many of the dissidents came here from other cities and states to join agitators in Los Angeles to set off a major riot, which was planned in advance . . . That the holocaust did not erupt into greater proportions is due to the bravery and tactics of the sheriff's deputies . . . Those arrested should be prosecuted to the fullest extent of the law. Precautions must be doubled to prevent a recurrence of such criminal irresponsibility." The continued existence of the Hearst Examiner explains a lot about the mentality of Los Angeles—and also, perhaps, about the murder of Ruben Salazar.

So the only way to go was to reconstruct the whole thing on the basis of available eyewitness testimony. The police refused to say anything at all—especially to the press. The sheriff said he was saving "the truth" for the official coroner's inquest.

Meanwhile, evidence was building up that Ruben Salazar had been murdered—either deliberately or for no reason at all. The most damaging anti-cop testimony thus far had come from Guillermo Restrepo, a 28-year-old reporter and newscaster for KMEX-TV, who was covering the "riot" with Salazar that afternoon, and who had gone with him into the Silver Dollar Cafe "to take a leak and drink a quick beer before we went back to the station to put the story together." Restrepo's testimony was solid enough on its own to cast a filthy shadow on the original police version, but when he produced two *more* eyewitnesses who told exactly the same story, the sheriff abandoned all hope and sent his scriptwriters back to the sty.

Guillermo Restrepo is well known in East L.A.—a familiar figure to every Chicano who owns a TV set. Restrepo is the outfront public face of KMEX-TV news . . . and Ruben Salazar, until August 29, 1970, was the man behind the news—the editor.

They worked well together, and on that Saturday when the Chicano "peace rally" turned into a Watts-style street riot, both Salazar and Restrepo decided that it might be wise if Restrepo—a native Colombian—brought two of his friends (also Colombians) to help out as spotters and de facto bodyguards.

Their names were Gustavo Garcia, age 30, and Hector Fabio Franco, also 30. Both men appear in a photograph (taken seconds before Salazar was killed) of a sheriff's deputy pointing a shotgun at the front door of the Silver Dollar Cafe. Garcia is the man right in front of the gun. When the picture was taken he had just asked the cop what was going on, and the cop had just told him to get back inside the bar if he didn't want to be shot.

The sheriff's office was not aware of this photo until three days after it was taken—along with a dozen others—by two *more* eyewitnesses, who also happened to be editors of La Raza, a militant Chicano newspaper that calls itself "the voice of the East L.A. barrio." (Actually, it is one of several: The Brown Berets publish a monthly tabloid called La Causa. The National La Raza Law Students' Association has its own monthly—Justicia O! The Socialist Workers Party covers the barrio with The Militant and the East L.A. Welfare Rights Organization has its own tabloid—La Causa de los Pobres. There is also Con Safos—a quarterly review of Chicano Art and Literature.)

The photographs were taken by Raul Ruiz, a 28-year-old teacher of Latin American studies at San Fernando Valley

State College. Ruiz was on assignment for La Raza that day when the rally turned into a street war with police. He and Joe Razo—a 33-year-old law student with an M.A. in psychology— were following the action along Whittier Boulevard when they noticed a task force of sheriff's deputies preparing to assault the Silver Dollar Cafe.

Their accounts of what happened there—along with Ruiz's photos—were published in La Raza three days after the sheriff's office said Salazar had been killed a mile away in Laguna Park, by snipers and/or "errant gunfire."

The La Raza spread was a bombshell. The photos weren't much individually, but together—along with Ruiz/Razo testimony— they showed that the cops were still lying when they came up with their second (revised) version of the Salazar killing.

It also verified the Restrepo-Garcia-Franco testimony, which had already shot down the original police version by establishing, beyond any doubt, that Ruben Salazar had been killed, by a deputy sheriff, in the Silver Dollar Cafe. They were certain of *that*, but no more. They were puzzled, they said, when the cops appeared with guns and began threatening them. But they decided to leave anyway—by the back door, since the cops wouldn't let anybody out of the front—and that was when the shooting started, less than 30 seconds after Garcia was photographed in front of that shotgun barrel on the sidewalk.

The weakness in the Restrepo-Garcia-Franco testimony was so obvious that not even the cops could miss it. They knew nothing beyond what had happened *inside* the Silver Dollar at the time of Salazar's death. There was no way they could have known what was happening *outside*, or *why* the cops started shooting.

The explanation came almost instantly from the sheriff's office—once again from Lt. Hamilton. The police had received an "anonymous report," he said, that "a man with a gun" was inside the Silver Dollar Cafe. This was the extent of their "probable cause," their reason for doing what they did. These actions, according to Hamilton, consisted of "sending several deputies" to deal with the problem . . . and they did so by stationing themselves in front of the Silver Dollar and issuing "a loud warning" with a bullhorn calling all those inside to come outside with their hands above their heads.

There was no response, Hamilton said, so a deputy then fired two tear gas projectiles into the bar through the front door. At this point two men and a woman fled out the back and one of the men was relieved by waiting deputies of a 7.65 caliber pistol. He was not arrested—not even detained—and at that point a deputy fired two more tear gas projectiles through the front door of the place.

Again there was no response, and after a 15-minute wait one of the braver deputies crept up and skillfully slammed the front door—*without entering*, Hamilton added. The only person who actually entered the bar, according to the police version, was the owner, Pete Hernandez, who showed up about half an hour after the shooting and asked if he could go inside and get his rifle.

Why not? said the cops, so Hernandez went in the *back door* and got his rifle out of the rear storeroom—about 50 feet away from where Ruben Salazar's body lay in a fog of rancid CS gas.

Then, for the next two hours, some two dozen sheriff's deputies cordoned off the street in front of the Silver Dollar's front door. This naturally attracted a crowd of curious Chicanos, not all of them friendly—and one, an 18-year-old girl, was shot in the leg with the same kind of tear gas bazooka that had blown Ruben Salazar's head apart.

This is a fascinating tale . . . and perhaps the most interesting thing about it is that it makes no sense at all, not even to a person willing to accept it as the absolute truth. But who could possibly believe it? Here, in the middle of a terrible riot in a hostile ghetto with a Chicano population of more than a million, the

Los Angeles sheriff's department had put every available man
on the streets in a vain attempt to control the mass looting and
arson by angry mobs . . . but somehow, with the riots still running in high gear, at least a dozen deputies from the elite Special Enforcement Bureau (read TAC Squad) are instantly
available in response to an "anonymous report" that "a man
with a gun" is holed up, for some reason, in an otherwise quiet
cafe more than ten blocks away from the vortex of the actual rioting.

They swoop down on the place and confront several men trying to leave. They threaten to kill these men—but make no attempt to either arrest or search them—and force them all back
inside. Then they use a bullhorn to warn everybody inside to
come out with their hands up. And then, almost instantly after
giving the warning, they fire—through the open front door of
the place and from a distance of no more than 10 feet—two
highpowered tear gas projectiles designed "for use against barricaded criminals" and capable of piercing a one-inch pine board
at 300 feet.

Then, when a man carrying an automatic pistol tries to flee
out the back door, they take his gun and tell him to get lost.
Finally, after firing two more gas bombs through the front
door, they seal the place up—without ever entering it—and
stand around outside for the next two hours, blocking a main
boulevard and attracting a large crowd. After two hours of
this madness, they "hear a rumor"—again from an anonymous
source—that there might be an injured man inside the bar
they sealed off two hours ago. So they "break down the door"
and find the body of an eminent journalist—"the only Chicano
in East L.A.," according to Acosta, "that the cops were really
afraid of."

Incredible as it seems, the sheriff decided to stick with this
story—despite a growing body of eyewitness accounts that
contradict the police version of "probable cause." The police say
they went to the Silver Dollar Cafe to arrest that "man with a

gun." But eight days after the killing they were still trying to locate the source of this fatal tip.

Two weeks later at the coroner's inquest, the sheriff's key witness on this critical point mysteriously appeared. He was a 50-year-old man named Manuel Lopez who claimed all credit for the tip with his tale of having seen two armed men—one with a revolver and one carrying a rifle in the port arms position—go into the Silver Dollar shortly before Salazar was killed. Lopez quickly "motioned to" the sheriff's officers stationed nearby, he said, and they responded by parking a patrol car directly across the six-lane boulevard from the Silver Dollar's front door. Then using a loud bullhorn, the deputies gave two distinct warnings for everybody in the bar to "throw out their weapons and come out with their hands over their heads."

Then, after a five- or ten-minute wait, Lopez said, three rounds of tear gas were fired at the bar, with one projectile glancing off the front doorway and two whooshing through a black curtain that was hanging a couple of feet back from the open doorway. It was too dark to see what was happening inside the bar, Lopez added.

By his own admission at the inquest, Lopez' behavior on the afternoon of Saturday, August 29th, was somewhat singular. When the riot broke out and mobs began looting and burning, Mr. Lopez took off his shirt, donned a fluorescent red hunting vest and stationed himself in the middle of Whittier Boulevard as a volunteer cop. He played the role with such zeal and fanatic energy that by nightfall he found himself famous. At the height of the violence he was seen dragging a bus bench into the middle of the boulevard in order to block all traffic and divert it off to side streets. He was also seen herding bystanders away from a burning furniture store . . . and later, when the riot-action seemed over, he was observed directing a group of sheriff's deputies toward the Silver Dollar Cafe.

Indeed, there was no arguing with his claim two weeks later

that he had been right in the middle of things. His testimony at the inquest sounded perfectly logical and so finely informed that it was hard to understand how such a prominent extroverted witness could possibly have escaped being quoted—or at least mentioned—by the dozens of newsmen, investigators and assorted tipsters with access to the Salazar story. Lopez' name had not even been mentioned by the sheriff's office, which could have saved itself a lot of unnecessary public grief by even *hinting* that they had a witness as valuable as Manuel Lopez. They had not been reluctant to display their other two "friendly" witnesses—neither of whom had seen any "men with guns," but they both backed the Lopez version of the actual shooting sequence. Or at least they backed it until the cops produced Lopez. Then the other two witnesses refused to testify at the coroner's inquest and one of them admitted that his real name was David Ross Ricci, although the police had introduced him originally as "Rick Ward."

The Salazar inquest rumbled on for 16 days, attracting large crowds and live TV coverage from start to finish. (In a rare demonstration of non-profit unity, all seven local TV stations formed a combine of sorts, assigning the coverage on a rotating basis, so that each day's proceedings appeared on a different channel.) The L.A. Times coverage—by Paul Houston and Dave Smith—was so complete and often so rife with personal intensity that the collected Smith/Houston file reads like a finely-detailed non-fiction novel. Read separately, the articles are merely good journalism. But as a document, arranged chronologically, the file is more than the sum of its parts. The main theme seems to emerge almost reluctantly, as both reporters are driven to the obvious conclusion that the sheriff, along with his deputies and all his official allies, have been *lying* all along. This is never actually stated, but the evidence is overwhelming.

A coroner's inquest is not a trial. Its purpose is to determine the circumstances surrounding a person's death—not who might have killed him, or why. If the circumstances indicate foul play, the next step is up to the D.A. In California a coroner's jury can reach only two possible verdicts: That the death was "accidental," or that it was "at the hands of another." And in the Salazar case, the sheriff and his allies *needed* a verdict of "accidental." Anything else would leave the case open—not only to the possibility of a murder or manslaughter trial for the deputy, Tom Wilson, who finally admitted firing the death weapon; but also to the threat of a million-dollar negligence lawsuit against the County by Salazar's widow.

The verdict finally hinged on whether or not the jury could believe Wilson's testimony that he fired into the Silver Dollar—at the *ceiling*—in order to ricochet a tear gas shell into the rear of the bar and force the armed stranger inside to come out the front door. But somehow Ruben Salazar had managed to get his head in the way of that carefully aimed shell. Wilson had never been able to figure out, he said, what went wrong.

Nor could he figure out how Raul Ruiz had managed to "doctor" those photographs that made it look like he and at least one other deputy were aiming their weapons straight into the Silver Dollar, pointing them directly at people's heads. Ruiz had no trouble explaining it. His testimony at the inquest was no different than the story he had told me just a few days after the murder. And when the inquest was over there was nothing in the 2025 pages of testimony—from 61 witnesses and 204 exhibits—to cast any serious doubt on the "Chicano Eyewitness Report" that Ruiz wrote for La Raza when the sheriff was still maintaining that Salazar had been killed by "errant gunfire" during the violence at Laguna Park.

The inquest ended with a split verdict. Smith's lead paragraph in the October 6th Times read like an obituary: "Monday the inquest into the death of newsman Ruben Salazar ended. The 16-day inquiry, by far the longest and costliest such affair in county history, concluded with a verdict that confuses many, satisfies few and means little. The coroner's jury came up with two verdicts: death was 'at the hands of another person' (four jurors) and death was by 'accident' (three jurors). Thus, inquests might appear to be a waste of time."

A week later, District Attorney Evelle Younger—a staunch Law & Order man—announced that he had reviewed the case and decided that "no criminal charge is justified," despite the unsettling fact two of the three jurors who had voted for the "death by accident" verdict were now saying they had made a mistake.

But by that time nobody really gave a damn. The Chicano community had lost faith in the inquest about midway through the second day, and all the rest of the testimony only reinforced their anger at what most considered an evil whitewash. When the D.A. announced that no charges would be filed against Wilson, several of the more moderate Chicano spokesmen called for a federal investigation. The militants called for an uprising. And the cops said nothing at all.

There was one crucial question, however, that the inquest settled beyond any reasonable doubt. Ruben Salazar couldn't possibly have been the victim of a conscious, high-level cop conspiracy to get rid of him by staging an "accidental death." The incredible tale of half-mad stupidity and dangerous incompetence on every level of the law enforcement establishment was perhaps the most valuable thing to come out of the inquest. Nobody who heard that testimony could believe that the Los Angeles County sheriff's department is capable of pulling off a delicate job like killing a newsman *on purpose*. Their handling of the Salazar case—from the day of his death all the way to the end of the inquest—raised serious doubts about the wisdom of allowing cops to walk around loose on the street. A geek who can't hit a 20 foot wide ceiling is not what you need, these days, to pull off a nice clean first-degree murder.

But premeditation is only necessary to a charge of *first de-*

gree murder. The Salazar killing was a second-degree job. In the terms of Section 187 of the California Penal Code and in the political context of East Los Angeles in 1970, Ruben Salazar was killed "unlawfully" and "with malice aforethought." These are treacherous concepts, and no doubt there are courts in this country where it might be argued successfully that a cop has a "lawful" right to fire a deadly tear gas bazooka point-blank into a crowd of innocent people on the basis of some unfounded suspicion that one of them *might* be armed. It might also be argued that this kind of crazed and murderous assault can be accomplished without "malice aforethought."

Maybe so. Maybe Ruben Salazar's death can be legally dismissed as a "police accident," or as the result of "official negligence." Most middle-class, white-dominated juries would probably accept the idea. Why, after all, would a clean-cut young police officer deliberately kill an innocent bystander? Not even Ruben Salazar—ten seconds before his death—could believe that he was about to have his head blown off by a cop for no reason at all. When Gustavo Garcia warned him that the cops outside were about to shoot, Salazar said, "That's impossible; we're not doing anything." Then he stood up and caught a tear gas bomb in his left temple.

The malignant reality of Ruben Salazar's death is that he was murdered by angry cops for no reason at all—and that the L.A. sheriff's department was and still is prepared to defend that murder on grounds that it was entirely justified. Salazar was killed, they say, because he happened to be in a bar where police thought there was also a "man with a gun." They gave him a chance, they say, by means of a bullhorn warning . . . and when he didn't come out with his hands up, they had no choice but to fire a tear gas bazooka into the bar . . . and his head got in the way. Tough luck. But what was he doing in that place, anyway? Lounging around a noisy Chicano bar in the middle of a communist riot?

What the cops are saying is that Salazar got what he deserved—for a lot of reasons, but mainly because he happened to be in their way when they had to do their duty. His death was unfortunate, but if they had to do it all over again they wouldn't change a note.

This is the point they want to make. It is a local variation on the standard Mitchell-Agnew theme: Don't fuck around, boy—and if you want to hang around with people who do, don't be surprised when the bill comes due—whistling in through the curtains of some darkened barroom on a sunny afternoon when the cops decide to make an example of somebody.

The night before I left town I stopped by Acosta's place with Guillermo Restrepo. I had been there earlier, but the air was extremely heavy. As always, on stories like this, some of the troops were getting nervous about The Stranger Hanging Around. I was standing in the kitchen watching Frank put some tacos together and wondering when he was going to start waving the butcher knife in my face and yelling about the time I Maced him on my porch in Colorado (that had been six months earlier, at the end of a very long night during which we had all consumed a large quantity of cactus products; and when he started waving a hatchet around I'd figured Mace was the only answer . . . which turned him to jelly for about 45 minutes, and when he finally came around he said, "If I ever see you in East Los Angeles, man, you're gonna wish you never heard the word 'Mace,' because I'm gonna carve it all over your fuckin body.")

So I was not entirely at ease watching Frank chop hamburger on a meat block in the middle of East L.A. He hadn't mentioned the Mace, not yet, but I knew we would get to it sooner or later . . . and I'm sure we would have, except that suddenly out in the living room some geek was screaming: "What the hell is this goddamn gabacho pig writer doing here? Are we fuckin *crazy* to be letting him hear all this shit? Jesus, he's heard enough to put every one of us away for five years!"

Longer than that, I thought. And at that point I stopped worrying about Frank. A firestorm was brewing in the main room—between me and the door—so I decided it was about time to drift around the corner and meet Restrepo at the Carioca. Frank gave me a big smile as I left.

A man police say preyed on elderly women was charged Tuesday with one count of murder and 12 of robbery. Frazier De-Wayne Brown, 44, a 6-foot, 2-inch, 230-pound former Los Angeles county sheriff's deputy, was arraigned in the same Hall of Justice courtroom where he once worked as a bailiff. Police had long been seeking a man who befriended elderly women at bus stops and later attacked and robbed them. Evidence against Brown included possessions taken from victims of strong-arm robberies and found in his home.

L.A. Times 3/31/71

Several hours later we came back. Guillermo wanted to talk to Oscar about putting pressure on the KMEX-TV management to keep him (Restrepo) on the air. "They want to get *rid* of me," he explained. "They started the pressure the day after Ruben was killed—the next fuckin day!"

We were sitting on the floor in the living room. Outside, overhead, the police helicopter was looping around in the sky above Whittier Boulevard, sweeping the neighborhood with a giant searchlight beam that revealed nothing—and served no purpose except to drive the Chicanos below into a seething rage. "Those sons of bitches!" Acosta muttered. "*Look* at that goddamn thing!" We had all gone out in the yard to stare up at the monster. There was no way to ignore it. The noise was bad enough, but the probing searchlight was such an obvious, outrageous harassment that it was hard to understand how even a cop could explain it away as anything but deliberate mockery and provocation.

"Now *tell* me," said Acosta. "*Why* are they doing a thing like this? Why? You think they don't *know* what effect it has on us?"

"They know," said Restrepo. He lit a cigarette as we went back inside. "Listen," he said, "I get about fifteen telephone calls every day from people who want to tell me stories about what the police have done to them—*terrible* stories. I've been hearing them for a year and a half, every goddamn day—and the funny thing is, I never used to believe these people. Not completely. I didn't think they were *lying*, just exaggerating." He paused, glancing around the room, but nobody spoke. Restrepo is not entirely trusted in these quarters; he is part of the establishment—like his friend, Ruben Salazar, who bridged that gap the hard way.

"But ever since Ruben," Restrepo continued, "I *believe* these stories. They're true! I realize that, now—but what can I do?" He shrugged, nervously aware that he was talking to people who had made that discovery a long time ago. "Just the other night," he said, "I got a call from a man who said the cops killed his cousin in the yail. He was a homosexual, a young Chicano, nobody political—and the police report said he hung himself in his cell. Suicide. So I checked it out. And, man, it made me sick. This guy's body was *all bruises*, black and blue marks all over him—and right across his forehead he had 16 fresh stitches.

"The police report said he tried to escape so they had to dominate him. They got him sewed up at the hospital, but when they took him to yail, the warden or yailer or whatever they call the bastard wouldn't *accept* him, because he was bleeding so bad. So they took him back to the hospital and got a doctor to sign some paper saying he was OK to be put in the yail. But they had to *carry* him. And the next day they took a picture of him hanging from the end of the top bunk with his own shirt tied around his neck.

"You *believe* that? Not me. But you tell me—what can I *do?* Where do I look for the truth? Who can I ask? The sheriff? Goddamn, I can't go on the air with a story about how the cops killed a guy in the yail unless I *know* something for proof! Jesus Christ, we all *know*. But just to know is not enough. You understand that? You see why I never made that story on TV?"

Acosta nodded. As a lawyer, he understood perfectly that evidence is *necessary*—on the air and in print, as well as in the courtroom. But Frank was not convinced. He was sipping from a quart of sweet Key Largo wine, and in fact he didn't even know who Restrepo was. "Sorry, man," he'd said earlier. "But I don't watch the news on TV."

Acosta winced. *He* watches and reads *everything*. But most of the people around him think The News—on the TV or radio or newspapers or wherever—is just another rotten gabacho trick. Just another bad shuck, like the others. "The news," to them, is pure propaganda—paid for by the advertisers. "Who pays the bill for that bullshit?" they ask. "Who's behind it?"

Who indeed? Both sides seem convinced that the "real enemy" is a vicious conspiracy of some kind. The Anglo power structure keeps telling itself that "the Mexican problem" is really the work of a small organization of well-trained Communist agitators, working 25 hours a day to transform East L.A. into a wasteland of constant violence—mobs of drug-crazed Chicanos prowling the streets at all times, terrorizing the merchants, hurling firebombs into banks, looting stores, sacking offices and massing now and then, armed with Chinese sten pistols, for all-out assaults on the local sheriff's fortress.

A year ago this grim vision would have been a bad joke, the crude ravings of some paranoid hysterical Bircher. But things are different now; the mood of the barrio is changing so fast that not even the most militant of the young Chicano activists claim to know what's really happening. The only thing everybody agrees on is that the mood is getting ugly, the level of tension is still escalating. The *direction* of the drift is obvious. Even Gov. Reagan is worried about it. He recently named Danny Villanueva, one-time kicking specialist for the Los Angeles Rams and now general manager of KMEX-TV, as the

Governor's personal ambassador to the whole Chicano community. But, as usual, Reagan's solution is part of the problem. Villanueva is overwhelmingly despised by the very people Reagan says he's "trying to reach." He is the classic *vendido*. "Let's face it," says a Chicano journalist not usually identified with the militants, "Danny is a goddamn pig. Ruben Salazar told me that. You know KMEX used to be a good news station for Chicanos. Ruben was the one who did that, and Danny was afraid to interfere. But within 24 hours after Ruben was murdered, Villanueva started tearing up the news department. He wouldn't even let Restrepo show films of the cops gassing people in Laguna Park, the day after Ruben died! Now he's trying to get rid of Restrepo, cut the balls off the news and turn KMEX-TV back into a *safe* Tio Taco station. Shit! And he's getting away with it."

The total castration of KMEX-TV would be a crippling blow to the Movement. A major media voice can be an invaluable mobilizing tool, particularly in the vast urban sprawl of Los Angeles. All it takes is a sympathetic news director with enough leverage and personal integrity to deal with the news on his own terms. The man who hired Ruben Salazar, former station director Joe Rank, considered him valuable enough to out-bid the blue-chip Los Angeles Times for the services of one of that paper's ranking stars—so nobody argued when Salazar demanded absolute independence for his KMEX news operation. But with Salazar dead, the station's Anglo ownership moved swiftly to regain control of the leaderless news operation.

Guillermo Restrepo, Salazar's heir apparent, suddenly discovered that he had no leverage at all. He was muscled into a straight newscaster's role. He was no longer free to investigate any story that he felt was important. . . . If the Chicano Moratorium Committee called a press conference to explain why they were organizing a mass rally against "police brutality," for instance, Restrepo had to get permission to cover it. And Chicano activists soon learned that a two-minute news feature on KMEX was crucial to the success of a mass rally, because TV was the only way to reach a mass Chicano audience in a hurry. And no other TV station in L.A. was interested in any kind of Chicano news except riots.

"Losing Ruben was a goddamn disaster for the Movement," Acosta said recently. "He wasn't really *with* us, but at least he was interested. Hell, the truth is I never really liked the guy. But he was the only journalist in L.A. with real influence who would come to a press conference in the barrio. That's the truth. Hell, the only way we can get those bastards to listen to us is by renting a fancy hotel lounge over there in West Hollywood or some bullshit place like that—where *they* can feel comfortable—and hold our press conference there. With free coffee and snacks for the press. But even then, about half the shitheads won't come unless we serve free booze, too. Shit! Do you know what that *costs?*"

This was the tone of our conversation that night when Guillermo and I went over to Oscar's pad for a beer and some talk about politics. The place was unnaturally quiet. No music, no grass, no bad-mouth *bato loco* types hunkered down on the pallets in the front room. It was the first time I'd seen the place when it didn't look like a staging area for some kind of hellish confrontation that might erupt at any moment.

But tonight it was deadly quiet. The only interruption was a sudden pounding on the door and voices shouting: "Hey, man, open up. I got some *brothers* with me!" Rudy hurried to the door and peered out through the tiny eyewindow. Then he stepped back and shook his head emphatically. "It's some guys from the project," he told Oscar. "I know them, but they're all fucked up."

"God *damn* it," Acosta muttered. "That's the last thing I need tonight. Get rid of them. Tell them I have to be in court tomorrow. Jesus! I *have* to get some sleep!"

Rudy and Frank went outside to deal with the brothers. Oscar and Guillermo went back to politics—while I listened, sensing a downhill drift on all fronts. *Nothing* was going right. The jury was still out on Corky's case, but Acosta was not optimistic. He was also expecting a decision on his Grand Jury challenge in the "Biltmore Six" case. "We'll probably lose that one, too," he said. "The bastards think they have us on the run now; they think we're demoralized—so they'll keep the pressure on, keep pushing." He shrugged. "And maybe they're right. Shit. I'm tired of arguing with them. How long do they expect me to keep coming down to their goddamn courthouse and begging for justice? I'm *tired* of that shit. We're *all* tired." He shook his head slowly then ripped the poptop out of a Budweiser that Rudy brought in from the kitchen. "This legal bullshit ain't makin it," he went on. "The way it looks now, I think we're just about finished with that game. You know at the noon recess today I had to keep a bunch of these goddamn *batos locos* from stomping the D.A. Christ! That would fuck me for good. They'll send me to the goddamn pen for hiring thugs to assault the prosecutor!" He shook his head again. "Frankly, I think the whole thing is out of control. God only knows where it's heading, but I know it's going to be heavy, I think maybe the real shit is about to come down."

There was no need to ask what he meant by "heavy shit." The barrio is already plagued by sporadic fire-bombings, explosions, shootings and minor violence of all kinds. But the cops see nothing "political" in these incidents. Just before I left town I talked on the phone with a lieutenant at the East L.A. sheriff's office. He was anxious to assure me that the area was totally pacified. "You have to remember," he said, "that this has always been a high-crime area. We have a lot of trouble with teen-age gangs, and it's getting worse. Now they're all running around with .22 rifles and handguns, looking for fights with each other. I guess you could say they're sort of like the

Blackstone Rangers in Chicago, except that our gangs are younger."

"But they're not into politics like the black gangs in Chicago?" I asked.

"Are you kidding?" he replied. "The only political thing the Blackstone Rangers ever did was con somebody out of a federal grant for a lot of money."

I asked him about some of the stories I'd heard about bombings, etc. But he quickly dismissed them as rumors. Then, during the next half hour of random talking about things that had happened in the past few weeks, he mentioned one dynamiting and a building burned down at East Los Angeles College, and also the firebombing of a local *vendido* politician's real estate office. "But they hit the wrong guy," the Lt. said with a chuckle. "They bombed another realtor who happened to have the same name as the guy they were after."

"Que malo," I mumbled, lapsing into my own dialect. "But aside from all that, you people don't see real trouble brewing? What about these rallies that keep turning into riots?"

"It's always the same bunch of troublemakers," he explained. "They take a crowd that's gathered for other reasons, and then they subvert it."

"But that last rally was called to protest *police brutality*," I said. "And then it turned into a riot. I saw the films—50 or 60 police cars lined up bumper to bumper on Whittier Boulevard, deputies firing shotguns into the crowd. . . ."

"That was *necessary*," he replied. "That mob was out of control. They *attacked* us."

"I know," I said.

"And let me tell you something else," he went on. "That rally wasn't *really* about 'police brutality.' The guy who organized it, Rosalio Munoz, told me he was just using that slogan to get people out to the park."

"Well, you know how they are," I said. Then I asked him if he could give me the names of any Chicano leaders I should talk to if I decided to write an article about the scene in East L.A.

"Well, there's Congressman Roybal," he said. "And that real estate man I told you about . . ."

"The one who got fire-bombed?"

"Oh no," he replied. "The other guy—the one they *intended* to firebomb."

"OK," I said. "I'll write those names down. And I guess if I decide to look around the barrio you guys could help me out, right? Is it safe to walk around out there, with all these gangs running around shooting at each other?"

"No problem," he said. "We'll even let you ride around in a radio car with some of the officers."

I said that would be fine. What better way, after all, to get the inside story? Just spend a few days touring the barrio in a cop car. Particularly right now, with everything calm and peaceful.

"We see no evidence of any political tension," the Lt. had told me. "We have a great deal of community support." He chuckled. "And we also have a very active intelligence bureau."

"That's good," I said. "Well, I have to hang up now, or I'll miss my plane."

"Oh, then you've decided to do the story? When will you be in town?"

"I've been here for two weeks," I said. "My plane leaves in ten minutes."

"But I thought you said you were calling from San Francisco," he said.

"I did," I said. "But I was lying." (click)

It was definitely time to leave. The last loose end in the Salazar case had been knotted up that morning when the jury came back with a "guilty" verdict for Corky Gonzales. He was sentenced to "40 days and 40 nights" in the L.A. County jail for possession of a loaded revolver on the day of Salazar's death. "We'll appeal," said Acosta, "but for political purposes this case is finished. Nobody's worried about Corky surviving 40 days in jail. We wanted to confront the *gabacho* court system with a man the whole Chicano community knew was technically innocent, then let them draw their own conclusions about the verdict.

"Hell, we never denied that *somebody* had a loaded pistol in that truck. But it wasn't Corky. He wouldn't dare carry a goddamn gun around with him. He's a *leader*. He doesn't have to carry a gun for the same goddamn reason Nixon doesn't."

Acosta had not stressed that point in the courtroom, for fear of alarming the jury and inflaming the gringo press. Not to mention the cops. Why give them the same kind of flimsy excuse to shoot at Gonzales that they already used to justify shooting Ruben Salazar?

Corky merely shrugged at the verdict. At 42, he has spent half his life gouging Justice out of The Man, and now he views the Anglo court system with the quiet sort of fatalistic humor that Acosta hasn't learned yet. But Oscar is getting there fast. The week of April Fools Day, 1971, was a colossal bummer for him; a series of bad jolts and setbacks that seemed to confirm all his worst suspicions.

Two days after Corky's conviction, Superior Court Judge Arthur Alarcon—a prominent Mexican-American jurist—rejected Acosta's carefully-constructed motion to quash the "Biltmore Six" indictments because of "sub-conscious, institutional racism" in the Grand Jury system. This effort had taken almost a year of hard work, much of it done by Chicano law students who reacted to the verdict with a bitterness matching Acosta's.

Then, later that same week, the Los Angeles Board of Supervisors voted to use public funds to pay all legal expenses for several policemen recently indicted "for accidentally" killing two Mexican nationals—a case known in East L.A. as "the murder of the Sanchez brothers." It was a case of mistaken identity, the cops explained. They had somehow been given the wrong address of an apartment where they thought "two Mexican fugitives" were holed up, so they hammered on the door and shouted a warning to "come out of there with your hands over your head or we'll come in shooting." Nobody came out, so the cops went in shooting to kill.

But how could they have known that they'd attacked the wrong apartment? And how could they have known that neither one of the Sanchez brothers understood English? Even Mayor Sam Yorty and Police Chief Ed Davis admitted that the killings had been very unfortunate. But when the Federal D.A. brought charges against the cops, both Yorty and Davis were publicly outraged. They both called press conferences and went on the air to denounce the indictments—in language that strangely echoed the American Legion outcry when Lt. Calley was charged with murdering women and children at My Lai.

The Yorty/Davis tirades were so gross that a District Court judge finally issued a "gag order" to keep them quiet until the case comes to trial. But they had already said enough to whip the whole barrio into a rage at the idea that Chicano tax dollars might be used to defend some "mad dog cops" who frankly admitted killing two Mexican nationals. It sounded like a replay of the Salazar bullshit: same style, same excuse, same result—but this time with different names, and blood on a different floor. "They'll put me in jail if I won't pay taxes," said a young Chicano watching a soccer game at a local playground, "then they take my tax money and use it defend some killer pig. Hell, what if they had come to my address by mistake? I'd be dead as hell right now."

There was a lot of talk in the barrio about "drawing some pig blood for a change" if the Supervisors actually voted to use tax funds to defend the accused cops. A few people actually called City Hall and mumbled anonymous threats in the name of the "Chicano Liberation Front." But the Supervisors hung tough.

They voted on Thursday, and by noon the news was out: The city would pick up the tab.

At 5:15 PM on Thursday afternoon the Los Angeles City Hall was rocked by a dynamite blast. A bomb had been planted in one of the downstairs restrooms. Nobody was hurt, and the damage was officially described as "minor." About $5000 worth, they said—small potatoes, compared to the bomb that blew a wall out of the District Attorney's office last fall after Salazar died.

When I called the sheriff's office to ask about the explosion they said they couldn't talk about it. City Hall was out of their jurisdiction. But they were more than willing to talk when I asked if it was true that the bomb had been the work of the Chicano Liberation Front.

"Where'd you hear that?"

"From the City News Service."

"Yeah, it's true," he said. "Some woman called up and said it was done in memory of the Sanchez brothers, by the Chicano Liberation Front. We've heard about those guys. What do *you* know about them?"

"Nothing," I said. "That's why I called the sheriff. I thought your intelligence network might know something."

"Sure they do," he said quickly. "But all that information is confidential."

Rolling Stone, #81, April 29, 1971

The Kentucky Derby
Is Decadent and Depraved

I got off the plane around midnight and no one spoke as I crossed the dark runway to the terminal. The air was thick and hot, like wandering into a steam bath. Inside, people hugged each other and shook hands . . . big grins and a whoop here and there: "By God! You old *bastard! Good* to see you, boy! *Damn* good . . . and I *mean* it!"

In the air-conditioned lounge I met a man from Houston who said his name was something or other—"but just call me Jimbo"—and he was here to get it on. "I'm ready for *anything,* by God! Anything at all. Yeah, what are you drinkin?" I ordered a Margarita with ice, but he wouldn't hear of it: "Naw, naw . . . what the hell kind of drink is that for Kentucky Derby time? What's *wrong* with you, boy?" He grinned and winked at the bartender. "Goddam, we gotta educate this boy. Get him some good *whiskey* . . ."

I shrugged. "Okay, a double Old Fitz on ice." Jimbo nodded his approval.

"Look." He tapped me on the arm to make sure I was listening. "I know this Derby crowd, I come here every year, and let me tell you one thing I've learned—this is no town to be giving people the impression you're some kind of faggot. Not in public, anyway. Shit, they'll roll you in a minute, knock you in the head and take every goddamn cent you have."

I thanked him and fitted a Marlboro into my cigarette holder. "Say," he said, "you look like you might be in the horse business . . . am I right?"

"No," I said. "I'm a photographer."

"Oh yeah?" He eyed my ragged leather bag with new interest. "Is that what you got there—cameras? Who you work for?"

"*Playboy*," I said.

He laughed. "Well, goddam! What are you gonna take pictures of—nekkid horses? Haw! I guess you'll be workin' pretty hard when they run the Kentucky Oaks. That's a race just for fillies." He was laughing wildly. "Hell yes! And they'll all be nekkid too!"

I shook my head and said nothing; just stared at him for a moment, trying to look grim. "There's going to be trouble," I said. "My assignment is to take pictures of the riot."

"What riot?"

I hesitated, twirling the ice in my drink. "At the track. On Derby Day. The Black Panthers." I stared at him again. "Don't you read the newspapers?"

The grin on his face had collapsed. "What the *hell* are you talkin about?"

"Well . . . maybe I shouldn't be telling you . . ." I shrugged. "But hell, everybody else seems to know. The cops and the National Guard have been getting ready for six weeks. They have 20,000 troops on alert at Fort Knox. They've warned us—all the press and photographers—to wear helmets and special vests like flak jackets. We were told to expect shooting. . . ."

"No!" he shouted; his hands flew up and hovered momentarily between us, as if to ward off the words he was hearing. Then he whacked his fist on the bar. "Those sons of bitches! God Almighty! The Kentucky Derby!" He kept shaking his head. "No! *Jesus!* That's almost too bad to believe!" Now he seemed to be sagging on the stool, and when he looked up his eyes were misty. "Why? Why *here?* Don't they respect *anything?*"

I shrugged again. "It's not just the Panthers. The FBI says busloads of white crazies are coming in from all over the country—to mix with the crowd and attack all at once, from every direction. They'll be dressed like everybody else. You know—coats and ties and all that. But when the trouble starts . . . well, that's why the cops are so worried."

He sat for a moment, looking hurt and confused and not quite able to digest all this terrible news. Then he cried out: "Oh . . . Jesus! What in the name of God is happening in this country? Where can you get *away* from it?"

"Not here," I said, picking up my bag. "Thanks for the drink . . . and good luck."

He grabbed my arm, urging me to have another, but I said I was overdue at the Press Club and hustled off to get my act together for the awful spectacle. At the airport newsstand I picked up a *Courier-Journal* and scanned the front page headlines: "Nixon Sends GI's into Cambodia to Hit Reds" . . . "B-52's Raid, then 2,000 GI's Advance 20 Miles" . . . "4,000 U.S. Troops Deployed Near Yale as Tension Grows Over Panther Protest." At the bottom of the page was a photo of Diane Crump, soon to become the first woman jockey ever to ride in the Kentucky Derby. The photographer had snapped her "stopping in the barn area to fondle her mount, Fathom." The rest of the paper was spotted with ugly war news and stories of "student unrest." There was no mention of any trouble brewing at a university in Ohio called Kent State.

I went to the Hertz desk to pick up my car, but the moon-faced young swinger in charge said they didn't have any. "You can't rent one anywhere," he assured me. "Our Derby reservations have been booked for six weeks." I explained that my agent had confirmed a white Chrysler convertible for me that very afternoon but he shook his head. "Maybe we'll have a cancellation. Where are you staying?"

I shrugged. "Where's the Texas crowd staying? I want to be with my people."

He sighed. "My friend, you're in trouble. This town is flat *full*. Always is, for the Derby."

I leaned closer to him, half-whispering: "Look, I'm from *Playboy*. How would you like a job?"

He backed off quickly. "What? Come on, now. What kind of a job?"

"Never mind," I said. "You just blew it." I swept my bag off the counter and went to find a cab. The bag is a valuable prop in this kind of work; mine has a lot of baggage tags on it—SF, LA, NY, Lima, Rome, Bangkok, that sort of thing—and the most prominent tag of all is a very official, plastic-coated thing that says "Photog. Playboy Mag." I bought it from a pimp in Vail, Colorado, and he told me how to use it. "Never mention *Playboy* until you're sure they've seen this thing first," he said. "Then, when you see them notice it, that's the time to strike. They'll go belly up every time. This thing is magic, I tell you. Pure magic."

Well . . . maybe so. I'd used it on the poor geek in the bar, and now, humming along in a Yellow Cab toward town, I felt a little guilty about jangling the poor bugger's brains with that evil fantasy. But what the hell? Anybody who wanders around the world saying, "Hell yes, I'm from Texas," deserves whatever happens to him. And he had, after all, come here once again to make a nineteenth-century ass of himself in the midst of some jaded, atavistic freakout with nothing to recommend it except a very saleable "tradition." Early in our chat, Jimbo had told me that he hasn't missed a Derby since 1954. "The little lady won't come anymore," he said. "She just grits her teeth and turns me loose for this one. And when I say 'loose' I do mean *loose!* I toss ten-dollar bills around like they were goin' outa style! Horses, whiskey, women . . . shit, there's women in this town that'll do *anything* for money."

Why not? Money is a good thing to have in these twisted times. Even Richard Nixon is hungry for it. Only a few days before the Derby he said, "If I had any money I'd invest it in the stock market." And the market, meanwhile, continued its grim slide.

The next day was heavy. With only thirty hours until post time I had no press credentials and—according to the sports editor of the Louisville *Courier-Journal*—no hope at all of getting any. Worse, I needed *two* sets; one for myself and another for Ralph Steadman, the English illustrator who was coming from London to do some Derby drawings. All I knew about him was that this was his first visit to the United States. And the more I pondered that fact, the more it gave me the fear. How would he bear up under the heinous culture shock of being lifted out of London and plunged into a drunken mob scene at the Kentucky Derby? There was no way of knowing. Hopefully, he would arrive at least a day or so ahead, and give himself time to get acclimated. Maybe a few hours of peaceful sightseeing in the Bluegrass country around Lexington. My plan was to pick him up at the airport in the huge Pontiac Ballbuster I'd rented from a used-car salesman named Colonel Quick, then whisk him off to some peaceful setting that might remind him of England.

Colonel Quick had solved the car problem, and money (four times the normal rate) had bought two rooms in a scumbox on the outskirts of town. The only other kink was the task of convincing the moguls at Churchill Downs that *Scanlan's* was such a prestigious sporting journal that common sense compelled them to give us two sets of the best press tickets. This was not easily done. My first call to the publicity office resulted in total failure. The press handler was shocked at the idea that anyone would be stupid enough to apply for press credentials two days before the Derby. "Hell, you can't be serious," he said. "The deadline was two months ago. The press box is full; there's no more room . . . and what the hell is *Scanlan's Monthly* anyway?"

I uttered a painful groan. "Didn't the London office call you? They're flying an artist over to do the paintings. Steadman. He's Irish, I think. Very famous over there. Yes. I just got in from the Coast. The San Francisco office told me we were all set."

He seemed interested, and even sympathetic, but there was nothing he could do. I flattered him with more gibberish, and finally he offered a compromise: he could get us two passes to the clubhouse grounds but the clubhouse itself and especially the press box were out of the question.

"That sounds a little weird," I said. "It's unacceptable. We *must* have access to everything. *All* of it. The spectacle, the people, the pageantry and certainly the race. You don't think we came all this way to watch the damn thing on television, do you? One way or another we'll get inside. Maybe we'll have to bribe a guard—or even Mace somebody." (I had picked up a spray can of Mace in a downtown drugstore for $5.98 and suddenly, in the midst of that phone talk, I was struck by the hideous possibilities of using it out at the track. Macing ushers at the narrow gates to the clubhouse inner sanctum, then slipping quickly inside, firing a huge load of Mace into the governor's box, just as the race starts. Or Macing helpless drunks in the clubhouse restroom, for their own good . . .)

By noon on Friday I was still without credentials and still unable to locate Steadman. For all I knew he'd changed his mind and gone back to London. Finally, after giving up on Steadman and trying unsuccessfully to reach my man in the press office, I decided my only hope for credentials was to go out to the track and confront the man in person, with no warning—demanding only one pass now, instead of two, and talking very fast with a strange lilt in my voice, like a man trying hard to control some inner frenzy. On the way out, I stopped at the motel desk to cash a check. Then, as a useless afterthought, I asked if by any wild chance a Mr. Steadman had checked in.

The lady on the desk was about fifty years old and very peculiar-looking; when I mentioned Steadman's name she nodded, without looking up from whatever she was writing, and said in a low voice, "You bet he did." Then she favored me with a big smile. "Yes, indeed. Mr. Steadman just left for the racetrack. Is he a friend of yours?"

I shook my head. "I'm supposed to be working with him, but I don't even know what he looks like. Now, goddammit, I'll have to find him in that mob at the track."

She chuckled. "You won't have any trouble finding him. You could pick *that* man out of any crowd."

"Why?" I asked. "What's wrong with him? What does he look like?"

"Well . . ." she said, still grinning, "he's the funniest looking thing I've seen in a long time. He has this . . . ah . . . this *growth* all over his face. As a matter of fact it's all over his *head*." She nodded. "You'll know him when you see him; don't worry about that."

Creeping Jesus, I thought. That screws the press credentials. I had a vision of some nerve-rattling geek all covered with matted hair and string-warts showing up in the press office and demanding *Scanlan's* press packet. Well . . . what the hell? We could always load up on acid and spend the day roaming around the clubhouse grounds with big sketch pads, laughing hysterically at the natives and swilling mint juleps so the cops wouldn't think we're abnormal. Perhaps even make the act pay: set up an easel with a big sign saying, "Let a Foreign Artist Paint Your Portrait, $10 Each. Do It NOW!"

I took the expressway out to the track, driving very fast and jumping the monster car back and forth between lanes, driving with a beer in one hand and my mind so muddled that I almost crushed a Volkswagen full of nuns when I swerved to catch the right exit. There was a slim chance, I thought, that I might be able to catch the ugly Britisher before he checked in.

But Steadman was already in the press box when I got there, a bearded young Englishman wearing a tweed coat and RAF sunglasses. There was nothing particularly odd about him. No facial veins or clumps of bristly warts. I told him about the motel woman's description and he seemed puzzled. "Don't let it bother you," I said. "Just keep in mind for the next few days that we're in Louisville, Kentucky. Not London. Not even New York. This is a weird place. You're lucky that mental defective at the motel didn't jerk a pistol out of the cash register and blow a big hole in you." I laughed, but he looked worried.

"Just pretend you're visiting a huge outdoor loony bin," I said. "If the inmates get out of control we'll soak them down with Mace." I showed him the can of "Chemical Billy," resisting the urge to fire it across the room at a rat-faced man typing diligently in the Associated Press section. We were standing at the bar, sipping the management's Scotch and congratulating each other on our sudden, unexplained luck in picking up two sets of fine press credentials. The lady at the desk had been very friendly to him, he said. "I just told her my name and she gave me the whole works."

By midafternoon we had everything under control. We had seats looking down on the finish line, color TV and a free bar in the press room, and a selection of passes that would take us anywhere from the clubhouse roof to the jockey room. The only thing we lacked was unlimited access to the clubhouse inner sanctum in sections "F&G" . . . and I felt we needed that, to see the whiskey gentry in action. The governor, a swinish neo-Nazi hack named Louie Nunn, would be in "G," along with Barry Goldwater and Colonel Sanders. I felt we'd be legal in a box in "G" where we could rest and sip juleps, soak up a bit of atmosphere and the Derby's special vibrations.

The bars and dining rooms are also in "F&G," and the clubhouse bars on Derby Day are a very special kind of scene. Along with the politicians, society belles and local captains of commerce, every half-mad dingbat who ever had any pretensions to anything at all within five hundred miles of Louisville will show up there to get strutting drunk and slap a lot of backs and generally make himself obvious. The Paddock bar is probably the best place in the track to sit and watch faces. Nobody minds being stared at; that's what they're in there for. Some people spend most of their time in the Paddock; they can hunker down at one of the many wooden tables, lean back in a comfortable chair and watch the ever-changing odds flash up and down on the big tote board outside the window. Black waiters in white serving jackets move through the crowd with trays of drinks, while the experts ponder their racing forms and the hunch bettors pick lucky numbers or scan the lineup for rightsounding names. There is a constant flow of traffic to and from the pari-mutuel windows outside in the wooden corridors. Then, as post time nears, the crowd thins out as people go back to their boxes.

Clearly, we were going to have to figure out some way to spend more time in the clubhouse tomorrow. But the "walkaround" press passes to F&G were only good for thirty minutes at a time, presumably to allow the newspaper types to rush in and out for photos or quick interviews, but to prevent drifters like Steadman and me from spending all day in the clubhouse, harassing the gentry and rifling the odd handbag or two while cruising around the boxes. Or Macing the governor. The time limit was no problem on Friday, but on Derby Day the walkaround passes would be in heavy demand. And since it took about ten minutes to get from the press box to the Paddock, and ten more minutes to get back, that didn't leave much time for serious people-watching. And unlike most of the others in the press box, we didn't give a hoot in hell what was happening on the track. We had come there to watch the *real* beasts perform.

Later Friday afternoon, we went out on the balcony of the press box and I tried to describe the difference between what we were seeing today and what would be happening tomorrow. This was the first time I'd been to a Derby in ten years, but before that, when I lived in Louisville, I used to go every year. Now, looking down from the press box, I pointed to the huge grassy meadow enclosed by the track. "That whole thing," I said, "will be jammed with people; fifty thousand or so, and

most of them staggering drunk. It's a fantastic scene—
thousands of people fainting, crying, copulating, trampling each
other and fighting with broken whiskey bottles. We'll have to
spend some time out there, but it's hard to move around, too
many bodies."

"Is it safe out there? Will we *ever* come back?"

"Sure," I said. "We'll just have to be careful not to step on
anybody's stomach and start a fight." I shrugged. "Hell, this
clubhouse scene right below us will be almost as bad as the infield. Thousands of raving, stumbling drunks, getting angrier
and angrier as they lose more and more money. By midafternoon they'll be guzzling mint juleps with both hands and vomiting on each other between races. The whole place will be
jammed with bodies, shoulder to shoulder. It's hard to move
around. The aisles will be slick with vomit; people falling down
and grabbing at your legs to keep from being stomped. Drunks
pissing on themselves in the betting lines. Dropping handfuls of
money and fighting to stoop over and pick it up."

He looked so nervous that I laughed. "I'm just kidding," I
said. "Don't worry. At the first hint of trouble I'll start pumping
this 'Chemical Billy' into the crowd."

He had done a few good sketches, but so far we hadn't seen
that special kind of face that I felt we would need for the lead
drawing. It was a face I'd seen a thousand times at every Derby
I'd ever been to. I saw it, in my head, as the mask of the
whiskey gentry—a pretentious mix of booze, failed dreams and
a terminal identity crisis; the inevitable result of too much inbreeding in a closed and ignorant culture. One of the key ge-
netic rules in breeding dogs, horses or any other kind of
thoroughbred is that close inbreeding tends to magnify the
weak points in a bloodline as well as the strong points. In horse
breeding, for instance, there is a definite risk in breeding two
fast horses who are both a little crazy. The offspring will likely
be very fast and also very crazy. So the trick in breeding thor-
oughbreds is to retain the good traits and filter out the bad. But

the breeding of humans is not so wisely supervised, particularly in a narrow Southern society where the closest kind of inbreeding is not only stylish and acceptable, but far more convenient—to the parents—than setting their offspring free to find their own mates, for their own reasons and in their own ways. ("Goddam, did you hear about Smitty's daughter? She went crazy in Boston last week and married a nigger!")

So the face I was trying to find in Churchill Downs that weekend was a symbol, in my own mind, of the whole doomed atavistic culture that makes the Kentucky Derby what it is.

On our way back to the motel after Friday's races I warned Steadman about some of the other problems we'd have to cope with. Neither of us had brought any strange illegal drugs, so we would have to get by on booze. "You should keep in mind," I said, "that almost everybody you talk to from now on will be drunk. People who seem very pleasant at first might suddenly swing at you for no reason at all." He nodded, staring straight ahead. He seemed to be getting a little numb and I tried to cheer him up by inviting him to dinner that night, with my brother.

Back at the motel we talked for a while about America, the South, England—just relaxing a bit before dinner. There was no way either of us could have known, at the time, that it would be the last normal conversation we would have. From that point on, the weekend became a vicious, drunken nightmare. We both went completely to pieces. The main problem was my prior attachment to Louisville, which naturally led to meetings with old friends, relatives, etc., many of whom were in the process of falling apart, going mad, plotting divorces, cracking up under the strain of terrible debts or recovering from bad accidents. Right in the middle of the whole frenzied Derby action, a member of my own family had to be institutionalized. This added a certain amount of strain to the situation, and since poor Steadman had no choice but to take whatever came his way, he was subjected to shock after shock.

Another problem was his habit of sketching people he met in the various social situations I dragged him into—then giving them the sketches. The results were always unfortunate. I warned him several times about letting the subjects see his foul renderings, but for some perverse reason he kept doing it. Consequently, he was regarded with fear and loathing by nearly everyone who'd seen or even heard about his work. He couldn't understand it. "It's sort of a joke," he kept saying. "Why, in England it's quite normal. People don't take offense. They understand that I'm just putting them on a bit."

"Fuck England," I said. "This is Middle America. These people regard what you're doing to them as a brutal, bilious insult. Look what happened last night. I thought my brother was going to tear your head off."

Steadman shook his head sadly. "But I liked him. He struck me as a very decent, straightforward sort."

"Look, Ralph," I said. "Let's not kid ourselves. That was a very horrible drawing you gave him. It was the face of a monster. It got on his nerves very badly." I shrugged. "Why in hell do you think we left the restaurant so fast?"

"I thought it was because of the Mace," he said.

"What Mace?"

He grinned. "When you shot it at the headwaiter, don't you remember?"

"Hell, that was nothing," I said. "I missed him . . . and we were leaving, anyway."

"But it got all over us," he said. "The room was full of that damn gas. Your brother was sneezing and his wife was crying. My eyes hurt for two hours. I couldn't see to draw when we got back to the motel."

"That's right," I said. "The stuff got on her leg, didn't it?"

"She was angry," he said.

"Yeah . . . well, okay . . . Let's just figure we fucked up about equally on that one," I said. "But from now on let's try to be careful when we're around people I know. You won't sketch them and I won't Mace them. We'll just try to relax and get drunk."

"Right," he said. "We'll go native."

It was Saturday morning, the day of the Big Race, and we were having breakfast in a plastic hamburger palace called the Fish-Meat Village. Our rooms were just across the road in the Brown Suburban Hotel. They had a dining room, but the food was so bad that we couldn't handle it anymore. The waitresses seemed to be suffering from shin splints; they moved around very slowly, moaning and cursing the "darkies" in the kitchen.

Steadman liked the Fish-Meat place because it had fish and chips. I preferred the "French toast," which was really pancake batter, fried to the proper thickness and then chopped out with a sort of cookie cutter to resemble pieces of toast.

Beyond drink and lack of sleep, our only real problem at that point was the question of access to the clubhouse. Finally we decided to go ahead and steal two passes, if necessary, rather than miss that part of the action. This was the last coherent decision we were able to make for the next forty-eight hours. From that point on—almost from the very moment we started out to the track—we lost all control of events and spent the rest of the weekend churning around in a sea of drunken horrors. My notes and recollections from Derby Day are somewhat scrambled.

But now, looking at the big red notebook I carried all through that scene, I see more or less what happened. The book itself is somewhat mangled and bent; some of the pages are torn, others are shriveled and stained by what appears to be whiskey, but taken as a whole, with sporadic memory flashes, the notes seem to tell the story. To wit:

Rain all nite until dawn. No sleep. Christ, here we go, a nightmare of mud and madness . . . But no. By noon the sun burns through—perfect day, not even humid.

Steadman is now worried about fire. Somebody told him about the clubhouse catching on fire two years ago. Could it happen again? Horrible. Trapped in the press box. Holocaust. A hundred thousand people fighting to get out. Drunks screaming in the flames and the mud, crazed horses running wild. Blind in the smoke. Grandstand collapsing into the flames with us on the roof. Poor Ralph is about to crack. Drinking heavily, into the Haig & Haig.

Out to the track in a cab, avoid that terrible parking in people's front yards, $25 each, toothless old men on the street with big signs: PARK HERE, flagging cars in the yard. "That's fine, boy, never mind the tulips." Wild hair on his head, straight up like a clump of reeds.

Sidewalks full of people all moving in the same direction, towards Churchill Downs. Kids hauling coolers and blankets, teenyboppers in tight pink shorts, many blacks . . . black dudes in white felt hats with leopard-skin bands, cops waving traffic along.

The mob was thick for many blocks around the track; very slow going in the crowd, very hot. On the way to the press box elevator, just inside the clubhouse, we came on a row of soldiers all carrying long white riot sticks. About two platoons, with helmets. A man walking next to us said they were waiting for the governor and his party. Steadman eyed them nervously. "Why do they have those clubs?"

"Black Panthers," I said. Then I remembered good old "Jimbo" at the airport and I wondered what he was thinking right now. Probably very nervous; the place was teeming with cops and soldiers. We pressed on through the crowd, through many gates, past the paddock where the jockeys bring the horses out and parade around for a while before each race so the bettors can get a good look. Five million dollars will be bet today. Many winners, more losers. What the hell. The press gate was jammed up with people trying to get in, shouting at the guards, waving strange press badges: Chicago Sporting

Times, Pittsburgh Police Athletic League . . . they were all turned away. "Move on, fella, make way for the working press." We shoved through the crowd and into the elevator, then quickly up to the free bar. Why not? Get it on. Very hot today, not feeling well, must be this rotten climate. The press box was cool and airy, plenty of room to walk around and balcony seats for watching the race or looking down at the crowd. We got a betting sheet and went outside.

Pink faces with a stylish Southern sag, old Ivy styles, seer-sucker coats and buttondown collars. "Mayblossom Senility" (Steadman's phrase) . . . burnt out early or maybe just not much to burn in the first place. Not much energy in these faces, not much *curiosity*. Suffering in silence, nowhere to go after thirty in this life, just hang on and humor the children. Let the young enjoy themselves while they can. Why not?

The grim reaper comes early in this league . . . banshees on the lawn at night, screaming out there beside that little iron nigger in jockey clothes. Maybe he's the one who's screaming. Bad DT's and too many snarls at the bridge club. Going down with the stock market. Oh Jesus, the kid has wrecked the new car, wrapped it around the big stone pillar at the bottom of the driveway. Broken leg? Twisted eye? Send him off to Yale, they can cure anything up there.

Yale? Did you see today's paper? New Haven is under siege. Yale is swarming with Black Panthers. . . . I tell you, Colonel, the world has gone mad, stone mad. Why, they tell me a goddam woman jockey might ride in the Derby today.

I left Steadman sketching in the Paddock bar and went off to place our bets on the fourth race. When I came back he was staring intently at a group of young men around a table not far away. "Jesus, look at the corruption in that face!" he whispered. "Look at the madness, the fear, the greed!" I looked, then quickly turned my back on the table he was sketching. The face he'd picked out to draw was the face of an old friend of mine, a prep school football star in the good old days with a sleek red Chevy convertible and a very quick hand, it was said, with the snaps of a 32 B brassiere. They called him "Cat Man."

But now, a dozen years later, I wouldn't have recognized him anywhere but here, where I should have expected to find him, in the Paddock bar on Derby Day . . . fat slanted eyes and a pimp's smile, blue silk suit and his friends looking like crooked bank tellers on a binge . . .

Steadman wanted to see some Kentucky Colonels, but he wasn't sure what they looked like. I told him to go back to the clubhouse men's rooms and look for men in white linen suits vomiting in the urinals. "They'll usually have large brown whiskey stains on the fronts of their suits," I said. "But watch the shoes, that's the tip-off. Most of them manage to avoid vomiting on their own clothes, but they never miss their shoes."

In a box not far from ours was Colonel Anna Friedman Goldman, *Chairman and Keeper of the Great Seal of the Honorable Order of Kentucky Colonels.* Not all the 76 million or so Kentucky Colonels could make it to the Derby this year, but many had kept the faith, and several days prior to the Derby they gathered for their annual dinner at the Seelbach Hotel.

The Derby, the actual race, was scheduled for late afternoon, and as the magic hour approached I suggested to Steadman that we should probably spend some time in the infield, that boiling sea of people across the track from the clubhouse. He seemed a little nervous about it, but since none of the awful things I'd warned him about had happened so far—no race riots, firestorms or savage drunken attacks—he shrugged and said, "Right, let's do it."

To get there we had to pass through many gates, each one a step down in status, then through a tunnel under the track. Emerging from the tunnel was such a culture shock that it took us a while to adjust. "God almighty!" Steadman muttered.

"This is a . . . Jesus!" He plunged ahead with his tiny camera, stepping over bodies, and I followed, trying to take notes.

Total chaos, no way to see the race, not even the track . . . nobody cares. Big lines at the outdoor betting windows, then stand back to watch winning numbers flash on the big board, like a giant bingo game.

Old blacks arguing about bets; "Hold on there, I'll handle this" (waving pint of whiskey, fistful of dollar bills); girl riding piggyback, T-shirt says, "Stolen from Fort Lauderdale Jail." Thousands of teen-agers, group singing "Let the Sun Shine In," ten soldiers guarding the American flag and a huge fat drunk wearing a blue football jersey (No. 80) reeling around with quart of beer in hand.

No booze sold out here, too dangerous . . . no bathrooms either. Muscle Beach . . . Woodstock . . . many cops with riot sticks, but no sign of a riot. Far across the track the clubhouse looks like a postcard from the Kentucky Derby.

We went back to the clubhouse to watch the big race. When the crowd stood to face the flag and sing "My Old Kentucky Home," Steadman faced the crowd and sketched frantically. Somewhere up in the boxes a voice screeched, "Turn around, you hairy freak!" The race itself was only two minutes long, and even from our super-status seats and using 12-power glasses, there was no way to see what was really happening. Later, watching a TV rerun in the press box, we saw what happened to our horses. Holy Land, Ralph's choice, stumbled and lost his jockey in the final turn. Mine, Silent Screen, had the lead coming into the stretch, but faded to fifth at the finish. The winner was a 16–1 shot named Dust Commander.

Moments after the race was over, the crowd surged wildly for the exits, rushing for cabs and buses. The next day's *Courier* told of violence in the parking lot; people were punched and trampled, pockets were picked, children lost, bottles hurled.

But we missed all this, having retired to the press box for a bit of post-race drinking. By this time we were both half-crazy from too much whiskey, sun fatigue, culture shock, lack of sleep and general dissolution. We hung around the press box long enough to watch a mass interview with the winning owner, a dapper little man named Lehmann who said he had just flown into Louisville that morning from Nepal, where he'd "bagged a record tiger." The sportswriters murmured their admiration and a waiter filled Lehmann's glass with Chivas Regal. He had just won $127,000 with a horse that cost him $6,500 two years ago. His occupation, he said, was "retired contractor." And then he added, with a big grin, "I just retired."

The rest of that day blurs into madness. The rest of that night too. And all the next day and night. Such horrible things occurred that I can't bring myself even to think about them now, much less put them down in print. Steadman was lucky to get out of Louisville without serious injuries, and I was lucky to get out at all. One of my clearest memories of that vicious time is Ralph being attacked by one of my old friends in the billiard room of the Pendennis Club in downtown Louisville on Saturday night. The man had ripped his own shirt open to the waist before deciding that Ralph was after his wife. No blows were struck, but the emotional effects were massive. Then, as a sort of final horror, Steadman put his fiendish pen to work and tried to patch things up by doing a little sketch of the girl he'd been accused of hustling. That finished us in the Pendennis.

Sometime around ten-thirty Monday morning I was awakened by a scratching sound at my door. I leaned out of bed and pulled the curtain back just far enough to see Steadman outside. "What the fuck do you want?" I shouted.

"What about having breakfast?" he said.

I lunged out of bed and tried to open the door, but it caught on the night-chain and banged shut again. I couldn't cope with the chain! The thing wouldn't come out of the track—so I ripped it out of the wall with a vicious jerk on the door. Ralph didn't blink. "Bad luck," he muttered.

I could barely see him. My eyes were swollen almost shut and the sudden burst of sunlight through the door left me stunned and helpless like a sick mole. Steadman was mumbling about sickness and terrible heat; I fell back on the bed and tried to focus on him as he moved around the room in a very distracted way for a few moments, then suddenly darted over to the beer bucket and seized a Colt .45. "Christ," I said. "You're getting out of control."

He nodded and ripped the cap off, taking a long drink. "You know, this is really awful," he said finally. "I *must* get out of this place . . ." he shook his head nervously. "The plane leaves at three-thirty, but I don't know if I'll make it."

I barely heard him. My eyes had finally opened enough for me to focus on the mirror across the room and I was stunned at the shock of recognition. For a confused instant I thought that Ralph had brought somebody with him—a model for that one special face we'd been looking for. There he was, by God—a puffy, drink-ravaged, disease-ridden caricature . . . like an awful cartoon version of an old snapshot in some once-proud mother's family photo album. It was the face we'd been looking for—and it was, of course, my own. Horrible, horrible. . . .

"Maybe I should sleep a while longer," I said. "Why don't you go on over to the Fish-Meat place and eat some of those rotten fish and chips? Then come back and get me around noon. I feel too near death to hit the streets at this hour."

He shook his head. "No . . . no . . . I think I'll go back upstairs and work on those drawings for a while." He leaned down to fetch two more cans out of the beer bucket. "I tried to work earlier," he said, "but my hands keep trembling . . . It's teddible, teddible."

"You've got to stop this drinking," I said.

He nodded. "I know. This is no good, no good at all. But for some reason it makes me feel better . . ."

"Not for long," I said. "You'll probably collapse into some kind of hysterical DT's tonight—probably just about the time you get off the plane at Kennedy. They'll zip you up in a strait-jacket and drag you down to the Tombs, then beat you on the kidneys with big sticks until you straighten out."

He shrugged and wandered out, pulling the door shut behind him. I went back to bed for another hour or so, and later—after the daily grapefruit juice run to the Nite Owl Food Mart—we had our last meal at Fish-Meat Village: a fine lunch of dough and butcher's offal, fried in heavy grease.

By this time Ralph wouldn't even order coffee; he kept asking for more water. "It's the only thing they have that's fit for human consumption," he explained. Then, with an hour or so to kill before he had to catch the plane, we spread his drawings out on the table and pondered them for a while, wondering if he'd caught the proper spirit of the thing . . . but we couldn't make up our minds. His hands were shaking so badly that he had trouble holding the paper, and my vision was so blurred that I could barely see what he'd drawn. "Shit," I said. "We both look worse than anything you've drawn here."

He smiled. "You know—I've been thinking about that," he said. "We came down here to see this teddible scene: people all pissed out of their minds and vomiting on themselves and all that . . . and now, you know what? It's us. . . ."

Huge Pontiac Ballbuster blowing through traffic on the expressway.

A radio news bulletin says the National Guard is massacring students at Kent State and Nixon is still bombing Cambodia. The journalist is driving, ignoring his passenger who is now nearly naked after taking off most of his clothing, which he holds out the window, trying to wind-wash the Mace out of it. His eyes are bright red and his face and chest are soaked with the beer he's been using to rinse the awful chemical off his flesh. The front of his woolen trousers is soaked with vomit; his body is racked with fits of coughing and wild choking sobs. The journalist rams the big car through traffic and into a spot in front of the terminal, then he reaches over to open the door on the passenger's side and shoves the Englishman out, snarling: "Bug off, you worthless faggot! You twisted pigfucker! [Crazed laughter.] If I weren't sick I'd kick your ass all the way to Bowling Green—you scumsucking foreign geek. Mace is too good for you . . . We can do without your kind in Kentucky."

Scanlan's Monthly, vol. 1, no. 4, June 1970

A Note on the Type

The principal text of this Modern Library edition
was set in a digitized version of Century Expanded,
a member of the Century family of typefaces.
It was designed in the 1890s by
Theodore Low DeVinne of the
American Type Founders Company,
in collaboration with Linn Boyd Benton.
It was one of the earliest types designed
for a specific purpose, the *Century* magazine,
because it was able to maintain the economics
of a narrower typeface while using stronger
serifs and thickened verticals.